# CONTENTS

# The
# Privileged Ape

## CULTURAL CAPITAL IN
## THE MAKING OF MAN

FRONTIERS OF THOUGHT
Series Editor Victor Serebriakoff

# The
# Privileged Ape

## CULTURAL CAPITAL IN THE MAKING OF MAN

J. Cohen

**The Parthenon Publishing Group**
International Publishers in Science & Technology

Casterton Hall, Carnforth,
Lancs, LA6 2LA, U.K.

120 Mill Road, Park Ridge
New Jersey, U.S.A.

Published in the UK by
The Parthenon Publishing Group Limited
Casterton Hall, Carnforth,
Lancs, LA6 2LA, England

ISBN 1-85070 144X

Published in the USA by
The Parthenon Publishing Group Inc.
120 Mill Road,
Park Ridge,
New Jersey 07656, USA

ISBN 0-940813-80-7

Printed and bound in Great Britain by
Redwood Burn Limited, Trowbridge, Wiltshire

# FOREWORD

*The Frontiers of Thought* series looks at some of the bounds of The Known. These are the interfaces between knowledge and ignorance where the scientists, and other thinkers, are advancing in today's world.

The constant forking proliferation of intellectual disciplines has divided them so that fruitful interaction between them is hardly possible today. It is the aim of this series to give the reader a chance to "walk the bounds" in the company of guides from the various fields.

The frontier of thought that has been making the most startling progress recently is biology.

Jack Cohen's theme arises from the enormously rapid developments in the biological sciences in the latter part of this century. In genetics, biochemistry, neurology, ethology and especially in developmental biology there have been startlingly great advances so that the time has come to look at the field holistically and ask some general questions. How do the elements of this growing knowledge base interact? What light do the discoveries in many new disciplines throw upon each other? Collectively, how do they change our views about those sciences which we have so far thought to be the "softest", anthropology, sociology and political science? Can the ideas arising from modern biology help us in predicting the future of the biosphere and of humanity? Sociobiology, as represented by Wilson, was one attempt but it excited much criticism and failed to guide politics and government. Cohen returns to the theme with a new approach; he shows how increasing knowledge from these disciplines may indeed guide economic, social and educational policy. These are the questions which, from a deep and lifelong professional but generalist interest in all of biology, Dr Cohen is asking. They are questions which have gone out of fashion for ninety years, since a few pioneers tried to apply the paradigms arising from Darwinism in the social sciences; Spencer, Marx, de Chardin, Haeckel and Darlington are examples.

These early speculations, even Darlington's, were supported by an inadequate database. One by one they have gone out of favour. But these writers were seeking, reasonably, to find sociological regularities, invariances, models and conceptual homologies from the developing fields of biology after Darwin. Perhaps they were premature, surely they were not mistaken in one sense. Surely study at the various levels in biology – at the level of the cell, the social cell assembly, the creature and the the social creature assembly, the tribe, colony, society – surely these must reveal echoes and similarities, throw light on each other and suggest more general laws and invariances. Indeed they appear to do so, if we may judge by Cohen's brilliant analysis.

Cohen does not follow the modern egalitarian paradigm in rejecting the concept of the Ladder of Life, the model which shows visible progression to more complex and more advanced informational forms. Accepting this he notices trends, as one moves up the ladder conceptually, that seem to have escaped general attention. He observes something very interesting about the later, complex life forms. In order to develop this complexity, flexibility and effective viability they have developed a greater use of what he fairly calls a heredity of privilege or capital. The more primitive forms pass on little but the genetic prescription and a "tape reader", the cytoplasm with the minimum of material as an inheritance. As he proceeds up the ladder of life, the privilege or capital passed from one generation to the next becomes greater and more important; the "investment" of each generation in the next – as material, care, knowhow – grows greater.

Looking at the most advanced life form from this point of view, human society – the "sociozoon" as I have called it – Cohen is able to show that the viability of many aspects of our civilisation is highly questionable. Using his biological model, he points to a new and relevant role for education, a subject whose aims and methods have been vague and uninformed; looked at through his lens this has worried him both as a biologist and as an educator. His conclusion is surprising in two ways. It is unexpected both in its message and in its plausibility. He has looked at the time, long gone, when animal life came out of the sea and occupied the great land masses. Now he raises his eyes to a future when the restless, questing, adventurous pressure of the Life Process moves off the Earth to occupy the solar system, and possibly even realms beyond that. So he sees the cultural counterpart of that paradigm in the enormous development and success of the literature of Science Fiction.

There is a great deal more in the book, which is packed with detailed stories, fables, parables and subtle metaphors coming from a man who is clearly a generalist polymath, and one with an impressive grasp of Mankind's enormous brand-new unexploited database, that arising from modern biology.

**By Victor Serebriakoff**
*Series Editor*
*Frontiers in Thought Series*

# 1

# PROLOGUE – HUMANITY IN A NEW EVOLUTIONARY CONTEXT

I hope that this book is an explanation. We, men and women and children, are puzzling creatures for biologists, and this is my attempt to explain both our successes and our failures from a new biological perspective. I do not intend to provide an "Explanation of Man", nor to imply that our behaviour is "Determined Biologically". Nor do I intend to prophecy. Science-fiction writers, among whom I count many close friends, have done that job well, and I believe it to be more important than we used to think. I present a new context in which to understand our evolution. Because it re-labels erstwhile heroes and villains, it enables all of us to take out our prejudices and re-examine them, give them a dusting over, perhaps replace them in the same mental category or a new one. It is an *interesting* new context, by which I mean that it has the potential to change minds. Some of you may even change your minds, and perhaps other people's too. That is my intention. Certainly this book will take your mind to new places. As with any package tour, I hope that you *are* changed and that you enjoy the excursion.

This first chapter is a prologue and an overview, a travel brochure and itinerary, to provide an introduction to my view of the problem and to serve as a guide to my way of presenting it. The thesis proper of the book starts in Chapter 2, and if you are the kind of person who skips Prologues and Introductions, or comes back to them later, I suggest you now go on to page 11.

I did originally intend only to provide a biological context for our cultural evolution, like so many other recent books, from Ardrey's *Territorial Imperative* to Dawkins' *Blind Watchmaker*. In the attempt, much of my biology fell into unaccustomed but attractive patterns. Some were anticipated, even sketched out, in my book *Reproduction* in 1977. That book was well-received by both colleagues and critics, so I have now built a rather more detailed account which I hope exposes both my reasoning and my prejudices to a wider audience, for further criticism. I trust that the design of this account will not upset the biologically informed layman, or the professional biologist, despite my (I hope confessed) unorthodoxy in some areas. Equally, I hope that my major points and arguments are accessible to those who are less informed about modern biology. I have given some of the biological examples in detail so that I can educate, inform, as well as persuade. Ideally, I would like to think that this

1

book will provide another "public" set of assumptions and principles, congruent with (some... ) modern biological thought, from which we may all find new understanding of, and new prescriptions for, some of the frustrations and indeed tragedies of our society.

I am a biologist who has specialised in the study of reproduction, particularly the development of animals from fertilisation to adulthood. I have for the last thirty or so years drawn a salary for teaching this. I have been employed at a large British university to teach it, mostly in a general zoological context, to undergraduates. During this time, I produced several text-books and many research papers and reviews, and trained a succession of post-graduates; by the standards of the profession, I was fairly successful. I now believe much of this task to be at worst nonsensical, and at least ill-conceived, and many of its relationships to be unethical, and have taken up other work instead. The chapter headings of this book suggest why.

However, I also gave many lectures to schools and public audiences, and became professionally involved with other areas, including science fiction. So I needed, while teaching, to explain to myself the paradox of the progressive withdrawal of my colleagues in the teaching profession from social involvement, which was very obvious during the term of my lectureship. The transmission of culture across the generations, like the transmission of genetic instructions or parasites, should be part of the professional concern of the reproductive biologist. So I observed the professor in his ivory tower, whose lectures frequently were totally divorced from his students' needs or interests, and the infant teacher whose children failed to acquire such socially necessary skills as reading. Both posed as transmitters of our culture across the generations – and I had to account for this, both in my reproductive biology and to my friends in other professions. Social irresponsibility of teachers was explained during the time of student unrest in the sixties, by such authors as Illich, Marcuse and Foucault, as the inevitable dropping of standards in any self-regulating profession, protecting the incompetents in its ranks. In contrast it seemed to me, a biologist not a sociologist, to form a necessary, pivotal process heralding a remarkable change in direction: I saw this disengagement of the vectors of education as part of our cultural evolution, not simply as social pathology. Indeed, it seemed to me that the progressive withdrawal of our cultural transmission from the "physiology" of our everyday competences might parallel the sequestration of hereditary material during three previous biological "revolutions". I would like to share this perspective with you, in the hope that any usefulness it may acquire can be translated into action, in design of cities and the rearing of children, rather than simply finding its way into new sociology books as an interesting fantasy.

Because I am concerned to give the story clearly, and to expose my arguments and bases as much as possible, I will give an outline of the "plot" here. Chapter 2 briefly looks at the origins and evolution of terrestrial life. What are the levels of organisation of life on this planet, and how long did it take for each organisation to evolve into the next? Are there general rules about such evolutionary steps, and how do we go about sorting them out? Because a bacterial grade of organisation dominated the first three quarters of Earth's history so far, and intelligence of our kind has been here for such a brief moment, can we pick out "likelihoods" or is it all just a matter of chance, of cookie-crumbling? Two lessons emerge from that greatest step in evolutionary advance, upward from the bacterial grade: that several disparate organisms *combined in a symbiosis* to produce the first eukaryote cells, and that *reproductive function was restricted to nucleus*, sequestered from the physiology.

I then proceed to reproductive issues. All organisms pass *much* more than simple genetic "instructions", DNA, to their offspring. Even the simplest forms of life, the viruses, do not have only genetic material, DNA, passing across the generations; proteins made according to maternal-generation instructions are provided for each viral particle, and are vitally necessary for the progeny to infect new cells. Similarly, bacterial daughter "cells" receive all the decoding machinery, all the metabolic machinery and "cell" walls, from the maternal organism, as well as their specific DNA ring. All this inherited machinery is necessary for the DNA to *say* anything at all. However, the converse view is usually found in biological popularisations, that DNA is *all* that is required to inform the new organism how to make itself. This issue is taken up in several places, both because it is interesting in its own right and because I need to show you how "higher" organisms inherit more and more, additional to DNA. "Extra-genetic evolution" is not a new phenomenon, then, invented only recently by our ancestors. Our remarkable form of it, cultural evolution, can be illuminated by comparison with other, simpler forms of extra-genetic inheritance, even by those of bacteria.

Higher organisms all pass biochemical machinery, working metabolism and, to a greater or lesser extent food material and other energy stores, to their offspring in addition to the genetic material DNA. These stores, represented by yolk, milk or even a paralysed spider left by a mother wasp for her progeny to eat, represent "profit" from the parents' physiological transactions with the environment, "invested" as "capital" for the offspring. I compounded this capitalist analogy, in my *Reproduction* book, by calling all such non-genetic but parentally-dependent inheritance "privilege", extending the use of this word from human to lower forms of animal life. Having made this extension of the concept of privilege out of the narrow cultural sense into a wider, more universal biological one, then the origin of culture itself can be explained in this wider context. Further, puzzles about the reproduction of cultures, and especially the *restriction of reproductive routes* within them, make a new kind of sense.

In nearly all animals, early development is entirely organised by informational molecules made on maternal patterns during the development of the egg cell in the mother's ovary. More complex organisms usually invest more in their offspring, and control their early development by more maternal instructions. The offspring's own genetics only takes over when development is well started, when the basic pattern has been roughed out. Early development is, of course, *fuelled* by parental donation as well as organised by it – embryos don't have to find their own food! Because the early development of complex organisms is privileged as regards both developmental instructions and food material, it can take developmental routes which would otherwise have been non-viable, just as the human baby couldn't make its own way but is "carried" through this helpless stage by adults. The trick of using parental abilities to cosset development, from the early organisation through viviparity into nests, allows further privilege to be exploited by helpless offspring: those mammals (and, of course, birds) which release helpless "late embryos" into nests permit *learning* by these juveniles from the parents, a new route of transmission of information across the generations. This sensori-motor route has many of the advantages a Lamarckian genetic system might have: it can produce a one-generation adaptive response to a new predator trick, for example, or to a new food source, when parents *teach* offspring. (But it has few of the Lamarckian disadvantages: accumulation of the effects of all the traumas during the parental lifetime, and mandatory passage of this to the offspring, for example.) I look at several new ideas about the acquisition of culture by each human child, and promote the view that animal images in nursery and myth form a necessary framework for the construction of a cultured personality; while not integral to my main thesis, this view has its own attractions.

The reproductive view, furthermore, makes a consistent picture of the whole story of evolution of human culture, from this humble beginning right through to urban life with a separate educator cadre. It is certainly a viable alternative to the "Once upon a time there was a nerve cell.... flatworms have the faint beginnings of a brain ... and then we achieved Goethe ..." story. In order to tell this story in its new dress, however, I judged it important not to confuse the issues with contemporary anthropological argument and jargon, so I use the old Morgan "tribal" ("savage"), "barbarian", "citizen" series. I do this partly because it is a useful simplification, free of most modern associations. But mostly I do so because I picked up this idea from John Campbell Jr. (long-time editor of *Astounding Science Fact/Fiction*, later *Analog*), with whom I first discussed the questions of university ivory towers in these terms; he was committed to this old-fashioned Morgan view, and one should be true to one's sources.

The differentiation of roles within urban cultures has many seductive similarities to the differentiation of the cells, tissues, and organs of the metazoan body – we have built-in reinforcements to this view in word-and-idea usage ("head" of a firm, "arm" of government). I use this metaphor carefully, to define the "germplasm" of human cultures; this is a concept close to Coleridge's "clerisy" (his "National Church"), those cultured people who passed the best elements of a human culture down to the next generation. Dawkins, in his popular book *The Selfish Gene*, made an extended comparison of this very kind, inventing a name for the elements of this transmission, "memes", analogous to the "genes" of the more biological heredity. These memes are ideas and idea-complexes, catchy tunes or Christian ethics (and of course the "meme" idea itself ... ), which multiply, compete, and evolve using human culture as their substrate, their environment, their resource. Planting the idea that the cultural germplasm, transmitted by the clerisy, has many "selfish meme" elements which must be controlled, I then turn to the educational paradox. I use a variety of examples and arguments to show that this amazingly successful use of privilege/culture by human societies creates affluence, surplus and, *because the "clerisy" withdraws from the "working class"*, creates deprivation, lack of privilege, in every successful society.

De*priv*ation is a concept homologous, in this new view of biological privilege, to de*form*ation in lower organisms: genetic (or environmental) defect produces deformation; cultural/maternal (or environmental) defect produces deprivation. Both genetic and cultural (memetic) inputs are required to produce people. "What", I asked in my textbook *Reproduction*, "passes between the generations to reproduce a Frenchman"? The expected answer needed genes, biochemistry, care in a womb and a bassinet – but also myths, mores and manners.

The middle chapters examine the enormous and apparent, cultural and material, success of urban life from this reproductive viewpoint. They point to paradoxes, too, within its structures and associations which are more explicable in the new view: most notably, the deprivations of affluence are as manifest as those of poverty. They derive in part, in our society at least, from the progressive isolation of education from other professional and cultural activities. It is quarantined in schools and universities, away from the flow of life. "I can't teach Johnny to read," says his mother "it'll make it difficult for him at school with their proper new methods.....". At a higher level, dogfish (rejected as food, except as "rock salmon", so unknown to most people) are the classical biology textbook fish – not herring, cod or even goldfish, which everyone has *seen*. The educators retain their mystique thereby, excluding Johnny's mother but making the university biologist privy to the special ritual of the formalined, tail-less dogfish.....

By these tricks, this mystique, the educational cadre has succeeded in forcing (almost...) all of society to accept its special rules for status, acceptability. These, usually as Public Examinations, have now largely supplanted previous nepotic standards of acceptability ("My family is financially OK, and we'll look after you too, now you've married our Esther...."), at least in the U.K. and the U.S.A. As technical and material privilege increased, so the educational process became progressively sequestered and ritualised, emphasising and examining skills unrelated to the workings of the urban community in daily life. There are other less obvious but similar trends, which in several affluent societies can be seen to have separated a series of small-but-powerful professional elites. Ivan Illich called attention to this process in both medicine and education, and called for a "de-schooling" of society to free us from control by these cadres. "Schools" in the Illich sense divide professionals both from the majority of people and from the educational/cultural strands related to *their own professions*. So the lawyer cannot manage the mechanics of selling his own house, while his low-status secretary can, and you would be well advised to get yourself bandaged by the low-status nurse, not the high-status medical specialist.

I relate these paradoxical trends to deep-seated and basic cultural attitudes, with their roots in an ancient biological dissonance, the contradictions of sexual and survival necessities. Animals usually separate the reproductive processes from the rest of their living. The contradictions for animals are usually explicit: camouflage protects you from predators and prey, but also hides you from your mate and mother; protective spines or shell (as in porcupines or tortoises) promote survival, but make copulation very difficult! So animals usually separate reproductive and vegetative activities into different seasons or even different individuals (like queen bees). Likewise, human cultures have adopted different strategies to separate sexual/reproductive from economic activities. The complication here is that reproduction is sex but it's also teaching. For women, especially, the demands of cultural and sexual reproduction bring about peculiar contortions in different societies; as an example, the girl growing up in an Islamic enclave within a European city is taught to be sexually attractive but *not* available, while her school-friends in the majority culture take the converse solution to the social equation: they are available but not (in her terms) attractive. For all of us, sex-as-bond is confused by sex-as-recreation and especially by sex-in-economic-exploitation, further complicated by the high economic value of sex-as-recreation to most human beings. Sex-as-procreation, as child-production, has often been culturally overlaid with child-labour values and the inheritance of land use. Human sexual contradictions remain all over our societies. Think of the poor integration of the concubine and gigolo roles, for example, in other-than-Hollywood Western societies, and more seriously of the emancipation of women from child-minder roles.

These sexual examples, while evocative and attractive to a (male) reproductive biologist, could be misleading as paradigms just because they are so physiologically – and culturally – basic, tied to strong emotions. I have used these examples because much of my professional expertise is in this area, and I believe that much can be learnt of the interaction between human cultural and biological constraints by examination of these ancient, powerful patterns. In current Western literature, for example, there is a considerable pressure to avoid "sexist" language, to pretend so far as is possible that all human roles are equally open to both sexes. By using sexual-difference examples, perhaps to be expected in a reproductive biologist promoting a reproductive paradigm of human society, it could be that I have offended your sense of the "proper" in my argument. I have, for example, been rather naughty about sexual pronouns throughout. I was brought up on the "he includes she" rule, but don't like it a bit because of its asymmetry – I read the lovely series of articles putting "she" instead of "he" everywhere and found them very provoking. *But*, although I use plurals and some of the tricks, and have thrown in the occasional she-lawyer and he-secretary, these practices make it much more difficult for me to say what I mean. So don't be put off by my sexist language. I genuinely do regret the asymmetry. But I am not going to pretend that the human genders are in every sense the same. No woman could have written this book, because no woman could have had the experiences and hang-ups I've had about sex and reproduction, in my life, which has given me these views and these examples. Nor could a Welshman, or a Yoruba of either sex. I value difference, I *don't* avoid it or demote it.

The final position is optimistic. Our super-species has produced a vast cultural ecology, a sea of memes, in which the major influences on survival and change in each society come from *cultural* constraints within and without, *not* from the biological, geological or chemical worlds' substrates. The next, more stable level of organisation of our kind of organism is the multicultural association with many cultural clades, not only many specialities or many genetic ancestries (a clade is a branch of the family tree). Many kinds of simpler organisms – bacteria, protozoans, simple metazoans and simple colonial animals – can and do live autonomously *inside* the termite colony, which has an organisation one level higher. So, more primitive human social associations can and do co-exist with, even in, multicultural cladic societies, with advantages for both in the continued relationship. I show how some of the paradoxes, especially of education but also of sexual/social mores, disappear in truly multicultural societies. As we achieve yet higher levels of integration of social diversity, however, they will doubtless be replaced by other kinds of problems as yet unimagined.

The philosophical assumptions upon which this optimism are based depend upon analogy between different levels of organisation, and so are subject to Russell-Whitehead kinds of criticism: orchards, even bags of apples, have different rules from those used for one juicy pippin. The series prokaryote < eukaryote < multicellular organism < colony/pack < tribal community < urban community < multicultural symbiosis may usefully be thought of as having subset<set relationships at every level. That in itself does not guarantee that the emergent properties of the sets can ever be predicted from the subsets. But they might, I think, if we can discover common properties of *all* the steps of the whole series. So it might be a very useful explanatory strategy to present analogies between the successive jumps to new levels of living organisation. If, as I hope to show, there *is* real similarity at each level in such abstractions as "*differentiate subsets for different function*" and especially "*quarantine the hereditary material*", I could then claim real homology, a set of general rules for this kind of evolutionary step. Perhaps all morphostats (Serebriakoff), at whatever level, advance by such tricks. If, as I suspect, managerial courses have not tumbled to this yet, they also may have something to learn from philosophical biology.

The underpinning of the views presented in this book, then, is not a *theory*, for in truth I have no coherent idea why hereditary functions should so generally be sequestered. (Although I can see advantages when they *have* been.) Certainly it is not a *scientific* theory; it is a new scientific viewpoint, which I hope will generate theories. It is a sociological paradigm, too, informed by concepts from reproductive biology, especially the idea of reproductive stability. Bourdieu, a French sociologist, and Cohen, an English reproductive biologist, both produced books called *Reproduction*, within months of each other, in 1977 (his was an English translation of an older, 1971, book). We actually outlined very similar ideas within a kind of suspicion-of-education paradigm, but in sociology or biology. For all I know, Bourdieu may be writing a companion to this volume as I sit here!

Comparisons between nature and human nature are too often seen as between Nature and Human Nature, and to embody David Hume's "Pathetic Fallacy"; that is, in this context, to be *prescriptive*. You might assume that when I say something *is*, I mean that it *ought* to be – I often don't, however, so do try to keep the distinction open. For example, I try to show that the more advanced societies sequester their clerisy as the more advanced animals sequester their germ cells; don't suppose this to be approving of ivory towers, Church Latin and the exclusion of women from the clergy. Again, I guess that a multicultural city like Birmingham or New York is balanced by its *differences* of culture, rather than by the lowest-common-denominator philosophy of its political wards or educational establishments; I am *not* recommending black ghettos and the Klan persecution of ethnic minorities. As a further detailed example of this incorrect assumption of *ought* for *is*, consider the menstrual cycle of women. The normal physiological state of primitive, and so perhaps all, women was – and is – to alternate pregnancy and lactation, with very rare menstrual periods. This biological view does not contradict the (entirely valid) belief that modern Western women should not be like that. I show you that something *is* so. This is not prescriptive, but it should help put you, the reader, into a better position to be prescriptive successfully. Some of my attempts to present the facts use metaphors and far-fetched analogies; these are communication tools, not injunctions, moral statements or prescriptions. They should present you with new options, based in a new view of human reality.

I finish this book with a set of perspectives, presented as a set of alternate futures, and some questions. New insights into the importance of symbiosis in previous evolutionary advances seem to apply to this latest and greatest, cultural symbiosis on a world-wide scale. I do think that we are now at the most critical, the pivotal time for our human way of life. I mean *all* of us, in the West as our National Debts are being exposed, in Russia in this time of *glasnost*, in China now that the doors are creaking open to permit foreigners in, in the Pacific exploitation of electronic technology and of the mineral wealth of Australia. My new viewpoint of the mechanisms of human evolution puts all of us unambiguously at the threshold of a new Way of Life, and we have choices to make. I would like to see a variety of different choices actually made, in different places for different peoples, and I hope that no one will "win". We must each now *nominate* or *identify* a new clerisy, a sub-group of our people with the wisdom and stability to carry our ideals of the multi-cultural human society, with its cultures intact and reproducing, into our unknown future. This could form a new, stable reproducing entity, a real – but heterogeneous – *World Culture* which builds the strengths of all human cultures into its structure. However, Islam or democracy or communism could each prevent the attainment of a culture which permits *all* of them to flourish. The choice of transmitter of our disparate cultures into the future will determine how this next step is taken, how many sub-cultures survive. Nominate the teachers of your children; act now to guide your part of your society into your preferred future.

I have not listed the options here. I don't want you to consider these, my set of options, until you come to them with some idea of the reason for my choice. Initially I conceived the book as presenting the viewpoint and leaving *you* to list the options, but my editor persuaded me to take off the last veil during the performance, to give value for money. Continuing that analogy, it would of course be quite inappropriate to exhibit the most delicate and climactic feat at the end of the overture. I warn you here, therefore, that Chapter 15 has deliberately been made opaque from outside, but I hope transparent to the informed eye.

Sociology, like medicine, is a speciality within biology. I go to the doctor when I'm ill, and I go to the professional sociologist when I'm puzzled about civilisation. I am quite a good reproductive biologist, but I have to suppose that I am as poor at sociology – or medicine – as my sociologist colleagues are at reproductive biology. So, when my biological insights generate sociological statements, I must air them for criticism; this book is the outcome.

# 2

# THE FIRST ORGANISMS CAPTURE
# THE FUTURE – BY SYMBIOSIS

Once upon a time, long long ago, there were no stories. Symbolism and imagery are the necessary basis for all myths and stories, and they appeared for the first time on this planet when our own ancestors, primeval Man, constructed and expanded verbal language during the last five million years. Before that, some large-brained mammals may have communicated with their young about absent events, and chains of ideas may have had ephemeral existence. But before sixty million years ago, it is overwhelmingly probable that there were no ideas with an existence separate from the immediate stimuli which caused them to appear in brains and inform their owners. A thousand million years ago, there were no animals, few cellular organisms at all, certainly no ideas. Yet life had existed on Earth for three times that, three thousand million years, and had produced a great array of immensely complicated life forms – but these were only about as complex as modern bacteria. They showed many and diverse functions; they competed, and in their survival Purposes could be attributed to their Functions. Before that there was, briefly in those terms, *no* life on the planet; then, there were not even functions, nor purposes, no ideas and no stories. How did function, purpose, ideas and stories appear on the Earth?

The earliest living things were local reproducing patterns of the complex chemistry of carbon, hydrogen, oxygen, nitrogen, sulphur and phosphorus. They may have been organised, set up in their complicated workings, to further the preservation of competing patterns in the clay substrates which catalysed them[1], or they may have arisen in remarkable but common circumstances like molten volcanic lava pouring into the sea. In any event, they were no more interesting, then, than the myriads of other chemical reactions changing the surface of the early Earth. What distinguished the chemistry which led to life was circularity, feedback, recursion: each reaction affected some other process which led through a series of steps back to control of itself. This is by no means a strange property; chemists now realise that most of the ordinary "test-tube" reactions depend on catalysts, often scratches or dirt on the side of the tube and then circles within the reactions themselves. The special property of the pre-living chemistry was that these feedbacks were such as to *keep the set-up going*, instead of hastening it to some kind of completion or exhaustion. Several such

11

systems have been invented by chemists (and especially by the biologist Winfree[2]), and they share the same apparent necessities: an energy source (often one of the original compounds is broken down to yield energy which keeps the system going); a reaction whose rate is controlled by a product of a "later" reaction in the system; and an end product which diffuses away (carbon dioxide diffusing into air from a liquid, for example), or spontaneously decomposes.

A very familiar example of chemistry which shows all these is the rusting of wet iron; this is started by some very fancy electrochemistry: water with dissolved oxygen and carbon dioxide is split by electrochemical currents between different iron crystals, at the interface of water and iron. The system is powered by free oxygen combining with the iron, and then maintained by electrochemical complexes at the junctions of ferric and ferrous carbonates, hydroxides and oxides with the iron crystals. In today's world there are usually bacteria helping the process along, and taking their tithe of the energy transactions involved, but rust can "feed on itself" in sterile circumstances too. So the original pre-life chemistry, like the rusting of iron or Art Winfree's beautiful pattern-making solutions, showed *complexity arising from simplicity*: as the implicit rules of the simple system were twisted into loops and rings, recursions, by the energy powering the system, they produced both spatial and temporal patterns of great complexity *and stability*. This seems counter-intuitive, unbelievable to many people, and I urge them to look up Winfree's papers in *Scientific American*[2] or *Nature*[3], and preferably to collude with a chemist friend to actually *do* the experiments; the chemicals are cheap, the methods only involve simple mixing of solutions, the effects are robust, and the results are dramatic both in their beauty and in the change of philosophies which they induce!

There have been many plausible proposals about the looped pre-life chemistry which led to such marvellous things on this planet. I prefer the ideas of Graham Cairns-Smith, who has emphasised the "high-technology" nature of all the life forms living now, even the simplest. As a candidate for the original, primeval life-chemistry, he has suggested clays; these mineral structures have complex geometry and chemistry, and compete for many of the same substrates as they dissolve and re-form their complex crystal systems. He proposed that long organic polymers, perhaps both nucleic acids (RNA and DNA) and proteins were used by replicating *clay* systems to stabilise their structure[1]: those clay crystal structures which used, and perhaps catalysed the formation of, these long organic props to maintain their structures lasted longer, and were more successful in competition for their chemical substrates.

There are many clays today which show behaviour very close to this, and this inorganic version of proto-life is a very convincing picture. Cairns-Smith suggested that "genetic take-over" occurred, replacing or at least supplementing the inorganic heredities of the clays with sophisticated organic chemistry. I imagine large areas of slime-covered clays, in estuaries, and deep in the eroding rocks, and on the sea floor. Some kinds of such hereditary chemistry must have increased their kind, others failed. Those kinds which increased produced variants, because the heredity was not stable – replication of linear hereditary molecules may have been a late event – and because local conditions often favoured heterogeneity – diverse, disparate energy-sources would decrease competition, for example. Some of the newer, more heterogeneous systems came to include larger areas of slime-covered clay, or more oily droplets on the surface of the wet clay at the sea's edge. According to Cairns-Smith's scenario, the long organic molecules of most use in stabilising clay heredities were proteins and nucleic acids, and the clays would have catalysed this polymerisation *in the clay's interest*, not the organic molecule's. These molecules, initially the tools of the clays, began to partake of the catalytic processes too. Then the dual systems were progressively "taken over" by the organic components. There is a distinct resonance with the way *our* silicon-based tools are beginning to take over their own construction and design, isn't there? Perhaps, indeed, carbon-based life is just an interlude between silicon-based clays and silicon-based computers..... Whether or not, our story here is (initially at least) about the evolution of carbon-based life forms.

Eventually, some of these systems became/produced discrete organisms, which reproduced their kinds and competed with other, different or similar, organisms. Many plausible routes towards organised life have been suggested, and many were doubtless tried. An early invention was doubtless a set of proteins (or perhaps clay surfaces with adsorbed organic chemistry) which held on to rare molecules or ions, and sometimes catalysed reactions which promoted the local synthetic chemistry. Biological *function* had appeared, and from that time onward *purpose* could be ascribed to function; these words require, for their meanings, that we can distinguish success from failure. Even these most simple forms of life succeeded by breeding, or (usually) failed by becoming extinct. Some of these early organisms, for example, developed an oily membrane which kept the outside sea out and kept a special internal medium inside, with its rare, energetic or specially synthesised chemistry. This membrane had function, its purpose was to keep the media apart, and its degree of success at this task was measurable. Its prevalence was the contemporary measure of its success, wasn't it?

It is most important to understand that these functions, their purposes and their successes and failures, were the counters in the competition between these early organisms.   In pre-life chemistry, there had been competition for chemicals or energy between the arrays of chemical reactions, but there was no sense in which this *mattered*.  This simple substrate competition continued, of course, as part of the lowest level of competition between the new hereditary types.  But once function arose, with consequence for future competition and therefore with purpose, this new level became the major arbiter of success.  The functions, not atoms, compounds, or energy, were now the counters in an ever-complicating world of competition.   The determinants of more efficient function, carried by the more efficient organisms they prescribed, became the *genes*, which in turn largely determined the structure – and functional success – of the progeny of these organisms.

In the earliest true (carbon-based) organisms, these genes were probably a double linear series of nucleotides forming DNA (or more likely RNA) chains, much like those of modern viruses and even bacteria.  The gene-replicating machinery, and even the mechanisms by which the gene sequence influenced other properties of these earliest organisms, may have been *external* to the organismic system itself, in at least some of the organisms.  Catalytic clay crystal arrays, or other bits of organic chemistry, may have been needed. Modern viruses are certainly not modern unchanged descendants of these ancient forms.  But viruses, like these oldest life forms, only prescribe a few proteins (up to a hundred) from their own genes;  much of the replicating and protein-synthetic machinery is supplied from outside – in the case of viruses, from the host cell.  If the machinery could have been incorporated as part of the working primeval organism, more reliability would have been achieved. We now know that some sequences of RNA itself can serve as catalyst for rep-lication, splicing and excision reactions  of RNA chains.  Some people have imagined that RNA-organisms, doing it all for themselves like some kind of writhing, knotted replicating string, were an early step in our kind of life.  I don't find this homogeneous kind of model attractive, but I have no doubt that this self-catalysis property has been useful to our primitive ancestors at many stages.

There are, of course, many advantages to possessing your own tools, even if they're not of the highest quality.  Even less-good catalytic machinery, but *inside* the organism, could promote more reliable replication, and it could be functionally more co-operative with other functions.   Furthermore and most significantly, as soon as the prescription of this machinery becomes part of the internal heredity, it can be improved by the success of those organisms which have better versions, and the failure of the less effective systems. While it is outside, borrowed from the environment as it were, the organism can only take what's on offer. Internal, replication-dependent systems, *even if they are initially less effective*, can be improved over the generations (provided that the organisms concerned are not initially competing with others using the outside, better, system, of course). Furthermore, systems and sub-systems would arise which would give some control over *when* functions could be prescribed. Modern bacteria, like the ancient bacteria, exploit this encapsulation of replication and determination-of-function inside one envelope. Some modern bacteria, especially the so-called archaeobacteria[4], are direct and representative descendants of these early forms. Bacteria have many more genes than viruses, much more prescribing information in their heredity, and thousands of different proteins are made, including those involved in their protein-synthetic and their gene-replicating machinery. This produces a new level of recursion, more feedback mechanisms *inside* the system, which are involved in the control of *which* system is operating. For example, in most spore-forming bacteria reproductive and physiological options are complementary. That is to say, each is emphasised at the expense of the other: they breed *or* they feed. The suite of functions necessary for reproduction precludes the ordinary processes of living.

For three-quarters of the history of our planet so far, this relatively simple pattern was all the life there was, but in exorbitant, prodigious variety[4]. Already, there was some segregation of the reproductive functions from the ordinary physiological processes of living, and we shall see this in greatly exaggerated form in subsequent evolutionary advances. One such early form became *autotrophic*, providing its own special power "generator" from within its own chemical resources. (Like other systems we call "generators", this was really a transducer, turning one form of energy into another, more readily utilised, form.) It invented chlorophyll and its associated chemistry, using the energy of sunlight to power the cells' machinery and so becoming the first successful plants. Other organisms invented other light-traps or chemical-energy-traps, and some have survived to modern times by riding the surf of chemical reactions, especially those of sulphur and iron in anaerobic muds. In ancient seas, their similar ancestors probably exploited the reactions of oxide-containing rocks with the reducing atmosphere. It is some of the modern descendants of these forms which win energy by rusting our iron and steel artefacts. Their ancestors, however, were actually responsible for most of the high-quality iron ore from which we smelt the metal; not only that, but the original Iron-Age invention seems to have been dependent upon just this ancient iron-working bacterium!  So, when you regret the rust eating away at your car body so expensively, think of it as a small penalty to pay for having available iron in the first place.  Biotechnology preceded engineering!

Chlorophyll reactions, and perhaps others that released oxygen, were very successful, but they produced the greatest pollution the Earth has ever known: oxygen was – in that ecology – a violently reactive, poisonous gas, and when excreted by these early inventors must have caused the demise of nearly all other life forms!  The early Earth atmosphere must have been nearly oxygen-free;  certainly it was a reducing atmosphere, with nitrogen, methane, some hydrogen, carbon dioxide and a great variety of friendly not-very-reactive gases like ammonia and hydrogen cyanide (not friendly *now*, to *our* kinds of life!).  The oxygen pollution happened relatively slowly, however, and the forms which survived had either changed radically or were confined to environments where something like the old oxygen-free environments could be relied on, in black estuarine muds for example.  An interesting "conservation area" for these primeval archaeobacteria has been discovered, where Man has unwittingly recreated their old environment, free of oxygen and ripe with ammonia and methane.  They have been found, living their ancient life of ammoniated anaerobiosis, free from the polluting oxygen excreted by the upstart Plants – under the ancient(?) urinals of Caernavon Castle!

These early plants were immensely successful, and massive aggregations of them dominated the shallow seas of the early Earth.  They lived on tidal flats, as many modern algae do, in clumps which became coated with clays and muds;  then more algae were deposited on the growing lump, until great laminated masses, metres or even tens of metres across, were formed.  Successful as these early plants were – they make the most dramatic very ancient fossils, beds of stromatolites – they made themselves a very real problem.  Few organisms can live in an atmosphere of their own waste products, and they were forced to change in order to live in the progressively oxygenated environment.  Not only did they make (nearly) all other organisms change, become oxygen-tolerant;  they changed as well, to become the most successful autotrophs in the new aerobic environment too.

The way in which this was done is, I think, most instructive:  here beginneth the First Lesson.  Most biologists now agree that the most successful adaptation to this oxygen "pollution", *evolutionary symbiosis*, was instrumental in the origin of the eukaryote cell.

Before I sermonise upon this first important step in my story, I must make sure that both "symbiosis" and "eukaryote" are part of our common vocabulary. *Definition* of words, as we'll see later, is usually not useful;  here I'll *describe* what I mean by these two. ("Description" addresses the central, common part of the meaning, "definition" is concerned with the edges, with exclusion/inclusion.) Symbiosis means, literally, living together and it has had several usages in biology. Originally, and very recently, it has been used to cover *all* the ways in which organisms have lives which impinge upon each other – only food relations were not usually called symbiosis by most biologists, but all kinds of co-habiting from extreme and destructive parasitism to the use of a dead animal's shell, or a tree for a nest, have been called symbiosis. I *don't* want this wide usage, now adopted by professional ecologists. Popularly, and for most of the last hundred years among professional biologists too, it has been *contrasted* with parasitism, as a *benevolent* association. Lichens, formed by the association of an alga and a fungus (and *much* more hardy than either), were the classic example, but the bacteria living in cows' and termites' guts (which enable digestion of grass), the algal cells *in* the cells of animals as diverse as corals and giant clams (which enable them to make sugars in light), the anemones which live on whelk shells inhabited by hermit crabs, dogs in the household of Man – all have provided text-book examples. These, where both partners benefit, have been contrasted with parasitism, where one partner takes at the expense of the other; commensalism has been used for the casual associations to which neither partner gives much. I wish here to use the *popular*, not the recent ecological, meaning of symbiosis: benevolent association, at least in one direction, and usually and apparently benefiting both or all.

Now to our other word, eukaryote; this is biologists' jargon, but necessary jargon here because crucial to the understanding of my arguments. I must digress to explain it, because the very important distinction the word makes is not of explicit concern in most people's everyday life and language but is very necessary to my argument here. *Eu-karyote* means "proper-", or "genuine-" nucleus, and refers to the presence in (nearly) all cells of these organisms of a real nucleus. This contains the chromosomes, which have not only DNA but also many proteins and some other molecules; division of these cells to produce daughters (nearly) always employs a complicated process called mitosis which apportions the replicated chromosomes properly, (usually) equally into the daughters. We are eukaryotes, so are oak trees, so are *Paramecia*, malaria parasites, fishes, flies and lichens.

Bacteria, of all kinds, are not; they do *not* have chromosomes, they have a ring of (nearly) naked DNA attached to the wall of the organism, and no mitosis. Nor are cyanobacteria, blue-green bacteria (which used to be called blue-green algae) – they have no nucleus, no chromosomes; but they look like the eukaryote, thread-like algae which also infest farm ponds and tropical fish tanks, and were thought to be related to them, rather than bacteria, until the immense importance of "having a nucleus" was realised in the last twenty years or so.    Blue-green bacteria, pathogenic bacteria like *Streptococcus* which infects wounds (especially in hospitals in cities), spirochetes (most of which live innocuous, helpful lives in polluted water but one of which, *Treponema pallidum*, causes syphilis), *Archaeobacteria*, like the *Halobacteria* of hot saline ponds and the *Methanobacteria* (found with them in the hot sub-oceanic rift "smokers"), all the smaller, simpler creatures like *Rickettsia*'s, down to the grossly simplified viruses in all their variety, are called "prokaryotes".   This is certainly an "umbrella" word, covering a great variety of unlike things.   As "invertebrates" means "animals without backbones" – but with *nothing* else interesting in common – whereas "vertebrates" denotes a natural group of closely-related animals with a dorsal nerve cord, haemoglobin in the blood, and lots more in common, so "prokaryotes" aren't unitary, but "eukaryotes" could be.   It happens that we now think that the eukaryote condition arose several times by association of prokaryotes, so there are actually several kinds of eukaryote too.   Actinomycetes living in compost heaps, and the red algae so common on the sea-shore may be different "eukaryote" lines (different symbiotic associations from us and oak trees), with nuclei and a kind of mitotic cell division but very different in other respects.

The sloppiness comes in the use of that vital biological word, *cell*.   So many biology text-books now write of the "bacterial cell" or the "bacterial cell wall" or even the "bacterial chromosome" when they don't mean that at all, that it is certainly hopeless to try to reform the professional usage.   Let us at least be correct here.   "Cell" refers to the nucleated mass of cytoplasm, with mitochondria and other organelles, which is a part of a multi-cellular eukaryote animal or plant, and by extension to eukaryote protozoans like *Amoeba* and uni-cellular eukaryote plants like *Chlamydomonas. It should not be used to refer to any of the prokaryotes listed in the last paragraph!* They are not cells, do not have cells, and have a quite different kind, indeed different grade, of organisation from cells.   This is important to my argument, because the symbiosis by which prokaryotes produced cells has much to teach us about evolutionary advancement, and about grades of organisation.   So, more than the biochemistry or "Cell" Biology text-book, we must be clear when we mean "cell" (= eukaryote) and when we mean prokaryote.    Now let's get back to the evolutionary story.

The extraordinary complexity which later generated ideas and stories, and whose genesis we are chasing in this chapter, arose in organisms with a eukaryote, or "cellular" way of making themselves.   It was previously believed that the original eukaryotes arose by evolution from a particularly adventurous and forward-looking bacterium. But now, largely due to promotion by Lynn Margulis[4], there is a consensus that a *community* of bacterial-grade organisms formed early mixed colonies. Cells arose as *communities, prokaryotes in symbiosis*; some prokaryotes (which became modern mitochondria) dealt with oxygen metabolism and kept intra-cellular levels low, others became involved in locomotion, yet others specialised in reproducing this whole community structure and imported mitosis. Plant cells had, and have, self-reproducing prokaryote organisms – which we now know as chloroplasts – in their cells to exploit light energy; in so doing, they excrete their waste product – oxygen – on which all we animals are now so dependent.

In modern eukaryote cells like ours, the oak's and the *Amoeba*, there are several components which reflect their ancestry (but a major function, reproduction, which does not). The *mitochondria*, self-reproducing bacteria-like structures with their own DNA system, oxidise sugars and produce energy as the high-energy compound ATP (adenosine tri-phosphate) which has become an almost universal energy-currency in cellular organisms. *Centrioles* (whose replication is still mysterious) regulate part of the contractile protein system, and are concerned with functions as diverse as cilia and flagella, the mechanism of movement of chromosomes at cell division, and the reception of light by sensory elements. *Chloroplasts* are mentioned above (and we have now found modern prokaryote organisms which must be very like the old free-living chloroplast, and are closely related to them). Perhaps even the *centromeres* of chromosomes, which don't carry protein-synthesis messages but are concerned with chromosome integrity, are descendants of an ancient symbiotic viral-grade organism.

There are many prokaryotes (non-cellular organisms without a nucleus, like viruses, bacteria, and blue-green "algae") which have *not* teamed up with anyone else, but have adapted *solo* to the modern aerobic (oxygen-rich) existence. But nearly all of the successful forms of life today are based on that evolutionary symbiosis we call the Cell. Some biologists think that other successful forms, the red algae and the actinomycete "fungi" for example, are descendants of other symbiotic associations; their "cells" have different components from those of *Paramecium*, potatoes or people. Some amoebae, too, are not as closely related to other amoebae as their classification with them in the Phylum *Protozoa* would suggest. *Amoeba proteus* is one of a family of fairly big amoebae (0.1mm-0.3mm, just discernible to the naked eye), which live on the bacterial film which gives the reflective layer on the surface of undisturbed mud in old ponds; and there are hundreds of kinds of much tinier amoebae in the same ponds. All of these seem to share much the same lot of symbionts as you, me and the oak tree. But there are some giant amoebae (sometimes millimetres long) like the giant *Chaos* (*Pelomyxa*) and some of the "slime moulds", which use ordinary free-living species of bacteria instead of mitochondria. Several other protozoans have also got odd prokaryotes performing some of their cellular functions, and again some of these very same prokaryotes are found free-living. This "evolutionary symbiosis" trick was not a one-off, then, but has happened very many times in the past, and is even happening around you as you read this. The evolutionary advantages of symbiosis between very unlike partners will turn up again, in the last chapters of this book, and the evolutionary ubiquity of this trick must be emphasised here. It happened many times, and similar symbioses, even of eukaryote cells being incorporated into other eukaryotes, are going on right now on coral reefs, in saline desert and rain-forest floor.

Surprisingly, the function that does *not* show its symbiotic origins, in any of these modern eukaryote organisms, is reproduction. There are structures, ancient symbionts, concerned with many of the ordinary processes of life, and with some of the addenda of reproduction (like lugging chromosomes about). But the reproductive - especially the *hereditary* - apparatus is nearly always *isolated* in the *nucleus*, in all the kinds of eukaryotic symbiosis which have survived to the present. Red algae, actinomycete "fungi", perhaps other fungal groups, even *Chaos* are all derived from different gangs of symbionts, but all have nuclei of some kind – *Chaos* has thousands in each organism! Even many of the genes thought originally to have been on our mitochondrial DNA, and some of those essential for the working of the plants' chloroplasts, are now to be found in the cell's nucleus. *It is as if there were a positive advantage to keeping heredity out of the way of ordinary life processes.* We shall find this theme again and again, at each step of the evolutionary ladder. The organisation of the single unstructured cell, with its ancient symbionts trading abilities within the membrane, but with its heredity tucked away in its nucleus, does allow a full and active life; ask any amoeba....! Most animals, however, have divided the body up into parts associated with different functions – even most "single-cell" protozoa do so (but not *Amoeba*, of course). *Paramecium* is the classic, with different parts of its body structure specialised for feeding (gullet, oral groove and mouth), locomotion (the ciliated surface), excretion and osmotic-regulation (the contractile vacuoles) and perhaps for overall chemical control (the macro-nucleus) – but there are many which are much more complicated than her. Some of the more complicated protozoans, indeed, have a much more specialised body-structure than some of the simpler cellular creatures.

The most successful eukaryote way of specialising bits of the body, though, was to multiply the nucleus and to divide the original body into many cells, each with its own nucleus. These multicellular (perhaps more elegantly "cellular") animals are called *Metazoa*. The kinds we have around us now arose in several different ways, very early in the eukaryote evolutionary story. Many other ways of becoming cellular were probably tried, but have died out (just as several attempts at being a eukaryote were made, and only some survive). Usually (but not always) the parts are themselves made of cellular structures, specialised for specific function but all with the *same* nuclear instructions. So muscle cells make up muscles and hearts, nerve cells make ganglia and brains, gut tubes have a cellular lining specialised for digestion and absorption, and so on. This has several major advantages. A larger size becomes possible, useful for catching food, for controlling internal environment and for protection. There is the possibility of continuous production and loss of expendable cells in difficult situations like the skin and the gut lining. Most important, some cells can be specialised for reproduction, and the animals can reproduce several times – most protozoans can only reproduce once, into two similar (or four or eight different) daughter "cells".

The way in which the same instructions in each cell of a metazoan results in different properties, different function, is a story in itself. Here we should only note that in most metazoa the *germ cells*, which will produce the reproductive cells themselves and so carry the important hereditary information for future generations, are *segregated* in the gonads, testis or ovary, away from the specialised functions of the rest of the body. Unlike the situation in bacteria or simple non-cellular animals like *Amoeba* or *Paramecium*, a metazoan can breed many times, whereas the simpler forms can only divide their body once to produce daughter bacteria or protozoans. But the metazoan has a price to pay: the body, or *soma*, of the metazoan can have no future; only the germ cells contribute to the genetics of the progeny and the body *must* die. There is a sense, of course, in which the non-nuclear part of a protozoan, or even the "cell" membrane or wall of a bacterium, has no future; only the genes go on. Dawkins has exposed and exploited this view of reproductive biology in his book *The Selfish Gene*[6], as Weissmann[7] earlier had made the point about the germ cells and the soma.

I want to emphasise the converse here; there is indeed segregation, apartheid, within each metazoan body, allocating function to all of the parts but setting aside a harem-within-the-household for that hereditary material which might go on to its progeny. In contrast, note that the animal's body's *own* hereditary material in its somatic cells isn't treated specially. Even in the coelenterates (jellyfishes, anemones and their relatives), animals in which the different parts, though cellular, are not specialised into organs, most of them *do* have segregated gonads. In addition, coelenterates which form colonies usually have special parts of the colony which *only* reproduce; then the other polyps or bells serve the other, so-called *vegetative*, functions. Some protozoans, too, have co-operating colonies, and here again it is usually found that some of the members only reproduce while the others take care of the business of living. *Volvox* is a well-known example of such a protozoan colony; they are spherical colonies of single cells embedded in a jelly, each with two whip-like flagella and chloroplasts, except for a little colourless group which reproduce the colony.

Many kinds of metazoa form co-operative colonies of separate individuals and here, again, there is usually a *segregation of reproductive function* to a few individuals. This segregation is at the "next level up" from coelenterates or *Volvox*, with their germ cells. Each individual of these colonies may have potentially effective gonads, with germ cells segregated from their somas, but only a few actually are breeders, "germ individuals". In animals as different as Portuguese Man-of-War (one of the coelenterates mentioned above), bees and termites, naked mole rats and wolves, only a few animals in the colony breed, and the others are all relegated to vegetative (non-reproductive) functions[7]. In wolf and wild dog packs, only the dominant female and her consort(s) have effective breeding (though other animals may mate), and the others bring food for the one lot of cubs. Why should breeding be confined to what seems to be a *minimum* number, in animals as different as these? Surely, and according to early genetic orthodoxy, the breeding of the largest number should contribute more offspring to the future?

The segregation has been effected in different ways in each of our examples: the vegetative functions are distributed according to caste in termites, to phases of worker life-history in bees, to versatile intelligent hunters in dogs. Can this tell us anything about evolutionary "pressures" towards this odd regularity, *segregation of reproductive function*, performed differently but effectively at the various levels? I want to show that it can, but I need to contrast the "Ladder of Life" view I have given above with the more usual physiological one, and then introduce some more concepts in reproductive biology, before I can usefully proceed to a synthesis which "justifies" the evolutionary origins of intelligence, of ideas and stories, in a new way.

# References

References in full are to be found from page 243 onwards. Below are listed names of authors and dates of publication.

1. Cairns-Smith (1985)
2. Winfree (1974)
3. Winfree and Strogatz (1984)
4. Margulis and Sagan (1987)
5. Dawkins (1976)
6. Weissmann (1904)
7. Cohen (1977)

# 3

# ORGANISMS PASS MORE TO THEIR OFFSPRING – PRIVILEGE

The classical way of getting to You, up the Ladder of Life from its Origin, was to emphasise progressive control of the environment by more and more complex nervous systems. *Amoeba* was dismissed as having "taxes" or something equally boring, then *Hydra* was introduced with a flourish of "Once upon a time there was a nerve cell .... then a nerve *net*...". Worms showed a head end with ganglia, so they knew which way was front and could concentrate sense organs there. Insects were much further along the same road, but had given up versatility for programmed *multum in parvo* – lots in a little space: "Show your designer of programmed inter-continental missiles an ant, to keep him humble... ". Birds were also programmed, with a predilection for *imprinting* on German biologists; but mammals had got it right, with *versatility* and all the other virtues of Western civilisation that would inevitably produce Einstein, Marilyn Monroe and You. Unfairly short, but I think the picture is encapsulated passably.

There is another way of viewing such an "evolutionary" series from simple metazoans to complex colonies and versatile individuals, and that is to see it as increase in the sophistication of the *reproductive* strategy. Instead of starting the series "Once upon a time there was a nerve cell... " and working our way up through more and more complicated nervous systems till we get to Man, the cleverest animal, I propose to look again at something we all take for granted philosophically, the processes of reproduction.

Before I do so, however, just a small aside about the word "evolutionary" at the beginning of the last paragraph. Such a series is *not*, of course, evolutionary, for the same reason that you can't build up *your* family tree only using your relatives who are alive now. The series from which examples are being drawn is not the series of *ancestors*. It is the series of living forms, arranged with the simplest at the beginning of the book, or near the entrance to the museum display. The most complicated, the "highest", come towards the end of the biology book, or at the far right of the museum display. This "series of created forms" is known as the *Scala Naturae*[1], the Ladder of Life and it is not about ancestors.

It is a very common tactic, however, in biological "explanations", to pick out a series of contemporary forms and arrange them in a series, to demonstrate the steps in an evolutionary *conceptual* series.  What this does is to show that each step in the series *could have been viable*, so it's OK to postulate something of that kind in an ancestor.  If the series also uses progressively more complicated animal examples, because we're selecting our examples progressively further right on the *Scala*, further along in the Zoology book – so much the better, it's "well known that" earlier ancestors were simpler than later ones ....  I did just that in the last chapter, and I think it's a philosophically OK exercise;  I shall do it again several times in this book.  Bear in mind that I'm just showing you examples of organisms doing the kind of steps I'm suggesting.  I'm not telling you that the left-most examples turned into the right-most examples *via* the ones in the middle!  Now let's get back to increase in the sophistication of re-productive strategies.

Reproduction is *not* the same as breeding, though many authors seem to regard the words as synonymous.  Reproduction is the re-production of what one starts with: a population of parents producing a similar population in the next generation, or an egg producing another egg.  A cat having kittens is not reproducing, only breeding;  only when two of their kittens have replaced the parents, have *become* a pair of parents, can reproduction be said to have occurred.  It is fashionable today to concentrate on the genes as the most important link between the generations, and to describe reproduction in terms of the DNA of which the genes are made.  However, this is only part of the story; the non-genetic inheritance is in many respects of more consequence.  Let us consider *all* of what is passed from parents to offspring to accomplish reproduction[2].

All organisms pass more than DNA between the generations; even the simplest organisms, viruses, wrap the progeny DNA in protein coats (coded for by virus DNA of previous replications) so that a virus particle's infectivity is determined not by its own DNA sequence, but by those of a previous generation.  Bacterial daughters also receive a whole working biochemistry, and an effective "cell" wall, from the parent, as well as a DNA ring (bacteria are *not* cells, remember, they are equivalent to *bits* of cells – like mitochondria). Eukaryote non-cellular (unicellular) creatures like *Paramecium* or *Amoeba* inherit a whole cytoplasm-full of working mitochondria (or in *Chaos* "wild" bacteria with the same functions).  They also receive centrioles, which organise the chromosomal endowment to daughter cells and also organise cilia, and a variety of other symbionts ancient and modern.  All the eukaryote plant cells, algae and higher plants too, receive a kit including chloroplasts.  Some animals such as *Paramecium bursaria*, most *Hydra*s, corals, and giant clams have symbiotic plants, usually eukaryote algal cells, in some of their own cells, and these are usually received in the egg cell (but some baby flatworms who need symbiotic algae have to find "wild" ones and "eat" them). Many insects (including *Drosophila*) and a surprising variety of other animals (including some fishes) receive special symbiotic bacteria in the egg, which "mark" that area which will become the germ cells. In *Drosophila*, different geographic races of fruit-flies have rather different germ-line bacteria, with different viruses infecting them. So some laboratory crosses produce odd sex ratios, or sterile offspring (sometimes in the *second* generation!) because one strain's germ-line symbionts have caught a disease from the other strain's gametes! I relate these examples to emphasise just how much, *in addition to the nuclear DNA in the chromosomes*, is necessary to start off most animal embryos. There are a whole lot of different symbiotic organisms, all with (much of) their own DNA and their own reproductive systems, in each eukaryote egg.

In nearly all sexually reproducing metazoans (*cellular* animals) the egg begins development without involving the embryo's own genes, in its own cell nuclei, until the ground plan of the embryo has effectively appeared in the multicellular structure[2,3]. This ground plan arises from structure and chemistry set up by the *maternal* system, that one mother's germ cell which became the egg-cell (oocyte) in mother's ovary. The special architecture and biochemistry of the egg's cytoplasm is *necessary* to turn on the developing embryo's genes in the right cells at the right time, just as a tape player is necessary to express the magnetic patterns on a tape; the DNA cannot express itself, its own linear information, any more than a tape can. This egg architecture, and informational molecules coded for by the maternal set of genes in the mother's ovary, are the most basic non-genetic inheritance of virtually every animal. The embryo's own nuclei do not prescribe important proteins until development is well under way. Only then do the similar genes in each cell nucleus, segregated into different parts of the original cytoplasm, express a rather different spectrum of proteins so that the different chemistry, and the different functions, of skin, liver or kidney cells is initiated. But there is much more non-genetic inheritance, in addition to this most basic structural ground-plan which in effect acts as a very structured tape-player.

No animal provides *only* DNA and read-out mechanism to its progeny, even a tape player needs an energy source as well as a tape. Energy and building materials (usually as yolk), complex instructions for early development in the egg cytoplasm, time, place and season of egg-laying, parental care of various kinds are each a necessary part of the inheritance of most animal eggs[2,4]. Different parents of the same species may provide more or less well in *these* ways for each offspring, just as they may provide more or less useful genes for them. Just as for the genetic endowment, an organism must choose its parents carefully to maximise its *non*-genetic endowment.   Conversely, the non-genetic endowment by the parents may influence their contribution to the future of the species as much as, or in "higher" animals more than, the chromosomal genes they pass on.  This non-genetic inheritance is, initially at least, independent of the chromosomal genes received by each embryo. Later, of course, different genes will affect each embryo's ability to benefit by different endowment from its parents, from the time its *own* genes get turned on during embryology and throughout its life.   So the genetic endowment continually affects usage of non-genetic endowment, and the non-genetic endowment (privilege) affects the expression, and the necessities, of the genome.   As an example, mammals differ (even within species, as well as between species) in the provision of proteins, sugars, vitamins and minerals in milk;   because the offspring have different biochemical (mostly genetic) requirements for these chemicals, quite complicated sums must be done to quantify heredities.

Yolk and milk are in most ways the simplest form of this endowment. They can both easily be seen as energy and food, surplus to the mother's needs, won from the mother's transactions with the environment as a kind of profit.  The mother, whose success is measured by the extent of her contribution to her progeny's reproductive success, "invests" this profit in her offspring to give them a start in life.  Clearly, well-provided-for offspring will compete more successfully and are more likely to be the breeders in the next generation.  So mothers who provide well will be represented in the future, and mothers who don't make a profit, or who enjoy it rather than giving it to their offspring, will not inherit the Earth.   Genetic programmes which direct excess into "packed lunch" for offspring will compete successfully with other programmes which direct it into fat or excrete it.   Offspring which receive more of it will be *"privileged"*, as we say of human children in the same situation, while those not getting the normal amount will be *"deprived"*.  This usage of "privilege" and "deprivation" can apply to most of the non-genetic endowment, not just to material and energy like yolk and milk.  Nestling birds in a smaller-than-usual brood are privileged, well-fed but also better cared for in other ways than others of the same species from larger clutches.  Contrariwise, a child born to a human mother who is starved, or who smokes heavily, may properly be said to be under-privileged.  For any population, there is a norm of privilege, and usually there is considerable deviation in both directions. These usages of "privilege" and "deprivation" are different from the usual, and are those introduced in my book *Reproduction*[2].   Privilege is assumed there to be absolutely measurable rather than relative, and "deprivation" should not suggest something taken away, but the state of being inadequately supplied – see Chapter 8.

Privilege may be seen to increase in nearly all the classical "evolutionary series", which are usually set up according to quite different criteria: advancement in some specialty (horses), control of internal environment (crustaceans), increase of size through time (most text-book examples). Primitive organisms in these series – and in the rest of the animal kingdom, too – gave, and modern ones still give, little to their offspring. Advanced organisms of any group invest more by way of material (yolk), energy (in nest-building and courtship), and time (in offspring care, protection and perhaps education). Genes have been selected which programme for a good start for the young *independently of their own genetics*. Although "orthogenesis" (evolution along prescribed paths) does not occur, nevertheless there is a sense of "pulling oneself up by one's own bootstraps" in many of these classical evolutionary series. However, the concept of advancing reproductive strategies, especially with increasing privilege, clarifies the philosophical problems raised by such apparently guided evolution. If we see it in this new way, we don't need to worry about who (or Who) guides it!

Contrast, for example, frog eggs in a temperate pond with guppy eggs developing inside the female fish. The frog eggs vary in temperature, perhaps from 5°C to 25°C daily in an English Spring, and their very complicated developmental processes must remain coupled together over this wide range (different chemical processes change rate differently with temperature!). The "same" tadpole results from different circumstances. Because of the developmental versatility required, the developmental programme must be basically simple, with much of the genetic instructions devoted to buffering and redundancy ("if temperature 20-25°...then use enzyme version #5; if 10-15°, use #2 which is faster, etc....." routines). In contrast, guppy eggs are carried within the female; her sophisticated nervous system *avoids* heat or cold, predators or low oxygen levels and so keeps the eggs away from these disturbing influences too.

In principle, with the same quantity of DNA a more complex organism could be prescribed, more reliably, by the guppy genome than by the frog genome. This more complex organism could then, with its more sophisticated control and avoidance systems in the adult female, provide a *more* controlled environment for development of *its* offspring, in turn. The developmental environment has become internal in this way in many evolutionary lines, not only in guppies and mammals; tse-tse flies, some sharks and salamanders, and adders all develop inside the mother, and birds provide a good substitute by incubation in a nest.   This controlled environment, in turn, permits reliable construction of a still more complex parent.   The early development of the later embryos can be very different from that of their ancestors' embryos, because a mutation which  would have killed the ancient, unprivileged embryo can be pampered in the descendant.   A lost function can be compensated by its mother's care, because its mother has taken over many of the embryo's functions, dealing with its necessities ever more competently as the generations pass[2,4.]

There is a capitalist analogy to this improvement as the generations pass. The improvement of technology, so that later factories can produce better goods more reliably and with less man-power because they come to rely on stability in their suppliers, is a good metaphor for this evolutionary increase in living standards.   Just as yolk or milk can be seen as capital transfers across the generations (justifying my use of the word "privilege"), so the change of value of capital, and even the pampering of recipients of much capital from previous generations, have their animal equivalents.   The evolutionary improvement I've sketched above is just like the progressive acquisition of more capital by a human family.   Think of it as represented by stability-providing networks of factories, and enough income to provide an excellent education, and investments, for each successive generation of children.   Later children will not need to do any of the early pioneering, and the family will have lost, by pampering, many of the early abilities, but will still be successful.   At least in major part, this will be because the children are, as we say, privileged.

Mammals form a late term in just such a series.   They have even lost yolk from their eggs, replacing it by dependence on mother's continuing provision during pregnancy;  the egg forms the nutritionally essential embryonic mem-branes even before the embryo itself appears.   The mammalian embryo is peculiarly sensitive to temperature variations, and requires exquisite control of this and many other physiological parameters for normal development to occur.   This is dependent on highly-evolved maternal control mechanisms, both physiological and behavioural.   Such a very advanced form of reproduc-tion, with embryonic functions not required because relegated to mother's abilities, has enabled the mammals to become very complicated homeostatic mechanisms, without using more DNA than frogs or much more than fishes. Their development is very peculiar, geared to a fastidious control of the embryonic environment and to a very precise re-production of this complica-tion in each generation.   Development is *simplified* so that it can make very pre-dictable complexity without *internal* checks and controls.   Paradoxically, this very precision permits a robustness of the developmental processes, controlled from without, much greater than that of any frog who controls it from within the genetic programme. It is this robust precision of development which enables the mammals to make versatile nervous systems, and so takes us into the realm of ideas and, later, stories.

Note again that it is *not* the mammalian embryo's genetic programme which is complex; it is the pampering developmental environment, controlled by mother's complicated physiology, which has freed the embryonic programme from many erstwhile necessities. We shall see how a very similar take-over of necessary functions, at a higher evolutionary level, has permitted urban children to lose abilities in a similar way. In order to illuminate further how this mammalian precision of privilege permits robust versatility, I shall use a couple of simple examples from outside the mammals themselves. Let's briefly contrast the privileged reproductive arrangements of the tarantula wasp and the goose, and see how both of them deal with the necessity of enabling offspring to recognise their mates.

The tarantula wasp spends all its larval life as a "maggot" in a burrow in the sand, excavated by mother, and she has provided a relatively enormous tarantula spider, paralysed, as food. The little maggot is programmed to eat the spider in such an order that the heart remains beating to keep the meat fresh – the vital organs are eaten last. After eating the spider, it finally moults to the adult winged form, tunnels out of the subterranean nursery, then mates. The female spends all her adult life digging burrows, catching and stinging tarantulas, dragging them to burrows and laying an egg on each. She does not feed, but performs her herculean tasks fuelled entirely by her larval gluttony on the spider provided by her mother. This is a beautiful example of extra-genetic endowment, what I have called privileged development. But there is a problem. The emerging female must immediately recognise her mate, he must recognise her, and mating must be accomplished; neither, remember, has seen anything but the burrow and the spider they've eaten. So both sexes must be "hard-wired" (provided with a pre-programmed neural circuitry) to recognise and respond to each other. Equally, of course, the female must be programmed to recognise tarantulas, disguise burrows, and so on. I don't know how many females sting and paralyse the males, then attempt to copulate with the spiders, but our biological experience would suggest the proportion to be very small! However, there must have been a lot of variation, and some versatility, in this neural programming, or evolutionary change to *produce* this wasp would have been impossible. Further, both the wasp shape *and* the circuitry to recognise this shape must evolve together. These spider-paralysing wasps are a very successful and diverse group, however, so those evolutionary constraints which required change of mate-image to evolve along with change of form or colour cannot have been stifling.

Geese, and many other birds, solve this problem very differently. The development is complicated, and nearly all of the construction of the young bird is fuelled by albumen and yolk in the egg. Development proceeds at nearly constant temperatures during incubation, arresting temporarily when the temperature drops (for example, when mother goes off to breakfast!). After hatching there are two vital components of the offspring's endowment still to be provided by parents: the continuation of food provision, increasing the privilege of *that* parent's offspring in comparison with competitors, is obvious. It is much less obvious that the other parental function is to programme the young bird for later mate-selection. Most young birds, but especially poultry, will "imprint" on any moving object seen (consistently) just after they have hatched, and will thereafter direct parent-oriented behaviour at it; Lorenz[5] and his geese are a well-known example. What is much less well known is that imprinting provides not only a "parent-image" in the young bird's brain, but also a "mate-image"; a goose that has imprinted on Lorenz cannot breed. Goose-parents have not reproduced unless the offspring have been provided with goose-imprints so that they can breed in their turn, and each goose *learns* it anew in each generation. This contrasts with the developmental rigidity, the "hard-wiring" of the tarantula wasp, which is controlled from *within* its developmental programme, and must have a lot of "if...thens", like frog development. The goose, on the other hand, receives instruction from without, as part of the parental endowment, like the outside control of mammalian development; it is as if a "photograph" of a mate image were given to each baby goose by its parents. One can imagine a whole line of such photographs, changing with the evolution of the geese, and running parallel to, indeed reflecting, the changing morphology as geese evolved. This allows much more versatility, but *controlled* versatility, in the evolution of goose development, of goose reproduction.

Let us return to the mammals with these two examples in mind, the privileged wasp with its programming from within the genome and the privileged goose with its programming from extra-genetic parental endowment. Of course, no mammal nervous system is as programmed as an insect's, indeed they work quite differently. But there are some mammals which have much of their behaviour set up while they are in the uterus, before birth, while others are like geese – and us – in that the parents must imprint, control, teach the juveniles.

Mammals like the gnu and the guinea-pig, and to a lesser extent cattle and horses, retain their offspring in the secure and stable developmental environment of the uterus so that they are born "mature", with most of the complicated behaviour required of the adult already wired up. Baby gnus are born while the mothers are migrating, and the new-born must be ready, within hours, to trek with the herd, to run and to recognise warning behaviour from adults. Baby guinea-pigs can eat a mixed diet, and discriminate among foodstuffs, within hours of birth; they can be taken from the mother at four days "old". Nearly all of the privilege has been conferred on these mammals *in utero*. The offspring's nervous system has had time to become completely programmed, very reliably, for a wide behavioural repertoire, while mother's nervous system is "minding the shop", supplying all the embryo's needs of energy, food material and especially stability.

Just as the behaviour of some mammalian adults is more functionally complex than that of any other natural system, so the mammalian uterine environment, designed (or at least improved) for the unperturbed development of mammalian embryos, may be the most imperturbable – homeostatic – physico-chemical system in terrestrial nature. Mammalian embryos have both gained and lost by this take-over of their developmental responsibilities by their mothers' physiology; the option taken up by the gnu and the guinea-pig for reproductive privilege is very successful, as is that of the tarantula wasp. However, in the next chapter we will see how an apparently opposite reproductive strategy can be derived from the same mammalian system, resulting in a basically new reproductive biology at whose heart is the idea and the story.

## References

Reference in full are to be found from page 243 onwards. Below are listed names of authors and dates of publication.

1. Lovejoy (1936)
2. Cohen (1977)
3. Davidson (1983)
4. Cohen (1979)
5. Lorenz (1981)

# 4

# THE SHARING OF PRIVILEGE – NESTS AND EDUCATION

We have seen that all organisms transmit more than genetic information across the generations to their offspring. Even "parent" viruses code for the protein coat in which to wrap their "offspring", which determines the off-spring's chance at infection of another cell. Most higher organisms provide yolk or other food store, milk or other processed maternal food; parental time is given to protection, and in general to stabilisation of the developmental environment. In this way the parental profit, from metabolic transactions with the environment, is passed on to offspring as a variable, *privilege*. Such a system has a peculiar evolutionary possibility, of building this privilege in each generation as a kind of capital investment, progressively giving each genera-tion a better start in life as the capital base increases. Mammals have benefited in this way, and our embryos have fewer demands upon their developmental versatility than other animals – so they can build complex, versatile *adults* reliably! The genetic survival value of such "investment" traits is clear, in Selfish Gene terms, and they provide an alternative reproductive strategy to the production of large numbers of poorly-provided-for offspring. The latter is shown by many fish; those few female cod which survive to breed produce tens of millions of eggs over several years. Bivalves usually do this too; a hundred million is not unusual for an oyster. It is a characteristic strategy of unpredict-able environments, and it has been called an "*r*" strategy by biologists (we need not worry why, but should remember this distinction). Most animals which produce few eggs and invest a lot in each (by way of food material, or care) live in a predictable environment, to which they are very well adapted and which they usually fill to saturation. This has been called a "*K*" strategy (again, never mind why but understand the distinction!). The mammals (and viviparous animals in general) provide their own predictable environment for develop-ment, inside the mother, and so can exploit unpredictable environments with well-started offspring – *privileged* offspring.

We would expect, then, that all higher forms of life on this planet (i.e. those whose physiological control systems keep them stable despite wide variations in the environment) would use viviparous mothers' abilities, to take offspring as far into the adult condition as can be managed. A variety of creatures obviously does this. Tse-tse fly mothers supply all of the energy and food

35

required for the single maggot to achieve full adult weight, while it is still in her oviduct – it moults to become the adult fly, without any more feeding, soon after birth (remember flies don't *grow* after adulthood – the tse-tse is born as big as it will ever be!). The fish parasite *Gyrodactylus* does even better – it actually has two or even three successive generations in its uterus when it is born from its mother, and so is already a grandmother at birth! Tarantula wasps, as we have seen (p. 31 ), provide all larval needs by parental abilities too. Gnu, guinea-pig and even perhaps goose (p. 32 ) can equally serve as prime examples, not perhaps going as far as tse-tse flies but using the maternal internal physiology to do the adult-making job pretty well.

However, some other mammals, like rats, cats and baboons, do not seem to have "understood" this privilege message at all; they have evolved what seems at first sight to be an opposite strategy, and have come up with a kitten instead of a calf. They have, as juveniles and even as adults, an adaptable, a versatile nervous system which contrasts with that of the gnu or even the guinea-pig. Anyone who has kept guinea-pigs and rats will immediately see the difference I'm referring to; both turn on our "little-and-cuddly" circuits (about which more on p.58), but guinea-pig babies are miniature adults, stoic and dumb, while baby rats are into any mischief within twenty feet of their nest! They, like kittens and baboons, are born *early*, very immature; then social interactions mould much more of the developing rat's brain than a mere imprinting of the photograph of a future mate. Parents ensure a continuation of the stability of the developmental environment by providing a *nest*, and milk as the food that makes least digestive demands on the baby. We should note, though, that a complex nervous/muscular programme must have been developed *in utero* to give the baby rat nipple-finding, latching-on and suckling reflexes. This must include all the circuitry which ensures (mostly) that the milk stream and the air stream don't get mixed up where they cross, flooding the lungs. There *are* many circuits already set up in these helpless, nest-dependent babies, just as in baby gnus or guinea-pigs – but the important thing is that there is *very much more programming to do*, in the nest and afterwards. This programming, like the goose imprinting, goes from behaviour of the parents into the sense organs of the offspring. It is the software being loaded into the little computers, which have been hard-wired while inside so that they may receive it properly. This is in one major respect *not* a very good analogy, because the "hard-wiring" is still going on in these infants, and some of the software is needed to make sure that it happens right. Indeed, some environmental cues are needed too, so that the animal can use the nest-received software to make itself successfully – but more of that later (pp 46, 58).

There is, in these nest building mammals, however, a whole new possibility – the *reciprocal* possibilities through the sensori-motor route can be, and are, exploited.   The gnu mother and fetus have reciprocal arrangements, too, of course, but they are physiological; the gnu baby *in the uterus* cannot learn from them about the outside world.   But the baby rat or baboon finds *mother* as part, the *major* part, of the outside world, and finds her behavioural programmes all designed to interact with its own behaviour and sensation.   Nearly all of their interactions are *via* the most sensitive parts of both animals – they have obviously *become* sensitive to exploit this;   eyes, ears, nose, tongue, lips, nipples all become involved in a new set of experiences, totally unlike the pre-birth, bland and muffled intra-uterine near-sleep.   We all get pleasure by eliciting signals from very young babies, especially that elusive smile, and we stimulate the baby in our turn with our cooings and cuddlings.   The actual cue to make babies smile is disappointingly simple:   babies will smile at a two-black-dots-for-eyes, and do better with an upward-curved mouth line under them.   By six weeks mother's face is a more reliable stimulus than other people's – but a simple drawing still works!   We can see two-eyes-and-a-mouth elicit smiles in week-old  human babies, but we can't see what subtle signs and signals pass between rat mothers and babies, and we can't even easily interpret baboon signals.   These, I suggest, are totally *unlike* the signals which gnu, giraffe or guinea-pig babies get and give – which are juvenile versions, perhaps, of adult-important signals.   The importance of the baby's smile is that it turns on the potentially rewarding *teaching* relationship to come.   The gnu had better know it all already, if it's to survive its first few hours.   It may develop more from intrinsic programme, or outside learning, later in life, but that is strictly individual enterprise.   It certainly doesn't persuade, incite, provoke its mother to teach it, like a rat, baboon or human baby does!

Social interactions now mould the developing brain, building on the hard-wired tricks (like the smile) which are built into baby and adult to foster this interaction.   We simply don't see these interactions and appreciate them for what they are, we are too used to them.   We are delighted to be manipulated by the baby's smile, and our pleasure in this, as in sexual interactions, is obviously functional.   It is still amazing to me how infants, or attractive members of the opposite sex, can elicit such dramatic and instant change-of-priorities;   even more amazing, though, is how resistant this change-of-motivation is to introspection.   We have all experienced the busy, efficient bossy business-man or woman who melts in these situations – and strenuously denies it afterwards!   I have interacted, but only as a father, with six baby humans; I seem to recall their differences from the beginning, and I can certainly be *sure* that the three boys were always more boisterous, out-going, mischievous than the three girls. Alas, it feels just the same to be sure *and wrong* ..... Psychologists have shown how baby-minders, or strangers, react differently to a two-week-old baby if told that it is "John" rather than "Joan"! Obviously, this experiment can't be done with the parents of the child, but we do actually have some data on cases in which the child was assigned the wrong gender at birth, because of abnormal external genitals. In these cases, the parents responded to the assigned gender, not the biological gender, and in some cases apparently found it more difficult to change than the child did! If you feel that this was socially-promoted behaviour, conditioned response in them, and in me to my children, as a result of our sexist society, I would completely agree. Then I would encourage you to wonder, with me, why it is so *easy* to condition us to behave specially to different babies.

Perhaps an example from the baby's side is more persuasive about just how very complicated the baby's internal hard-wiring is, and how complicated the signals are that it readily abstracts from its complicated environment and responds to. We see babies *copy* adult behaviour – in rats as well as in humans. We think that this is one of the simplest forms of behaviour, for it is something that people, like other primates – and parrots – do superbly well. But just think about it for a moment. A baby (or a parrot) must hear a sound, and analyse it *via* the external and middle ear apparatus, impinging on the transducer inner ear which translates it into a spatio-temporal set of nerve impulses .... into the brain ..... then a wholly different spatio-temporal set of nerve impulses goes to throat, tongue, diaphragm, jaw muscles, larynx (or, in the parrot, syrinx) which then *makes* a similar sound. *How* the result of a sound into the ear is a *similar* sound, but from the mouth, is *nothing at all* like a tape recorder mechanism. Because we have one word for it – "copy" – we think it's simple. It's not. Think of the *sight*, into the eye, of an arm moving, a mouth smiling, which results in the "same" movement in response ..... now try to think how to connect up a robot to mimic the *seen* actions of another robot? (If you are used to computers, think what "COPY A*.* B*.*" does – and how inadequate that is to go from stimulus to *equivalent* response!) These circuits are there in the young child, and in the young rat, "copying circuits". I suspect there are far fewer, if any, in the young giraffe, who doesn't need to copy because its responses are already in place, like the tarantula wasp's. Many of the young rat's noises and responses, of course, are as automatic as the giraffe's. But it has the extra abilities to turn on meta-responses – like "copy" – or even meta-meta-responses – like "learn that this is a time to copy ...... ". There is, then, a dynamic interaction between bitch and pups, queen (cat) and kittens, human mother and her baby which makes new kinds of events in brains, indeed new kinds of brains.

I must rehearse this difference again, and put it into evolutionary context (make what Stephen J. Gould calls a "Just So Story") because it is important to later argument.    Let us return to the contrast between calves and kittens. Calves are born already programmed to a large extent, kittens *learn* in the nest because their "hard-wiring" has given them less programming, enough to maintain life in the security of the nest, but only there – they are *helpless* babies. Associated with the take-over of fetal responsibilities by maternal physiology in early mammalian ancestors was a *loss* of embryonic functions;  just as the cave fish lost their eyes, so mammalian embryos lost temperature tolerance, yolk, digestive abilities and have come to rely on mothers' internal provision. When the fetuses were matured to functional organisms in the uterus (as I suspect the original mammals were – they were guinea-pig-like rather than rat-like[1]), this helplessness was covered by mother's physiology.   Now these babies are born "prematurely" into a nest, where mother's behavioural com-plexity continues to provide a *safe* environment.   One important advantage, to mother, of dumping the babies earlier was that she could hunt, climb, escape better and this was perhaps the primary evolutionary "reason" for earlier births. But the advantage to the baby, to each individual, was for the first time on this planet the possibility of *non-lethal* trial-and-error learning.   Errors had been fatal, not instructive, before parental care of helpless young in nests.

Sure, fishes had cared for their young, even some amphibia and reptiles had, and I'm sure some of the giant reptiles used privilege like gnus.   But it is instructive to contrast mammalian nest-babies with avian nestlings.   To a large extent, the mammals learn, change themselves, differently in each family, while the young nestling birds mature their abilities as they grow, program-ming from inside rather than from outside (except for imprinting....).   I don't think a mammalian "brood-parasite", like the cuckoo, *could* exploit otters, baboons, even rats; mother would find them out! Yet there are several different brood-parasite bird families, with many successful species (often parasitising several host species each, which underlines the point).

Baby mammals born into a nest, then, can make uncomfortable (so instruc-tive) mistakes, impossible to those still *in utero*;  therefore they can *learn*, and mother can *teach* them.   Again, contrast this with nestling birds.   These do not *learn* to fly, they became more and more able, and siblings prevented from "practising" with the mother do just as well.  They *do* learn birdsong, or at least the local variations of it, but there is even a computer-like element to that; they don't, like baby mammals, fall about the place and get it wrong lots of times, they just invent variations on the local birdsongs they hear. The human baby, the kitten, the puppy or the rat, in contrast to the baby fish, songbird or gnu, can make many non-lethal mistakes. They result in discomfort within the security of the nest, and perhaps in some conditioning, but not usually in death. Repetition of the discomfort may be actively useful, and maternal traits can be selected which make the most of this new information channel, using both its reward and its punishment options – watch mother cats.

This is a genuinely new information channel between the generations, and I cheated in using goose imprinting to lead you up to it; imprinting is one-way-only, like gene transfer. But mother-baby interaction in the nest is genuinely two-way, both in deep programmed structure – both mothers and babies have many built-in responses to facilitate the learning/teaching – and in the minute-to-minute playing out of each .... each what? I very nearly said "*idea*", because here for the first evolutionary occasion do we have communication between two organisms in the absence of the referent; when the baby fails at something that both mother and baby want to achieve, the goal is an idea in both minds, however primitively. Ideas came into the world in the nest, as in the nursery. I cannot believe the picture of some Lucy-like australopithecine faced with a problem, with a bubble over her head saying "IDEA!!!"; I can't see it for an early primate holding a stick to pick up termites. But I can easily picture mother insectivore bringing back a large fierce insect for the babies in the nest, a bit chewed for them to practise on. And for me that's so damn close to teaching, to transmission of an idea, that I nearly used the word back then.....

This new mode of information transfer between the generations has, I believe, *become* true communication, but its provenance, its history, gave no promise of that till the last step. The mammalian privilege strategy resulted in maternal take-over of the embryo's abilities, followed by cosseting of the embryos to late, almost-mature stage before release. This in turn resulted in more loss of embryo/fetal abilities, till even the almost-adult was still in the womb, like the fully-grown tse-tse fly maggot. At this time communication was all physiology, and no observer would have seen promise of education, any more than we see it in tse-tses or cattle. Some specialised mothers then found it advantageous to look after their young *outside*, perhaps for speed as in horses, weight as in elephants, agility in hunting as in carnivores. No mares' nests, nor elephants', but the early carnivores and perhaps the early arboreal primates dropped the helpless fetuses into nests instead of carting them about.

The early rat-type rodents (myomorphs) did similarly, but the porcupine-like ones (hystricomorphs) took the keep-'m-inside route and produced guinea-pigs ("K" strategists, p.35). The myomorphs probably "wanted" a fast turnover, and time in the uterus was at a premium; by getting the babies out and suckling they could have a much faster production line, and they've given us lemmings, mice, rats, hamsters, which are all "weeds" in the wild ("*r*" strategists, see p.35). This is a preferred explanation, too, for the reproductive success of the marsupial wallabies and kangaroos: they can have one early embryo in the uterus, a "fetus" in the pouch and an older joey suckling a late-milk teat in the pouch, all at the same time. This could have been the explanation, too, for the early mammals which dropped babies early[1] - it is romantic to think of mother leaving babies so she could be better at providing for them, but perhaps she simply dropped them so she could get some more started quickly. These helpless babies, in their nests, were a new thing on the Earth, but I can't believe that there was a Celestial Fanfare of Trumpets, which their potential deserved. This is the explanation which the reproductive view can give, but the "Once upon a time there was a nerve cell ... " story can't. Let's put it in context, its past and its future.

Helpless babies, cosseted in a nest, might well have seemed an aberrant, rather specialised reproductive trick to any Martian observer. There was no glowing neon sign which said "Here Be Einstein *in embryo*!". There had, after all, been a lot of kinds of insect nests, lots of mammals without nests, birds were getting round to making nests, and there may well have been mammals with pouches; there was nothing to mark out that particular reproductive trick as Having Great Potential. Just as an aside, we should notice that that is often true of great evolutionary advances: *Eusthenopteron*, perhaps the first fish to come out of the water, whose descendants were all the land vertebrates, was not re-markable; the first metazoa must just have seemed like multi-nucleate protozoans with a few internal partitions; even the first eukaryotes must have seemed like prokaryotes who kept strange company, or failed to digest their prokaryote food! The innovation made by these nest-using mammals was that they replaced the endocrine/metabolic/physiological interactions of mother and offspring by sense-organ/neural interactions; this suddenly put a premium on communication, ideas and brains. Perhaps the evolutionary "reason" was some clever locomotory adaptation, because a heavy pregnant mother was slowed down dangerously, and she could feed effectively earlier if she gave birth prematurely; or perhaps there was a need to have a rapid turnover of litters. Whatever the evolutionary "cause", a whole new set of reproductive rules appeared. It didn't matter why the fish came out of water, or why the prokaryotes associated into eukaryotes. The rules changed when they did. They changed again when mammals dropped their helpless young into nests. Learning and teaching had appeared on the Earth.

Contemporary mammals show a variety of exploitations of this new link between the generations, and because I am going to say that human use of it is odd, I'd better put a few other mammals into the same context. What have our cousins done with ideas, with teaching the young while they are helpless in the nest? Different mammals have done very different things, and we can find an evolutionary series starting with one-female-and-babies (like foxes, and domestic cats and dogs), *via* more social animals where several females and older siblings may be involved (as in rats, mongooses, lions) up to complex social groups where the babies may learn from many other animals (meerkats, wild dogs, savannah baboons, chimpanzees, "primitive" peoples).

Simple mother-to-offspring passage, as in cats, is not very interesting in our context – most people have seen this happening, anyway, and I don't want to use a deeper understanding of this than your observation will have shown you. Rats are in some ways more interesting than domestic cats, because there is a bit of a social life and several adults may be concerned with rearing the young. There is good evidence that sedated mothers produce incompetent young, and that handling of the young by people, or interaction with rats strange to the mother, produces much more capable, successful adults[2]. It is as if these animals need some of the rough-and-tumble, some of the frustrations, some *failure* of maternal placidity in order to become better rats (yes, this *should* console parents who lose their tempers with their offspring – it may not be the best way, but it may be good, not bad for the kids!). This is suggestive, but hardly clear, evidence for some of the advantages of this special mammalian kind of juvenile experience – they have got their adrenal glands going before they get out into the world. But this is not an argument restricted to helpless-young-in-nests; the same might be true for cattle, and even geese, or cichlid fish (which all care for their young, too). Some natural history of other, more social mammals can expand the point, however, and emphasise the particular strengths of learning and teaching, at all steps of an evolutionary progression.

Wolf and wild dog packs are, in most senses, family groups. Only one pair breeds, but all adults hunt and there is interaction and instruction of all cubs by all the adults. Different packs have different calls that can be recognised and distinguished, not only by the animals themselves but also by human ears. Such differences, consistent among the members of each pack, are very unlikely to derive from genetic differences; outbreeding is common, and genetic difference between packs is only of the same order as that within packs. Yet inherited vocal patterns, hunting techniques and other behaviour differentiate packs from each other and must contribute to their competition. Cubs born to each pack conform to the patterns and so inherit, extra-genetically, a life-style which they help pass on, even if they do not themselves breed. This is clearly a simple set of "traditions", ideas passing through the generations. So these new ideas have not only appeared ephemerally, they have a substrate in which they live, passing down the generations through time. But they are *not*, like the goose "photo", dependent on the biological substrate for their creation in each generation; they have their own lineage, ideas producing ideas. They are primitive memes (p.5).

In the wolf pack, the status hierarchy is fairly stable, with the reproductive female at the top, her preferred male(s) immediately below, then her current litter, then everybody else. Among primates, however, life is often more complicated[3,4]; lowland gorillas and hamadryas baboons do form essentially one-family groups, like wolves, but in the common savannah baboons, chimpanzees and humans the lines of transmission of ideas, primitive cultural traditions, are not so simple. In a multi-male baboon troupe there is more than a simple pair plus many helpers, and the inheritance of both tradition and more general privilege is more complex than in the dog pack. *Status* in the troupe is of crucial importance both for the genetic and the extra-genetic passage of information between the generations. In baboon troupes, there is a small group of high-status males, and most other males are totally excluded from access to females in oestrus – they form a band of "assistants" and scouts. Females each have a place in the social order, too, but this changes according to their reproductive state. Most mature females are pregnant or lactating, but at any time a few exhibit readiness to mate (oestrus), as they come up to ovulation as they wean a current baby (some may ovulate during lactation, too, it seems, like women). Because all the females get mated by several males when they are at peak oestrus, they very nearly always get pregnant. So menstruation is rare, fertilisation is usual, and most females are pregnant or lactating (this is true of most non-seasonal wild animals – people don't think of it because domestic and laboratory animals, like women, are in that rather strange state of being fertile but not reproducing!). Pregnant female baboons have a somewhat flexible social ranking, but when they give birth they rise in status as the baby receives attention both from the high-ranking males and their temporary consorts. These consorts are the few ovulating females, who are ready – eager – for copulation. During lactation the females join a coterie of nursing mothers, deferred to by the pregnant females but lower in rank than females at peak oestrus. As the babies are weaned the mothers begin a cycle again, and as they approach ovulation they rise in status until, at their peak of sexual receptivity, proceptivity and fertility they associate with one or more of the dominant males. Their offspring, now playing with a peer group but still spending more than half their time with their mothers, still receive much attention from the dominant males and the high-status female group. These "alpha" animals are much more patient with these juveniles than they are with lower-status adults; perhaps this is because they are *their* latest children, and may still reproduce, so it is *worth* investing time in them. (I contrast this, on pp 55-8, with the strange human habit of "putting up with", indeed even adopting, unrelated juveniles.)

In this social order the non-genetic inheritance includes not only tit-bits of food but grooming and education in the ways of that particular troupe. These primitive cultural traditions are passed to the young from many adults. Mother is the main transmission route, of course and, briefly, father (who probably *does* know which of the offspring are his, or at least which are likely to be). The baby also interacts with father's peer group of the other alpha males, a few other females fortuitously in oestrus, but *not* the low status adults unless and until the juvenile is demoted to their ranks. Some of the games played by young peer groups may be traditional too, so the young baboon's brain is programmed from a number of cultural sources, many of them not closely related genetically, as well as by regular or occasional, accidental events in the physical, chemical and biological environment. His reactions to thunderstorms, salt or alkaline waterholes, or snakes is conditioned largely by the cultural traditions of his group, and these differ greatly among groups. Some troupes are largely terrestrial and disregard trees as sources of food, or recreation, but others centre juvenile games around them – and use their thinner upper branches as look-outs, and refuges from big cats.

These cultural habits must be at least as important as genetic differences, with which they must interact, to determine reproductive success, survival and prosperity in their Darwinian world. A few baboon troupes have been transplanted to, or created in, zoological gardens or research institutes. These have developed a whole series of peculiar traditions, in relation to their human keepers or regular feeding, which could never have occurred in the wild but are nevertheless useful, adaptive in the new circumstances. We have changed the culture of some wild communal monkeys, too; probably the most famous example is that of those Japanese macaques who have developed a "swimming for recreation" culture relatively recently, and in which young animals play water-games, whereas other groups of the same macaques have the usual monkeys' suspicion of open water. Washing of sweet potatoes, left as food by observers, was initiated by one animal and has now spread to all but the most conservative old members of the troupe[5]. There is presumably no genetic basis for this difference between troupes – yet. It is probable that there soon will be, however, as certain genotypes arise by recombination which meet the new criteria more ably, and so result in higher status for their bearers. Perhaps challenges between males will occur more often in the water, directing attention to the face rather than the rest of the animal or emphasising swimming ability. However, it is important for us to realise that the cultural context may *avoid* selection for genetic differences in performance, substituting somewhat versatile behaviour in *every* successfully-programmed juvenile. And that thought brings us to the question of the peculiar kinds of natural selection, resulting from different *genetic* contribution to the future, on organisms with heredity additional to their genetics. Cultural heredity changes these rules too.

The genetic programme of these baboons, like that of many primates, myomorphs and carnivores, produces versatility rather than specific adaptations, ability-to-adapt rather than ability-to-perform. This is true of the programmes for nervous circuitry, too, goose rather than tarantula-wasp – super-goose, rather. Embryonic development guided by these programmes imposes some rigid behaviour, but also directs much ability-to-learn in specific areas. It "directs attention to", abstracts from the environmental "noise", some very specific behaviour of other organisms of the same species. Some behaviour is "meaningful", then, almost from birth (like cuddling, presentation of nipples) or later (male threats, female spankings). So behaviour of these other animals starts to programme the young brains into the societies of which they will be a part. Their juvenile responses (like the human baby's smile) then elicit behaviour from the other members of the juvenile society, which the juvenile recognises and responds to, or learns. This cascade process continues throughout the juvenile's development, and depends upon interaction with others *who were themselves programmed by the system*. This is the major reason why human-reared apes, monkeys and social carnivores cannot be "returned to the wild" successfully; the animal, we say correctly, has been denied its birthright. *We* simply cannot supply the traditional exercises and models which turn a versatile learning juvenile into a competent wild adult. We have no trouble releasing laboratory-reared tarantula wasps, little with geese if we're careful about what they imprint onto, but these human-reared social primates are as incomplete as a Lorenz-imprinted goose, or as a human without language. They are, in our sense, underprivileged, indeed deprived; they have been denied a part of their inheritance, and are as maimed as genetically defective organisms. A major part of the reproductive channel has been blocked, as surely as if the reproductive tubes had been clipped. We should not be surprised that the colonies we release into the wild do so badly; their cultural lines have been cut as seriously as those of the African slaves taken to America (p. 213)!

The human system of reproduction is the furthest advance along these lines to date. Because I wish, later, to dissect and inspect the human system of cultural inheritance I will give only a brief outline now, enough to link "ideas" up to "stories" and myths as the final step in the elaboration, the enhancement of our extra-genetic evolution. At this point of my argument I only want to set up the "primitive" human system of cultural transmission as the end term, the highest point in the evolutionary series of reproductive strategies which used tarantula wasp, goose, wolf and baboon as examples of rungs on the conceptual (but not of course the phylogenetic) ladder.

Human babies are born very immature, but with a large repertoire of already-programmed neuro-muscular circuits. At birth they can "root" for a nipple, they can suckle without choking, they can grasp firmly in response to palmar touch, they can cry. There are many other reflexes, whose purpose is not so apparent but which point to complex circuitry nevertheless: the "stepping-up" and "walking" movements, the Moro ("startle") reflex are some examples, but there is a whole suite of others, used by neurologists to check the normal functioning of the new-born's neuro-muscular systems. During further development, in any of the great variety of human home environments, they *become able* to crawl, to walk, to babble and to begin understanding spoken language. There is fairly good evidence that all these, and other developing abilities, result from continuing maturation of developing circuits. We are just beginning to understand how this maturation happens, and it is often, perhaps usually, the case that some elements of the outside world must impinge on the growing baby for the circuits to develop normally: structured images must fall on the retinas, structured sounds must impinge on the cochlea, for normal vision and the understanding of speech to appear later. (We know, for example, that the eye-brain connections of kittens do not develop properly if complex patterns do not fall on the retinas during critical periods.) On p. 58 I promote the theory that human babies *need* animal images (the teddy-bear is a familiar Western example) for the characteristic human thought-patterns to be constructed. This kind of suggestion, that human children need specific stimuli in order to develop specific mental abilities, is at a higher level than the physiological requirements of the retina's and the cochlea's connections, but still seems to be common to all people, in whatever society. However, most of the more interesting inputs to our children (and of course our own interactions with the changed children) differ from society to society, and during the history of some societies. This emphasises the versatility of this way of socialising one kind of animal, and our versatility of developmental response. It is very probable that the urban New Yorker, the Bushman, the Chinese peasant, the Scottish Highlander cculd all be made from the same human baby, by different sets of social interactions. These very different lives would qualify those living them as different species, perhaps, for our hypothetical Martian observer, and I am going to argue (pp 195-7) that there *is* something species-like about different human social modes. Yet all are made, in each generation, from the same versatile human substrate.

In all human societies (with very few exceptions, like the most radical kibbutzim, and some women's-liberation communes) babies are initially brought up by mother, aided (or hindered) by other sibs. Mothers determine the sights and sounds which babies see and hear, bye and large, and pass on to them a great variety of highly ritualised gestures and responses. Stories, lullabies, ritual phrases and toys start the post-uterine programming of babies so that they become children, the very various juveniles of our societies. By building on these, interacting with other sibs, parents, peers, the child acquires the basic mores of that particular society. Fathers are very often not at all involved, until the child has learned a comprehensible language and some of the manners of the social group – toilet habits, for example. In the many strictly monogamous societies it may be allowable for the father to exhibit (especially male) children; in Orthodox Jewish society of London's East End, and (so far as I can tell) in Birmingham-Pakistani society, this is barely permissible; but even then most males lose status by repeated and overt association with young children, even their own. Certainly males lose status by association with the offspring of other families, even in a professional capacity as schoolteacher or regular taxi-driver, or even regular school-bus driver. Yet women can usually find socially acceptable employment in a variety of child-related roles, from wet-nurse or nanny to spinster schoolteacher. (Several of our local school buses now have regular woman-drivers, but I cannot tell if that is simple permeation of women into male roles, or significant in this context.)

There is "division of labour" in all human societies, and most of our cultures segregate peer groups of juveniles to receive cultural instruction, more or less formally, from specialist *educators*. There is resemblance here to baboon society, in that a special "leisure-class" devotes time to this cultural transmission. Among baboons it is the dominant males and their high-status companions who play with the young juveniles (they are *not* children – see the next chapter), but in nearly all human societies those who instruct children are out of the cultural main-stream, and are generally very low-status. This contrast, once observed, is very striking. Leacock's "*Essays and Literary Studies*", especially "*The Lot of the Schoolmaster*"[6] are a dramatic and pathetic exposé of the real situation in fin-de-siècle small-town America, and we will find and examine this same situation in a variety of times and places, for it is at the core of our reproductive *cultural* strategy. Even where a group with pretensions to the role of Coleridge's "clerisy"[7] claimed the rights and responsibilities of transmission of the essential culture across the generations – like the medieval Church clerics – those "unfortunates" in day-to-day contact with children were always the novices, the simple or the aged. Even in our classical stories, and even for the children of highest status, their nurses and tutors were figures of fun, not reverence; Merlin represents the genre (*not* T H White's Merlin[8], though!). Even in our highest places of learning, university colleges and departments, teaching staff and teaching duties are always subordinate to the more prestigious scholarship, research and even administration! Just as we may say of savannah baboons that their culture comes through the dominant, high-status end of the culture, so we should say that it is characteristic of the transmission of human cultures that the non-parental adults involved are towards the bottom end of any social hierarchy.

This depreciation of the job of passing on our cultural privilege has, I believe, had the most unfortunate consequences and may be a major cause of present problems in Western societies. But I am *not* going to recommend giving educators higher status; that would be a grave mistake too. In order to explain why I think my previous colleagues should not be rewarded further, I must digress to what I see as a most remarkable reproductive phenomenon of all our human societies. It is something for which it is very difficult to invent "Just So Stories", evolutionary explanations or models. It is, however, that which I believe to be at the root of all of our success, our affluence: we share our privilege with other families' children!

## References

References in full are to be found from page 243 onwards. Below are listed names of authors and dates of publication.

1. Lillegraven, Thompson, McNab, and Patton (1987)
2. Hofer (1978)
3. Dunbar (1984)
4. Elia (1985)
5. Kawai (1965)
6. Leacock (1911?)
7. Coleridge (1938)
8. White (1939)

# 5

# THE STRANGE CHILDREN OF
# THE PRIVILEGED APE

It may seem only a small step from the passage of privilege, by parents to offspring, to the caring for children *by others* of the same species. But it actually runs counter to much of our understanding of the process. After all, the passage of privilege to your own children fosters, increases the chances for, just those genes that do the passing better; so it increases their representation in future generations at the expense of representation of less provident members of your species. Orthodox biology denies that caring for other's children can be a successful strategy, unless the sharing of privilege among close relations increases the overall survival of those genes (even if this is at the expense of the one doing the providing). I must digress briefly to explain this, for arguments of this form will form my basis for arguing that human beings are very peculiar and specialised *reproductively*, and that this is part of the secret of our intelligence and of our affluence.

This story is one that has been associated with the sociobiological school, but its origins lie much further back in the history of biology, at least as far back as the early 1940s. J.B.S. Haldane is reputed, for example, to have got involved in arguments about natural selection, selfishness, altruism, and the conditions under which behaviour would be selected *even if it was to the disadvantage of the behaver.* The story goes that he saw the point about helping those likely to share the same alleles, and declared himself willing to dive into the canal to save two siblings or four cousins! Altruism as a characteristic behaviour is very difficult to explain *as a character favoured by natural selection,* a trait which will help the altruist contribute more offspring to the future. A classical example is the songbird which calls a warning when a predator is seen; presumably this makes it more likely that *that* noisy bird will be eaten. It's good for the group, because on average they escape predators better, but this extra safety is bought at a great risk to the caller. Imagine all the group having the "alarm-giving" allele (an allele is one version of a gene – see pp 90, 187). I do know that there aren't alleles for individual acts – bear with me ... Now, any mutant bird without warning behaviour (or some of the offspring of one who "marries out") will get the benefit of being warned, but not the risk of warning others. On average, if the risks and benefits are as I've said, this "selfish" or "cheat" bird will be genetically "fitter", will contribute more offspring to the future.  Depending on the magnitude of the risks and benefits, the non-warning, selfish behaviour will take over sooner or later.  But there can be no doubt that, if I've given the whole story, such altruism will be subverted by natural selection – it *will* be taken over.

How, then, do biologists explain the occurrence of such behaviour, which is actually fairly common?  Altruism in general is explained by the concept of "inclusive fitness":  not only the survival of genes in the altruist but also the statistical promotion of "those" genes in his close relatives (who are likely to share them).  The fundamental example is the parent which gives up its own chances by investing food, energy, care, even its life, in its offspring.  The female scale insect, whose body forms a protective shell around her growing progeny as they eat her up, is doing her best by them and so passing her genes effectively.  Some male animals, from ptarmigan to guppies, have colours or behaviour that enable them to decoy predators away from the camouflaged female with their progeny.  Such "throw-away males" have more contribution to the next generation, we suppose, by saving this lot of young once than by living to have a chance at producing more young.

There is a vast literature on this kind of reproductive investment arithmetic[1]. We must distinguish such behaviour by parents, which directly contrives to help their own offspring, from the bird calling a warning – this must *reduce* the chances of, or for, its offspring!  There are several kinds of altruistic behaviour which can be explained in other ways, but the concept of "kin selection", added to the usual me-and-my-offspring natural selection concepts, produces the "inclusive selection" idea.  Can this kind of thinking help to explain why people share privilege so widely?

Let us look at some of this arithmetic.  Another classical example, worker honey-bees who help their mother produce more daughters instead of having them themselves, is explicable but only because of a peculiar relatedness among these hymenopteran insects.  The males are haploid (have only one set of chromosomes, unlike their mothers, sisters or us) so all the daughters get exactly the same genes from their father.  Like us, though, their chances of getting an allele (version of a gene) of which their mother has two different copies (is heterozygous for) is 50%.  So *their* chances of sharing an allele are 75% (whereas our chances of sharing a rare allele with our siblings is 50%). But a female bee's chances of sharing such an allele with its offspring, of passing it on, is only 50% (the haploid male's is 100%, if he breeds, of course). So the best tactic for such a rare allele to increase its representation in future generations, according to current dogma, is to help mother have more sisters (Dawkins' *The Selfish Gene*[2] put the popular argument best, but Hamilton's original paper is worth reading too[3]).  There are many criticisms of this basic argument, particularly as it applies to social hymenopterans: the other daughters your mother produces as a result of your efforts don't breed, so the effective representation of the rare allele is not increased (except as more helpful daughters, which is a different argument); other insects without male haploidy, notably the very successful termites, show the same sociality with most of the colony sterile; semi-social bees and wasps do the wrong things; and so on. Nevertheless this general pattern of explanation by "inclusive fitness" is very generally accepted in evolutionary biology, because it substitutes a "workable" natural selection advantage for a general "hand-waving" invocation of "the good of the species" or, in general, "group-selection" theories of natural selection. The computer models, mathematical consequences and worked-out examples of kin selection in real natural history have taken over professional journals of evolutionary studies in recent years, and have had many popular expositions too. Of these, Dawkins[4] is among the most readable, Wilson[5] gives a coherent biology based on this, and some of Gould's essays[6] oppose effectively and amusingly.  Sahlins[7], on the other hand, gives data on the extent of adoption (25-30% in Polynesia, combined with a high level of infanticide!), and makes clear that the naive sociobiology doesn't begin to explain it.  He doesn't give an anthropological answer either, but warns us that human lives are *socially* valuable rather than genetically valuable.

So I won't take further space here, except for a general warning about some very misleading "jargon" phrases in this literature, that must not be taken at face value.  By "gene" geneticists usually mean a very different thing from, for example, popular journalists.  They use the term, their subject's most fundamental "atom", to mean "genetic difference", that is to say "different alleles at the same genetic locus".  So, when they speak of siblings having a 50% chance of sharing the same genes, this is fine.  But it is very close to the altogether different "siblings share half their genes", which is also found commonly;  of course they do, siblings share nearly all of their genes, their genomes are very similar.  But the chances of their sharing a particular parental allele *which differs in the four parental chromosome sets* is in general 50%. For cousins the figure is 25%; so, in Haldane's example again, it is worth risking your life by jumping in to the canal to save two siblings – or four cousins – from drowning...... !  At least, if you possess a "gene for doing this" (whatever that can mean!) it will spread through the future of your breeding group if it encourages behaviour of this very selective kind.

I hope that it has now become clear that helping someone-else's offspring is a very peculiar thing for a species to do regularly.  Much more easy to understand is behaviour of the precisely opposite kind, and I will give examples of that so that the human peculiarity stands out. Bertram showed that when a pride of (female) lions is taken over by a new pair of males, the above rules seem to apply; the males are almost always brothers, always relatives, and the first thing they do when they have established their position is to kill all the young cubs, drive out older ones, and even cause females to abort. This ensures that as many as possible of the future progeny will be theirs, and that the maximum proportion of the prey will go to them. Hrdy has shown that the same kind of thing happens in the leaf-eating monkeys of India, langurs; males kill babies which are not theirs, and Hrdy[8] has interpreted will-ingness-to-mate among these (and other) primate females as a tactic to preserve their next offspring (whoever the father, the new dominant male will "think" it is his!). She even interprets the human female's concealment of ovulation time (and perhaps willingness to mate with higher-status males) in the same context. Our cousins the chimpanzees, she suggested, have multi-male mating of oestrous females so that all the males involved are then protective of all the young in the group – but they kill and eat young chimpanzees from other groups, without apparent inhibition! In the multi-male baboon troupe, the alpha males father most offspring, and the young males who serve as scouts are guarding their own siblings, so the arithmetic can work out. It is only a little more complicated than the situation in herd-living herbivores like horses or cattle, where one male sires all the offspring. Deer, and the gnu, have more complicated sex lives but this kind of kin-selective explanation seems to work for them too. It even makes foster-mothering, preparedness to give milk to others' progeny, explicable *if* the absent mother is a close relative. But it leaves us with no explanation of the very general cross-fostering, adoption, and in general privilege-sharing seen in all human societies[7]. We even share with other species, like cats and other less useful pets. And this, I hope to show, is our clue.

It has been argued above (p.39) that a cuckoo-like brood-parasitism could not arise among mammals, because the gnus and guinea-pigs, programmed internally like the birds, have no nests. On the other hand, carnivores, myomorph rodents and primates which *do* have nests also have more-or-less complex teaching/learning behaviour which probably can't be emulated by an outsider of a different species. And there's the catch: what about *within*-species "parasitism"? All the "genetic fitness" arguments would suggest that exploiting *another* parent's privilege could easily arise in this mammalian nest-baby set-up; it is rather puzzling that we don't see more of it among the mammals. We do indeed see exploitation of female privilege-giving by males, we even see males bringing up progeny which are not theirs, the results of adultery. Wild ducks show this, and wild coypus, and it has been argued that harem-keeping evolved several times because of the unbalanced, fragile relationships inherent in such pair-bond situations infected with occasional adultery. Irene Elia[9] sees the "mothering" circuits received in these species, by males as well as females, as opening the doors to a great variety of other exploitative situations. She also sees the positive, nurturing side of these peculiar mammalian strategies, but limits herself to description rather than theory. This is, I think, because the theory very soon gets lost in arithmetic which is much more precise, much more sensitive to tiny differences of advantage or risk, than we can know about in the wild situations; she and I have discussed such problems at length, and I think she has the right of it. Perhaps, I suggest and I think she agrees, we don't see examples of within-species-but-outside-family parasitism, outside our own species, because of such inherent instability, susceptibility to exploitation. Those who did it are extinct.

I do know of one very strange, zoologically remote example, however, and this is the little beadlet sea-anemone *Actinia,* the commonest anemone around our rocky coasts. The tiny ciliated larvae, produced from eggs fertilised inside the tissues of the mother, swim out of her mouth and locate another anemone of the same species. There is a suspicion that the larvae "choose" genetically dissimilar hosts, and there is certainly evidence that different hosts are variously receptive, some even digesting all larvae which try to establish themselves. Males and non-sexuals shelter – and nurture – the baby anemones too, and they are released at about 0.5-1cm across after some months of parasitism. Carter[10] has tried to make kin-selection sense out of this, but has only succeeded in exposing a great variety in the exploitative tactics of different strains, some of which favour fostering their babies at the cost of being receptive while others neither exploit nor receive. The only other case of within-species privilege-exploitation I can bring to mind occurs in some parasitic wasps, indeed hyper-parasites. Most of these wasps lay their eggs in larvae of other insects, but a few lay eggs in other parasite larvae inside the host larva; a few even lay male-producing (unfertilised) eggs in the female-producing larvae of their own species, probably laid by other females. This is best interpreted, I think, as competition-with-teeth, natural selection for nasty reproductive tactics. So within-species sharing of privilege outside the family is rare, and unlike the human case as it exists now. (However, while I was writing this, a paper appeared in Nature showing that cliff-dwelling sea-birds replace the eggs in other nests with their own – at the cost of having others do it to them when they leave their own nest to lay elsewhere[11]). Can we imagine a situation, or has one been documented, where our peculiar kind of out-of-the-family baby-sharing could have arisen?  I suggest below that this could have been adaptive in the peculiar situation of a large terrestrial primate living on the grassland, savannah, not in the scrub or forest more typical for large primates. But I think it arose in a way which has not so far been written about, even by so sensible a biologist as Foley.

Scenarios of the origin of Man as a new species with un-ape-like characters, especially well-based and rational ones like those in *Another Unique Species* by Foley[12], all seem to agree that the savannah was very variably productive in both space and time.  Long droughts caused places and periods of great hardship.  This was, it is generally agreed, mitigated by the opportunities for gathering and hunting over large areas.  However this occurred, similar periods of adversity in modern populations living so directly off the land show two phenomena which we accept, because we're so used to them, but which contrast greatly with other mammals, and especially with most other primates. The production of babies is unimpaired down to very low nutritional levels, in contrast to most mammals who stop breeding first (ask any zoo!).   In the women, ovulation ceases at about 65% of "normal" weight but pregnancies are maintained at lower levels even than that[13].   Most mammals miscarry a pregnancy as one of the first symptoms of malnourishment, but people often seem to become *more* baby-productive as they starve.  This is certainly untrue in situations of real starvation, and the arithmetic of human reproduction is also greatly complicated by our very *low* overall fecundity[14,15], but the high level of successful breeding in  conditions of severe deprivation is a surprising human character.  It is all the more surprising because we love our children so much: middle-class "yuppies" in affluent societies will choose not to have children because they "don't want to bring them into such an awful world", while refugee camps are overflowing.   The other phenomenon which is unique to people is our readiness to adopt the children of others:  from urban play-groups for working mothers, through wet-nurses sharing or giving their lactation, and the family-adoption practices of middle-caste Hindus, to full-scale adoption of children "as one's own", even children of another culture altogether – or, even harder to believe, the children of despised sectors of one's own culture[7].

It is very tempting to me to adumbrate a theory of the origin of "children", and of our adult responses which force such a new word for our juveniles, and I shall succumb. Let me try it out on you.   A very successful tactic on these early savannahs would have been the ability of orphaned, or even rejected, children to beg shelter, comfort, food.  Presumably loss of babies by loving, lactating mothers would have provided exploitable new homes for orphans, then as now. Even the infertile women could have accepted partly-weaned children; those infertile women with infected genital tracts would often have food surplus, while low-status (high-prolactin) women would perhaps lactate more readily in response to a suckling infant. Comfort would be given as well as got, both participants would benefit short-term. But how could natural selection have rewarded such mothers with a greater contribution of their own genes to the future? *Why are* we all such "suckers" now for all the child-like exploiters, from Disney, E.T. and kittens to street urchins? It is easier to see that it was to the advantage of the *child*, who is seeking parents. Everyone would be better represented in future generations if they produced "attractive" children who retained baby-like characters to turn on possible new parents; that was obviously one of the pressures towards "neoteny", the retention of juvenile characters. We do indeed retain many juvenile characters into adolescence, even adulthood, but I think the explanation for this neoteny is to do with growth rates, brain size, perhaps even standing up[16].

When we examine our own *adult* susceptibilities – as much a product of selection as the neoteny which complements it – it is at first tempting to dismiss them as necessary adaptation in a carnivore for protection of our own children. I would do so, too, if it were not so *exaggerated*. As *Actinias,* we beg to be parasitised by any young around; why do we so treasure the cuckoo's eggs, and our susceptibility to them? Carter, if he worked with us instead of *Actinia,* would expect to find resistance to being parasitised by other people's, other families', children. The "group-selective" explanation would be that those groups who cared for their children, even at their own expense, would do better than groups which took less care, were less turned-on. However, like nearly all group-selection arguments, there is the problem that such groups would inevitably be subverted from within, as less susceptible people got their babies looked after by others, but didn't look after other people's. They, the callous, would contribute *more* to the future gene (and culture) pool, and the group would evolve away from commitment. What kept us committed?

The suggestion has been made that the human menopause is a specific adaptation to deal with a new problem. Human children take a very long time to become "independent". Indeed this stage is never really reached in most human cultures, especially urban ones (pp122, 179). Because a large fraction of a woman's adult life must be taken up with rearing of children, the woman cannot be an effective adult – unless there are baby-sitters. The suggestion is that the menopause results in freedom from child-bearing in later years, freeing the woman for child-rearing. If the woman survives, her wisdom could make her the most valuable resource for her grandchildren; her input into the child-rearing necessities frees the mother and results in many more privileged, mature progeny. This would need, and could foster, the extension of "own" children to "related" children. But I don't see that it offers a good explanation for taking in "any" children. Geneticists have been arguing about "genes" for the behaviour, and I must agree that it is impossible to achieve more genetic representation in the future by taking in other folks' kids.

But there is an alternative, in the *other* part of our inheritance; the "habit" of taking in teachable offspring would certainly spread, if they learnt it in the new family. The *meme* would spread, where the *gene* would not. Let me try such a scenario on you. A few (or even I suppose, one.... ) of the mothers whose babies were killed, and who would therefore welcome orphans even *before* adoptive behaviour became common, may have taken in a child who was not closely related. This *may* have been rewarding both for her and the rest of her family, and as a story could have been passed on to other children in that and indeed other families. If such a scenario, the idea of adoption being rewarding, once got started then it could spread in a savannah environment where infant mortality and maternal accident rates were both high, provided that the cost was *not* high. In a vegetable tuber- or grain-gathering economy, or a small-animal hunting tradition, children are useful labour, at least, and adoptees would have been selected for survival abilities more stringently than the nest-reared "adoptive sibs", the natural children of the adopters. I could argue that this would bring real advantages in *genetic* fitness to adopters, because their own progeny (carrying their alleles, including "those for adopting") would be likely to mate with the stranger, at least in the second generation. Adoptees would probably on average have survived much more stringent tests, by disease (which may have killed their parents), by starvation, perhaps by injury, than nest-reared progeny. So adopters could recruit this hardy gene set by mixing their own progeny's genes with those of "disease survivors" from other groups (pp189-91) – and it may indeed have been so. But until we know more of the distribution of tissue types resistant to infection in hunter-gatherer groups (which do adopt, usually), or in chimpanzees and baboons (which don't), this kind of argument should be avoided.

I am not very convinced, either, by models of adoption which are related to male adoption of juvenile-looking female youngsters, for rearing and later contributing to a harem, as in hamadryas baboons (Irene Elia[9] favours this model). Early men *may* sometimes have seized baby girls to raise into wives, and one could homologize this with some modern social pathologies, of course; it is possible to pick out any of these models and find illustrative analogies (child-molestors) and criticisms (women should be *much* smaller and more baby-like..... ).  The point here is simply that there may be both advantage and a hereditary mechanism for passing on the advantage for adoption, but only in "nest" rearing, teaching/learning mammals with enough intelligence to provide a substrate for the ideas, the memes, concerned.  How it originally happened could have been any of the above, but it was *not* just a one-off; it spread as a cultural tradition.

We were talking recently at a science-fiction group meeting, and I mentioned this problem.  Helen Wake had just been reading about language acquisition in children, and proposed that language *developed* as child/mother and child/child communication – this conforms with my story here.  The conversation moved over to myths which would promote such practices, and we talked "child marriage", changelings and Snow White.  Then it was suggested that fairy folk, and indeed "travelling peoples", particularly the Romany Gypsies, had a reputation for stealing and/or changing babies.  Such a cultural practice would improve disease resistance of your second-generation offspring, which might appease geneticists.  But much more important culturally, young children (say from three to seven years old) would know the local vegetation, local dangerous species, local human tribes to beware of.  Taking in local children, with their language and culture available to your group as they learn your ways, would usually be immensely useful for the subsequent survival of your own offspring.  A language-and myth-bearing local child is a pre-literate's local Guide Book.  This was surely the earliest sexual system of our memes, how recombination of words and ideas was made possible and profitable.  Everyone *with language* who did it benefited.  That it should be Polynesians who adopted and cross-fostered so much (30% was not unusual, according to Sahlins[7]) would be expected, as the Pacific islands they inhabit must be amongst the most "patchy" of human environments; a local guide would contribute greatly to everyone's survival.

Once we *were* conditioned in each generation to want any baby, not just our own (for whatever evolutionary "reason"), this behaviour would have improved the child-rearing chances for those adults best at it.  Then genetic selection proper would have sorted out those genetic combinations with the best hormone/behaviour profiles to exploit this strategy: babies would become more appealing, and our stimulus-thresholds would drop.  We feel horrified now at the description of male chimpanzees killing and eating the progeny of another group with whom they had fought, don't we (see the description in Elia[9])?  We rarely see ourselves as that unique mammal which sees other mammals' babies as to-be-protected, like its own, instead of as easy-to-digest

food – crazy behaviour, in natural-selection terms, it seems!   This odd
behaviour of ours, our susceptibility to the little-and-cuddly of all kinds, has
all kinds of peculiar aspects.   The pet-keeping propensities of (perhaps especially) the English, the sales of tiny seal-toys (perhaps made from the skins of
culled seal-pups!), our need to keep the slaughterhouse remote from the
restaurant, the popularity of E.T. and (the later, more child-like[6]) Mickey
Mouse, the breeding of baby-like lap-dogs, all are aspects of this peculiar susceptibility.   It has two positive aspects, which are I think rather less obvious:
firstly, it led to domestication of carnivores, then herbivores; even more
important, according to Paul Shepard[16] (see below) it also meant that we could
"anthropomorphise" other mammals, and use them as symbols in our own
nursery world.

This change in attitude towards the babies of others, even other species, had
an unsought bonus, as so often in evolution: the young of other mammals were
not seen primarily as food, but as baby-substitutes.   After we acquired the
baby-addiction we now show, this must have led to the adoptions of young of
other mammals, and so to domestication of carnivores (probably dogs first[17])
then of the much less baby-like herbivore stocks (perhaps goats first).   This
emotional turn-on was certainly instrumental in the domestication of other
mammals; but it must have pre-dated it, have been promoted in our ancestors
for a previous advantage.   I have, then, invented a Just-So Story which bridges
from the chimpanzees eating other parents' progeny, *via* adopted children
sharing language and myths, to lap-dogs and Mickey Mouse.   It could account
for other oddities, too, like the amazing tolerance of some parents for teen-age
behaviour;   but I parade it here simply to show that there is a phenomenon
which needs explaining, and that explanation is in principle available. Sahlins[7]
documents the problem very well – Polynesians kill their own children and
adopt other family's – this must make sociological rather than genetical sense.
But he doesn't then suggest why it happens.   I have begun to do so.

So much for the basic problem of privilege-sharing, but I must also consider
the passage of culture across the generations.   Mothers giving children sights
and sounds, stories and smacks, has already been touched upon.   But there have
been new thoughts on this in recent years, and I want to rehearse these before
I go into my evolutionary explanations for adult human cultures.

There has recently been a most interesting suggestion about the requirements of human children for very specific images, based both in reality and in
myth, in order that they may create a structured universe of the mind.   In a book
very aptly titled *Thinking Animals*, Paul Shepard[17] tied together our use of
animals (like teddy bears or wombles) in the nursery and in "nursery tales", the

division of many tribes into totem allegiances to a variety of animals, and our history as a plains ape killing, butchering and *classifying* animals. Our use of animal similes ("like a lion on the fold") and metaphor ("he chickened out") refer to inhabitants of our mythical mind-world, not to real lions or chickens, and Shepard made an excellent case that we *need* animal images to learn to classify. Our later classification, assessment, of our fellows depends upon properties given to our animal images by the myths of childhood (we in the West all share the cunning fox, the brave lion, the timorous mouse, the wolf and the three little pigs... ). Totems are related directly to these, says Shepard, as we construct an "ecology" of our mind-creatures related to their behaviour in story, and the behaviour of their totem-people in sociology, with little relationship but only a dim ancestral congruence with the real ecology out there. The real ecology is irrelevant anyway, most people substitute the sociological set-up and believe they have left the animals behind in the nursery. The popularity of zoos is, when examined in a biological context, as peculiar as our getting turned on by puppies and kittens, or our dressing up our moral tales in fox-and-chicken garb. Zoos are unreasonably popular, if it were true that we "leave our teddy-bears in the nursery", and circuses with their animal caricatures are quite inexplicably attractive. These animal shows remind us of our childhood congruences, in Shepard's view, and reinforce our "pictures" of the animals in ways that are still a very necessary part of human thinking, however civilised.

The plains ape, according to Shepard, *needed* to classify the animals it found, and in *butchery discovered homology* – the *same* parts occurred in most animals! I have taught an evolution course to zoology students for many years, and have always had difficulty making them see how problematic was this concept of homology; they all just "knew" that a bat's wing was "the same as" their arm and a whale's flipper! Where was the problem[18]? It is my most difficult task, in this book, to show you that these attitudes, bits of knowledge, which we've all accepted without examination can be false-to-the-real-world, peculiar. This is like the accepted attitude to puppies and kittens; everyone – in the contemporary Western tradition – *knows* that small cuddly animal babies must be protected, and certainly not butchered ... obviously! (But talk to a Chinese cook ... ). You are probably less emotionally involved with homology, so let me try to persuade you that in this case too we are peculiar, and promote attitudes which are false-to-fact, then find it difficult to analyse them. Even after I had pointed out to biology students that the genes could be different, the structure could be different, the development could be different, and asked them to tell me what was the invariant that made them "the same thing"[18], they still couldn't see the point; they just *knew*, it was obvious! The idea that it was the relationship between the parts, or even the relations between relations, got to some of them. They all believed that the matter was obvious because it was really the same genes, and therefore really the same structure; the genes were for them, usually, a kind of Platonic ideal hovering behind the reality of the organism: the whale, the bat, the human being all exposed, made explicit, the "arm-ness" in different ways. They were variations on a theme, they thought, and the theme was written in DNA.

But then I used an apt invention of Wolpert's, designed to sever, or at least render tenuous, rigid conceptual links between genes and structure. "I ask this chick embryo", said Wolpert "What genes do you use to make this limb bud?". A very reasonable question, if you believe that it is possible to have a general causal mapping between genes and structure (which Wolpert and I mostly don't...). I paraphrase him: "It replies, 'Some of 22, a smidgen of 3a then a bit of 4c....', but now [19] he has the embryo reply: 'What do you mean, *wing bud* ? Point to it.......oh, you think that's *one structure*, do you? I think it's some of 22, a smidgen...etc' (I have not got his exact words here, but the meaning is faithful to his intention, I'm sure.)There is no reason why what we see as *one structure* should be one structure as far as its formation is concerned, is there? After telling that story to the students, I said "Paul Shepard knows why Wolpert thought 'a wing' was one coherent structure; it was because our ancestors have been 'jointing' carcasses for so long, tearing off 'the arms', 'the legs', that we now learn in the nursery to think of them as 'things' – we even think of the 'face', or the 'chin', as a thing". From the developmental point of view, the view of the creature who's *making* it, there isn't an "it" – the chin is only a mental construct, an abstraction with no relevance to embryology or anatomy in the real world outside our heads. But we learn, in all human cultures, to make the same abstractions, which have nothing to do with embryology, and precious little to do with functional anatomy faces, chins, "ears" ... Ask any cartoonist about this; they are expert at playing with these "bits" of mind, these ideas, which the rest of us classify without critical appreciation.

The above diversion into the concept of homology will be picked up later (pp 89, 105, 163 ), when I question our cultural abstractions in general, and criticise them for being based in this kind of un-examined, unreal mental biology; here it serves as one example of the ways our culture programs our minds as we grow. This differs quite a lot, of course, from culture to culture, and the Inuit's idea of foxiness is doubtless very different from mine. But I bet it's very different from the fox's, too, and much more like something in the Inuit's *social* environment.

The child growing up in its family shares common values, expressed as animal images to a large extent, and these build up each child into an adult with the characteristic culture of that group. It is not only its own family that contributes these images. Although it seems at first sight that the main cultural contribution to the very young human child is *via* the parents, as in the rat or cat family, there is necessary contribution to (nearly all) human family culture (as well as more material privilege) from many other adults and organisations in its human group. Traders, hunters, priests, farmers, shepherds all contribute to the development of all the children of their social groups, sometimes by being physically present but more often by attributed cultural norms: "Be grateful you've got meat today – one of the hunters was nearly killed by a leopard....", or "Say 'Thank you' to God – and the priests – before you go to sleep!". In our Western society, during the extended childhood and adolescence of our juveniles when they learn our myths and social skills, symbolic adult models are there in the family stories. Present in the background are the shadowy figures of the butcher, the baker, the electric-light maker as well as the soldier, the sailor, especially the policeman. They recur in the moral stories children are told, and are recognisable even in the emasculated versions which have survived as our "fairy stories" (pp 95). The assemblage of ideas into coherent packages for transmission to children is characteristic of all human societies, and they lay the foundation of the cultured personality.

What, then, of the reproduction in, and of, the cultures in which these children are growing up? We should have a brief, and prejudiced, look at some of the previous biological models of human culture before I can put this reproductive view into that context.

## References
References in full are to be found from page 243 onwards. Below are listed names of authors and dates of publication.

1. Greenwood, Harvey, and Slatkin (1987)
2. Dawkins (1976)
3. Hamilton (1963)
4. Dawkins (1986)
5. Wilson (1984)
6. Gould (1983)
7. Sahlins (1977)
8. Hrdy (1981)
9. Elia (1985)
10. Carter and Thorp (1979)
11. Davies (1988)
12. Foley (1987)
13. Prentice and Whitehead (1987)
14. Cohen (1984)
15. Short (1976)
16. Gould (1977)
17. Shepard (1978)
18. de Beer (1971)
19. Wolpert (1985)

# 6

# PRIVILEGE BECOMES CULTURE –
# TRIBESMEN, BARBARIANS AND
# CITIZENS

Recent attempts to "explain" human behaviour in terms more or less appropriate to that of other animals, to put our own life in biological context, have aroused approval, excitement – or anger. Wittily titled tomes, from *The Naked Ape* through *The Descent of Woman* to *Another Unique Species* have sold many copies, found their way on to many yuppy bookshelves, and provided fodder for the Sunday reviewers. Clearly they have both fostered, and benefited by, an increasing biological awareness in our society. This is manifested on the one hand by all the little shops selling wholemeal ties and homespun muesli, and on the other by biotechnology and the new techniques in human reproduction. There are many problems, verbal and moral, scientific and philosophical, even political[1], with attempts at explanation in this area (Marx' model was based explicitly on Darwin[1]). Usually, "highest common factor" arguments from selected contemporary practices, screened through anthropological theories of the time, have rather naively invented "best present practice" prescriptions. In our century these take the form of plausible ancestors for us, dressed up as explanations for what the author sees as puzzling human practices. Plausibility is a very unreliable critic, but there are rarely more incisive methods of criticism available for the "Just So Stories" of our evolutionary past.

Arguments have been simple-minded, usually with two major, and basic, conceptual errors: there is usually[2,4,5,7], confusion of "ultimate" (evolutionary) explanation with "proximate" (physiological) causation or indeed mechanism; and there is usually [2-5, 7] an antithesis set up between "genetic" *or* "environmental" causes for innovative structure or behaviour. This excludes most modern evolutionary theory, particularly that largest class of human reproductive tactics, the non-genetic inheritance discussed in Chapter 3, and its application to human upbringing in Chapter 5. This confusion is partly because a great assortment of human ancestors has been postulated, with roots in the prejudices of very disparate authors, and therefore with a great variety of practices, problems and populations. I have the strong impression that much time and imagination has been spent on the invention, but little on the rigour of the arguments. I intend to rehearse a few of these inventions, and criticise them, before building an alternative model. The three most appropriate to have a more critical look at, for our purposes here, are probably *The Naked Ape*[3], *The Noble Warrior*[4], and *The Sea-shore Woman*[5].

The Naked Ape was not entirely, and certainly not originally, Desmond Morris' invention, but he has certainly been its best proponent. The basic and most saleable tenet concerns our sexiness, which was considered to be tied to a pattern of family care; the male came back to his mate for sex, having hunted co-operatively with his buddies and achieved a high-protein share of the kill. Lures which returned males to their wives and offspring were a successful "genetic" device giving more successful mature offspring. The roots of this idea in Freud, in Wells (*The Outline of History*) and even in Rousseau are not difficult to locate. Their later modification by Morris himself (in *The Human Zoo*[6]) and by Tiger[7] and others, have produced attractive evolutionary "explanations" of male sexiness, chauvinism, aggression, and of female family-orientation, female breasts as bottom-mimics, and so on – each of these touches some resonance in all of us and reinforces the idea that Man's beginnings *must* have involved some of these steps, to make us as we are now.   This is the strength of such "Just So Stories", that they do give us new insights as the authors' prejudices are paraded.   We then find that evolutionary "explanations" of Man's beginnings which imply those insights seem very satisfying.   We go from "Yes, breasts do look a bit like buttocks, don't they ...... certainly more than monkey chests or a cow's udder ..... " to "What a good idea! Men *were* turned on by buttocks when we did it from the back (as *all* animals do) so there had to be a substitute when we acquired look-in-the-eye loving .... or he wouldn't have been turned on and we'd've died out ..... "!

There seems little doubt that some 20-23 million years ago, not long after the original diversification of the primates (into prosimians, New and Old World monkeys, and apes), a forest ape like *Dryopithecus* had a savannah-living cousin like *Ramapithecus*.   Both of these apes are fairly well known from fossils, and resemble each other closely (and are like other fossil apes of the times, such as *Proconsul*).   It was thought till quite recently that the *Ramapithecus/Dryopithecus* divergence was that point when the ancestry of the Great Apes and Man diverged, with the dryopithecines specialising into gibbons, chimps, orangs, and gorillas. This story, popular among professionals[8] until the early eighties, had the plains-living ramas specialising in running and thinking and becoming us.

However, that 16-20 million-year-old divergence story has been upset, in 1982-5, by the publication of some biochemical comparisons, of several proteins and DNA sequences, between modern primates.   Recent fossil finds, and the detailed biochemical resemblances, strongly hint that the divergence between Man and chimp/gorilla, at least, was much more recent. Further, the new view suggests that such divergences have been common in our history[9]. Probably the gibbons left first,about 18-20 million years ago, and specialised for their very successful brachiating (arm-swinging) locomotion in the trees. Then the dryopithecines and ramapithecines diverged in the India of 20-15 million years ago; the orang-utan is a very modified, modified for tree-clambering, dryopithecine. The basic stock continued in its versatile semi-arboreal habit, then the gorillas specialised into the trees – and are in process of coming down again as their size increases. This also has been a recurrent theme, larger herbivores specialising off the more versatile omnivorous stock. Most spectacular was the enormous *Gigantopithecus* (whose great molar teeth are highly prized indeed in the traditional Chinese pharmacopoeia!). The chimpanzee and Man represent a basic stock which has not specialised into the trees (although some people believe that the chimp has come down again). Man does not come from the apes or from monkeys; the converse is nearer to the truth.

There is time here for a little lesson in evolutionary theory, whose basis we owe to Clifford Dobell, writing in 1911[10] about what were then called "Protista" (nearly the equivalent of modern Protoctista, i.e. "unicellular" animals and plants). He was very concerned then that people saw The Amoeba as being Close to the Origin of Life, because it came at the beginning of the Zoology textbook, at the bottom rung of the Ladder of (animal) Life. People still do, of course. It's "primitive", after all, isn't it? Dobell pointed out that *Amoeba* is a contemporary of ours, a cousin not an ancestor. If we make the minimal assumption that because we've both had the same time to change since our common ancestor, then it's at least possible we've diverged equally far but in different directions. Consider the "ape-like ancestor of Man", said Dobell (he was actually criticising "Men came from Monkeys"); we get clues to what this animal looked like, equally, from the descendants we have now: it looked as much, or as little, like an ape as it did like a man. We argue from the descendants what the ancestor looked like, said Dobell, and call the ancestor by the name of the other descendant. The common ancestor of the apes and man was "the Man-like Ancestor of the Apes" just as much as it was the "Ape-like Ancestor of Man"! Equally, of course, we could – and he said that perhaps we should, if only to remind people – speak of "the Man-like ancestor of the *Amoeba*"! This is not (quite) as daft as it sounds; there have been many more generations (but mostly without sexual variation...OK) in its ancestry. *Amoebas* seem to need hundreds of chromosomes, lots of DNA, for their *multum in parvo*, all functions in one blob; while we have but twice 23 chromosomes, much less DNA. *Amoeba* (but not so much as its cousin *Chaos*) has quite different mitochondria from other eukaryotes, and in that respect (and much other biochemistry) Man is closer to, more representative of, the common ancestor than modern *Amoeba* is. And that is why I finished the last paragraph with that tendentious bit about the Great Apes being specialised and Man being primitive; there really does seem to have been a Man-like ancestor of the Gorilla, rather than the converse. So there.

Back to the idea of the sexy plains ape, *Ramapithecus* or, more likely, much more recent and much more chimp-and-man-like. I think we are probably right in assuming that the adaptations taken up by our ancestors were savannah, plains and meadow land specialities, and that we can speculate about the basis of their way of life from a knowledge of modern baboons. Morris' suggestion, that bands of dominant adult males hunted game animals and returned to their family "nests" for sexual pleasures, with meat for Mum(s) and kids, has a certain resonance with human habits we regard as "brutish" today. The family group has similarities to the Freud/Wells picture of the Old Man provider, bullying his wives and daughters and driving out his adolescent sons, and links the Naked Ape to the Noble Warrior (see below). Tiger[7] continues the story of the band of young excluded males, possibly hanging about peripheral to the family groups, developing practices from which both comradeship and "male-chauvinism" derive, and which lead on to other Warrior traits.

I don't want to examine each of these ideas in detail, just to hit a few high spots for us to build up a working vocabulary of the suggestions that have been made. Nice little subsidiary suggestions like Morris' pair of explanations for nakedness (fleas build up in the permanent un-primate-like nest; better to be less hairy if you have to *lose* heat by sweating all over when *running down* your prey) add to the story he gives, but could really add to our picture of *any* of the evolutionary stories. We must carefully distinguish the *basics* of a suggestion like Morris'. I take these to be: males acquire protein by running game down on the plains; frequent sex with large obvious sex organs, penis and breasts brings males back to the sedentary family group where the protein supplements his females' gathering of roots and fruits. Then we will find ourselves with a pile of "addenda" (like fleas and sweating, Lovejoy's suggestion of erect posture to see further over grasses and to carry babies, Tiger's adolescent comrades and so on). These may "add attractive verisimilitude to an otherwise bald and unconvincing narrative"[11], in Koko's words, but are not integral to the basic thought. They can in fact serve several of our "Just So Stories" and improve them; I will indeed use several of these for my own story. But we should be careful to judge the picture, the model of our evolution, by the grand design rather than the little attractive, persuasive details.

This is especially true of Noble Warrior models, because variations on the dominant male theme have been legion. The original (Rousseau) picture of the strong, Noble Savage fighting his best friend for the girl has had a long life in novels and on the silver screen, and you may think that this qualifies it for ancient roots as well as a lucrative future. The more complicated models have more to commend them as history, I think; they fabricate important, trendy history rather than individual stories. There have been suggestions that males kept territorial boundaries and hence were more aggressive (better food kept more of their babies alive), or that warfare between groups of Warrior males was the major evolutionary cause of the increase of brain size (losers don't breed[4]), or that competition for dominant, strong males made females sexier-looking (overlap into Naked Apes, here). All these have as basis a social structure in which a few dominant males have harems or wives and can breed, while other males, perhaps all younger males, form bands. In these gangs competition hones those social abilities which have come to dominate our society, and given it some (usually regrettable) character like violence on television or rape. The picture is not very different, actually, from that presented as the basis of "savagery" by the anthropologist Lewis Morgan[12] at the end of the nineteenth century, and to which we will return (pp73 *et seq.*). The most extreme Noble Warrior view was probably Bigelow's[4]; he suggested that male aggression (as organised warfare between competing groups, mostly) was the prime cause of our "sudden" increase in brain size and power, and finished his book with the climactic claim that the only final stability for Man can be found under the aegis, the protection of Great Warriors like Genghis Khan. (He thought we were nearly there, in 1965, because there were really only two great powers in the world, then, West and East, and the next War would give us just One Great Leader – some of us feared, then, that he might be right.....!)

There have been many unorthodox versions of our early history, usually with uncertain historical or biological connections. That is to say, it is not made clear whether it was *Ramapithecus*, australopithecines, *Homo habilis* or our own *H. sapiens* who took up the peculiar option whose modern results justify the author's prejudices about modern society. The best-known of such suggestions is probably Elaine Morgan's inflated version[5] of Sir Alister Hardy's question "Was man more aquatic in the past?"[13], and I will use this as the paradigm of all such odd special-pleading visions of our recent evolution. Originally, Hardy had made the curious point that many of Man's peculiarities as a primate resembled those of mammals which had returned to an aquatic existence: hairlessness, sub-cutaneous fat layer, readiness to swim at least as early as to walk, and even frontal copulation; hair pattern on the body, scalp hair for protection from the sea-side sun, floating breasts were part of his story. Hardy made the attractive suggestion that sea-shore life gave security, in the water, from the larger carnivores while providing many incentives for intelligent erect-posture tool-using, to use molluscs and crustaceans as food.

Elaine Morgan then produced a scenario on this basis, but with Woman as the protagonist and vehicle of evolutionary change[5]. Many other evolutionary suggestions have indeed failed to credit females with important roles. It is very probable that Man the Hunter, in whatever guise he may have existed, required the continued support of hard-working Woman the Provider, Collector, Storer and Preparer, especially for successful rearing of their children. Morgan emphasised the role of women on the sea-shore, but unfortunately spoiled her eminently sensible approach to an effective scenario by a series of wild sexual fantasies. These may have sold many copies of the book to those seeking ultimate explanations of male lust and female unfulfilment, but many of her suggestions were biologically unsound, even absurd. For example, she offered two explanations for our frontal copulation in the *Descent of Woman*. Firstly, that it is practised by all aquatic mammals like whales, otters and beavers. But these all have an enormous tail to get around, and would need a ?-shaped penis to succeed in sperm transfer from the rear – this explanation is simply not relevant to tailless apes like Man! Secondly, she suggested that sitting around on sandy rocks favours development of fleshy bottoms and the "higher" (anterior) vaginal opening. Then men developed larger penises, "chasing the retreating vaginal orifice as it moved...." anteriorly. Presumably the higher vaginal orifice got less sandy, too..... So "unnatural" (i.e. unsatisfactory to female) frontal sex became the preferred option for the stronger males.

In her second book in this area, *The Aquatic Ape*, Morgan[14] did much better. She used much better examples, like the water-loving and shore-living proboscis monkey and the Japanese macaques, rather than the general category "aquatic mammals" she'd used in the first book. Her biological thinking was much better, too, and she made great play of the observation (originally used by Hardy too) that human babies can kind-of-swim before they become able to walk. The front dust-jacket of the book has a very young human baby, underwater, turning its head in preparation for taking a breath at the surface. The remarkable assertion being demonstrated there was that human babies have a specific head-turning reflex as they approach the surface, which permits easy, non-emergency breathing to an infant being carried by a swimming mother. If this is true, and especially if other mammals don't show it (except, perhaps, proboscis monkeys and Japanese macaques!), it is a very strong argument for a previous set of adaptations for semi-aquatic life. She even convinced my wife and me to try this head-turning reflex on our two-week-old baby (carefully monitored by the other children, goggled underwater) and it worked. Like Elaine Morgan, I can find no other "function" for this trick, and am persuaded now of the viability of the basic elements of the aquatic story. That doesn't mean I think it's true; but it has made me much more receptive to theories which include Woman and Water.

If only she had made other "predictions" than the Afar triangle as the site where it all happened ...... does she think it was Johanson's "Lucy"[8] it happened to, I wonder? Those gracile (lightly-built) australopithecines of about four-to-five million years ago were already erect, and fairly intelligent. They were on the way to us, so far as one can see, and there wasn't enough time from then to "now" to put aside an unregistered couple of million years to make the radical hair/behaviour/sexual apparatus differences. Perhaps she's right and it didn't take that long. But the aquatic story was supposed to *explain* becoming erect, bipedal – all the pictures of Lucy show a creature that probably *did* copulate from the front. But our common ancestor with chimp (and perhaps even gorilla) was probably only a couple of million years before that, and these other descendants certainly *don't* show the suite of characters that Hardy, then Morgan, latched onto. So the common ancestor probably didn't, and our ancestors developed them later than that splitting. Perhaps we went into the water, or at least the shore-line, while our cousins went up into the trees. Elaine Morgan leaves open the possibility that the real "missing link", the aquatic ape, did just that at the north-east corner of Africa. If you are persuaded by this story, you would then ask what predator drove some of us into the trees and others into the water. Can we at least find a candidate for that?

I want to take you on this kind of imaginative excursion, so that I can give you the kind of deflating image I generate for myself. I want to communicate to you the attractive-but-silly feeling I have about these "Just So Stories". The best suggestion for this terrible predator that I've come across was that it was the *other* social predator, the wild hunting dog. You've probably seen footage of the modern Cape Hunting Dog packs on television, and there were bigger ones six million years ago! I can easily imagine our modestly-arboreal ancestors getting "treed" by such a dog-pack, and can easily envisage the advantage of being even marginally more limber in the trees, and becoming gorillas and chimps. But as soon as I try to imagine them chasing *our* ancestors down to the beach, the picture comes to pieces on me. I imagine the dogs running growling and barking down the beach, even swimming out into the water where mothers are swimming further out with their babies; I can see males throwing pebbles. But then, instead of tearing our putative ancestors apart, the dogs turn into Labradors and run barking back on to the sand, shaking sandy water off onto any nearby primate – especially warm dry ones! I can't keep this scenario emotionally serious. It keeps degenerating into the comic. Despite this, however, I can argue intellectually that wild dog packs could have been just that predator which took over the savannah from the Man-like Ancestor of the Apes, the Ape-like Ancestor of Man. Can I persuade you?

The only useful measure of evolutionary plausibility is the extent to which such suggestions satisfy readers. What is always tested, too, less explicitly, are the reader's and the author's shared perception and analysis of human societies. There is also, as I've tried to show, a point at which believability fails, or our imagination becomes subject to the inroads of humour-as-criticism; dogs may in truth have chased my ancestors into the water, but my imagination genuinely can't carry it. There is, however, another useful way to apply evolutionary principles to human societies (or to animal groups), which was successful in the hands of Galton[15] and Darlington[16], but which failed to convince (me...) in the hands of Rousseau[17] or Ardrey[18]. This is related to the use of such words as "primitive" and "advanced" in biology, instead of "ancestor" and "descendant"; it requires another diversion, to touch on a major issue in contemporary biology before we come back to human evolutionary models.

Many modern biologists are very unhappy with the rather casual classificatory systems which we have inherited from pre-evolutionary biology, and which carry with them all kinds of unacknowledged philosophical baggage. You may think that the practice of putting like animals close together in classificatory systems, and putting unlike ones further apart, is not controversial. Perhaps if we actually had every one of the ancestors documented, the immense task could be done and there would be little disagreement. The arguments are about many aspects of the way in which our imperfect classifying of organisms illumines or obscures our picture of their evolution. There is certainly an element of circularity in the way we assign fossil bits, because we only "recognise" them because we have a prejudice about the relationships of modern forms; this prejudice has its basis in *Scala Naturae*, of course, not in evolutionary history. Again, if it were always true that evolutionary lines diverged, so that the extent of the difference between two organisms was a reliable guide to their common ancestor (both "what" and "when"), biologists would argue less. But this is not so; apparently similar organisms have often "converged" because of the exigencies of the environment – think how similar are a dolphin and a fish!

In the general attempt to bring rigorous assignment into the textbooks, new words – and thought – have entered our practice. Words such as "plesiomorphic" and "apomorphic" are used by purists, especially "cladists", nowadays. Plesiomorphic means present in the common ancestor of the group you're trying to classify, so not much use for distinguishing sub-groups within the group – like "presence of hair" or even "nails" in apes and men. In contrast, apomorphies are the particular characters, like brachiating arms or walking hips, invented in the different lines. Cladists have rather different views and philosophic styles. (Self-styled "transformed cladists" even throw doubt on *any* building of evolutionary scenarios; they abominate the circular argument involved in assigning fossils to groups by using modern classificatory prejudice, then using the fossil to modify the prejudice! Most of us call this "reinforcement of the model", or "recursional phylogenetic argument", and do it happily.) All cladists, however, agree that attempts to attain real phylogeny must avoid using "grades of organisation", as I've done here in my Ladder of Life approach. The only way to attain a real family tree, they insist, is to keep your eye on the divergences; these are flagged by apomorphies – usually by groups of them. Such a suite of characteristic acquisitions by a diverged group is called a synapomorphy. Their rigorous arguments depend upon distinguishing suites of plesiomorphic characters (symplesiomorphies), and rejecting these characters as criteria. By using only apomorphies they can discover *clades*, groups of organisms having but one oldest ancestor in their class (being "monophyletic", in the old jargon). A beautiful precision of phylogeny can result, but this is frequently unworkable! Lungfishes, because their origin from early "fishy" stock presaged the amphibians and the other land vertebrates, are in that clade (with cows and us!) instead of with the rest of the "fishes". Cladistic classification does *not* make very good Field Guides! Unfortunately for this precision, too, there are a whole host of interesting and informative ideas in biology that depend on concepts like "reptiles", "trees", "fishes", "herbs"......, none of which are clades, of course.

I nearly forgot to add *Homo sapiens* as a major difficulty for the cladists – cladistic argument is very difficult to apply when we know so *much* about our recent ancestry[8,9]. We are, you see, not asking for the same end-point, the same satisfaction as the cladists. They want an evolutionary tree, with its uncertainties quantified; they've told us that man's line diverged from chimpanzee's about 5-6 million years ago, and that the gorilla's lot left a little before that. I, and I hope you, want to know why; we want the scenario (to use the jargon), not the detailed tree.    Foley and Johanson give us both;   Morris, Morgan, Bigelow, Ardrey give us scenarios.   All depend, however, upon contemporary examples, the so-called comparative studies so frowned upon by the cladists, because this is the major source of all scenarios of our origins.   This is, as I've shown, naughty by contemporary standards;   but it has a long and honourable history, and a good record in present practice - and I'll try to use it carefully.

Much modern anthropological thinking of this kind has its roots in Darwin's *Descent of Man*[19], then via Samuel Butler, Lewis Morgan[12], perhaps Galton[15] himself – Malinowski[20], up to Glynn Isaac[21] and Foley[9] today.   It does not depend upon fossil series, but upon comparative studies, and then upon argument to ancestral states based upon anthropological theory (in Foley's case, even upon ecological theory).   When this was attempted by Darwin, who used "savages" as his primitive models, or by Darlington[16] nearly a century later, who used hunter-gatherer Bushmen and other "primitive" human groups, the assumption was always made that "they" haven't changed, but "we" have immeasurably advanced!   Even Foley, in 1987, remarked that defining hunter-gathering as "primitive" tends to populate all of palaeo-archaeology with rather uniform populations of hunter-gatherers, even across species boundaries.   What he means is that our contemporary image of "the" hunter-gatherer is derived in large measure from a few kinds of Bushmen, so this restricted image gets painted onto all the extinct humanoids, from Lucy upwards, who we think hunted or gathered!   But then he denies that anything can be done about this circularity.   Apparently, we must just learn to live with the idea – we must continue to assume that modern "primitives" are like ancient peoples, and vice versa.

However, Dobell sorted us out about the man-like ancestor of the apes (p 65), and nearly all evolutionary biologists have now learned that lesson.  *Some* characters of each of the descendants can inform about the ancestors (the plesiomorphies and apomorphies should indeed be distinguished), but comparative studies can tell us what new questions to ask about the life-styles, the ecology, the overall biological plausibility of the ancestors we dream up.   If I were a modern anthropologist I would try *not* to confuse the *Scala Naturae* with the sequence of real, actual history – *Amoebae*, and !Kung bushmen, are our cousins not our ancestors.   But I would not be a cladist either, throwing the baby out with the *Scala* bath-water;   there is much of real value, many rational and useful scenarios, in the variety of Naked Ape-type guesses about our history which I'm criticising here.   A biologically biased anthropologist might widen his comparative base by looking at the television-watchers of my own civilisation, as well as the Bushmen, to see how early agricultural, comparatively affluent peasants spent their time!

I'm not an anthropologist; I'm a reproductive biologist with no desire to get caught up in modern anthropological stances. So I want to use a very "Noddy" anthropological model, so that we do not get side-tracked by contemporary fashions in anthropology. I'll take a manifestly simple-minded anthropological model and ride that, knowing that we'll not be tempted into thinking it's *true*. The model I'll use is a rather peculiar version of the nineteenth century Lewis Morgan's[12]. His book *Ancient Society* was immensely popular all over the world, and was translated into Russian, German, Spanish – my copy is a 2nd reprint, in 1958, of the Indian reprint of 1902! Nearly all of the associations we now have with words like "savages", "barbarian", and so on have been tinted by the great influence of this book three generations ago. Nearly all the television programmes showing "primitive" humanity take a stance, and feed attitudes in the audience, both rooted firmly in this book. Like all of the above it finds "grades" of human society, rather than phyletic lines ("clades"). It attempts to explain increase of societal complexity by finding processes which operate in the simpler, more primitive society to raise it to a more complex, higher, state. I shall do the same, but in a manner informed by the new biologies. This is not by any means a new kind of enterprise for a biologist. The geneticist Darlington[16], for example, interpreted many of the progressive events of recent human history as the results of different races coming to live together and forming symbioses, because of artisan immigration or occupation by a conquering force with different technology and mores. We will return to his very scholarly and fruitful suggestions later (pp 183, 186).

A very potent suggestion, rooted in Lewis Morgan, was made by Campbell in 1961[22], and this is the simple version I'll use for our models of human cultures; it is manifestly too simple to be taken very seriously. He suggested that human societies, and to some extent human actions, could be seen as falling into one of three categories: "tribal", "barbarian" or "civic". "Tribesmen" were much nearer to the "savages" of Morgan than the tribesmen of Sahlins[23]; "barbarians" was close to modern usage, with its associations with vandalism and with sport; and "citizens" were Platonic, as civic society had been for Morgan too, but Campbell gave them a strong American accent! This view of kinds of complexity in human societies is simple-minded, but it does permit a new, illuminating view of the sharing of human privilege and of the functioning of educational transmission of culture. It will be expanded here in the belief that, because it is so simple and without present authority, I can't hide false argument behind it. In rough outline, then, Campbell's societal levels can be expanded usefully as follows.

In tribal society, nearly every customary action is ritualised, fitting into family patterns of expectation; almost all possible actions are either mandatory or forbidden by custom.   Juveniles are punished ritually for transgression of such custom, and thus the culture is reproduced in each generation as individuals learn to conform to customary roles.   Not only "savage" tribes, but also modern examples like contemporary orthodox Judaism (especially in Jerusalem, but also in city ghettos like Manchester or Boston) exemplify such a culture in a particularly explicit form (or perhaps I just understand the language ...).   I will go on to argue that Judaism has survived precisely because it has the written instructions and admonitions of the Torah and Talmud as its basis, with their central instruction "...and you shall teach them diligently to your children...".   There must be a joke which ends *"This*, you call it a *privilege?"*.   Yes.

Tibetan culture up to the Chinese take-over, at least as portrayed in film and television documentary, and some of the poor South American Catholic cultures also conform closely to this pattern; and studies of Pacific Islanders and Australian aboriginals seem to depend upon just this kind of rigidly-controlled behaviour for their conclusions.   Rank in these societies is usually hereditary, frequently related to marriage-kinship system (and thus indirectly, if at all, to genetic kinship) or a system of tribal division which is at its base totemic (as in many American Indian groups, and perhaps also the Hebrew "tribes").

There is usually a system of puberty or "manhood" rituals, "rites of passage", which show a pattern of great relevance to the transmission of culture in that society, and probably to the selection of the breeding group during the development of all human cultures.   Such puberty rituals commonly have a painful experience for the aspirants:   ritual laceration of facial skin, genitals, or other sensitive areas is often part of the ceremony, and there is usually additional pain caused by fasting, emetic or otherwise noxious drugs, and frequently physical abuse.   There is often an explicitly sexual, often homosexual part of the ritual too.   It has been suggested that such practices, by giving the aspirants experience of pain, enable them to feel empathy with other members of the tribe and so participate more fully in later social interaction[23.] By introspection, because they have the memory of this ritual event, reinforced by observation of others undergoing the pain, they learn to "live for others".   To a biologist, these ceremonies parade both social and biological pathology, and I incline to a more evolutionary view.

The ceremonies have been described for many primitive peoples.   The New Guinea Bena-Bena[24] have a succession of painful episodes:   boys' ears are pierced at 5 or 6 years old, nasal septum at 9 or 10, then the major series of events occurs, prior to puberty, at about 12. During these they are forbidden to contact women at all, especially their mothers, even to walk on a path where a woman has been! Food is restricted to banana, and they must learn to swallow thin canes (which are also used to beat them for transgression of mystical constraints –which they don't yet know); boys doing this together become very close, and this is retained into future life. The climax of initiation occurs in a secret place, usually in a riverbed. They are roughly tied up, and abrasive leaves are pushed into their nostrils, causing much bleeding. Miniature stone-tipped arrows are shot repeatedly into their tongues and into their urethras, again causing much pain and blood loss. During this ritual special flutes are played, representing ancestral deeds and lands which the boys gain allegiance to; the nama, a bird-like but invisible creature, is believed by all to be conducting the ceremony.

Colin Turnbull's famous account[25] of the initiations in the tribes he lived with in Central Africa also emphasise the painful nature of the procedure for the initiates (for the Bantu – the pygmies took the whole business more lightly, apparently); his language is less explicit, as one would expect in a popular account written in the fifties. Margaret Mead's girls in Samoa[26] also had a difficult time, socially rather than physically painful, but all we learn of the boys is that they were circumcised in pairs; they were themselves responsible for finding an elder to perform the ceremony. Ritual circumcision of Islamic and Jewish children is not (usually) at puberty, but soon after birth; Jewish boys (and more often, now, girls as well) have a Bar Mitzvah (Bat Mitzvah) at about 13 at which they must read some Hebrew. The requirement that it be ritually sung, and that the supplicant must take part of the service and explain the biblical text for the week, has been dropped in most communities (I still feel unreasonably proud of having done it – examinations held little terror thereafter!).

John Campbell[27] suggested another interpretation of the events surrounding puberty rituals. He believed, with some evidence, that the ritual pain is always balanced against a ritual requirement, a mythical compulsion, a verbal instruction. The aspirant must balance his fear of the pain, his "instinctive" reaction to the dangerous situation, against a symbolic requirement that he submit to it. Campbell made the point that only if the symbolic instruction was stronger than the instinctive fear was the candidate "human", "one of us" and permitted to breed. Campbell in conversation would choose a variety of persuasive (but poorly-referenced) contemporary practices to justify his position; nevertheless, Mead's Samoan boys exemplify it well, as do the Bena-Bena and Bantu.

Because comparable practices are widespread today among "primitive" peoples (and in sophisticated cultures too), I think that Campbell was right that we can argue for the existence of at least one similar practice in our own ancestors, and for its great selective value during early human history. Selective, because those who failed, who leapt up from the symbolic restraints and fled the pain, were not granted adulthood, community or breeding rights among the humans. Campbell may have been right that in many cases they were killed and ritually eaten, that the failures contributed to the manhood feast, but I doubt it was the general case. If such processes did occur among our ancestors, they surely mediated the change from pre-man to man, perhaps from *H. erectus* to *H. sapiens*; if so, then the acquisition of a super-ego was the critical step in our evolution.

This suggestion enables resolution of one of the most frightening social paradoxes of modern times. This is the negation of all the "higher social faculties" – compassion, responsibility, judgement – in a civilised man or woman who is obedient to authority. We saw this exposed during the trial of Eichmann, whose defence was that he had only obeyed his orders; but it was exposed even more starkly – and much more informatively – by the experiments of Milgram[28]. He set up a series of situations in which volunteers were instructed to hurt others, who they thought were volunteers too – but who were in fact actors, miming the pain. When instructed to do so by the white-coated "experimenter", most subjects gave "shocks" to the (apparent) victims without such question as would stop the "experiment"; few refused, despite the screams of the "victims", when told that there would be no permanent damage! Milgram explained our willingness to do others' bidding, when the bidders were Authority Figures, by saying that we dropped into "agentic mode"; this is fine as a description, but as explanation it is useless (and his other attempts are not much better, for me). We need explanation of this peculiar trait in our characters, so contrary to our expressed beliefs. Any evolutionary scenario which purports to explain our Greatness, our Intellect, our Art must also explain our Eichmanns. This suggestion by Campbell does so, by making us see the pubertal rites of passage as selecting for Obedience to Authority – the title of Milgram's book.

I grew up in a "tribal" Jewish culture, and was required to perform my Bar Mitzvah near my 13th birthday, reading (or rather chanting) the portion of the Torah for that week, and the blessings, on the sabbath morning before the whole congregation in the synagogue. This is closer to an explicit pubertal rite of passage than most of you will have had, but we have all suffered "tests" by peers, at school, by parents' friends at that time. "Becoming a man", "becoming a woman", always seems to require a peculiar deference to authority; we all feel that those – few – who will not give that deference are not our brothers and sisters, are a race apart. At that time, perhaps more than at any other, we require acceptance by our culture. I find it completely believable that rituals have been selected which elicit this most effectively, but differently, in different cultures and at different social levels in each culture. Further, and nearer to classical sociobiology, I find it believable that these cultural filters have, in the past, rejected as unfit, unacceptable, the uncouth individual who spits in the priest's eye. In the tribe, in my youth, the priest had the ultimate sanction; in my tribal history, he did not permit the disrespectful to breed. The system is reproductively stable; it is fostered, promoted and organised by those older men who endured the rites in their youth of long ago, but all of the group collude in their practice; a woman's sons will bring disgrace upon her if they do not pass with honour, after all. Jews have replaced the physical/emotional trauma of pubertal circumcision (now reduced to an infantile, but still explicitly tribal-accepting ritual) by the intellectual/emotional test of the performance-under-stress before all one's relatives and peers. In our ancestors a variety of such institutionalised practices, over the whole spectrum from gross physical trauma to subtle emotional intimidation, formed the central element of the build-a-tribesman cultural kit. This has left us with a stable hierarchy, with super-egos, with respectability in its several senses, with "inner" standards but with Eichmann.

The Campbell view of "barbarian society", in contrast, has very little traditional ritual *action*; but much is built on traditional *values* (and in this it greatly departs from the original Morgan[12]!). Barbarian society is rooted in the transmission and maintainance of "manly virtues" like honour, bravery, patriotism, chastity. Barbarian cultures have a much "looser" structure than tribal systems, with leaders (= heroes) and adulthood rituals with quite different emphasis. These involve action, usually the fulfilment of a task (e.g. dragon-slaying) rather than submission to authority. Males are always dominant (but Amazons were a persistent myth) and females use sexuality as the major social currency (Helen of Troy, and the biblical Ruth and Jezebel, were good examples). Male children take male heroic models, and girls have dreams related to the favours of this male hierarchy. Perhaps a leader forms an apex towards which juvenile aspirations are directed (e.g. a Khan); but even if not, the young men form groups (gangs) maintained around honour systems which are self-perpetuating. That is how these systems, too, can show reproductive stability as a variety of human cultures. These gangs, with their own internal honour-systems, contrast with Mead's Samoan tribal gangs, which were apparently constrained by traditional, adult-derived prohibitions and fears.

Tiger[7] has made a good case for barbarian systems (in our rather naive, restricted sense) evolving from the bands of young males excluded from whatever constituted ancient agricultural, or even ancient hunter/gatherer society.   That behavioural repertoire would succeed which gave the best chance of ... not *offspring* to the excluded males as Tiger suggested, but juveniles that they could "teach" – "impress" would be a better word, in both its senses.   Such a gang system would have succeeded, especially if it gave food/sexual rewards and was reproductively stable as a culture; even if there was no genetic passage (as in most "street gangs" now) cultural reproduction could use rejected males as substrate.   Rejected males are a necessary consequence of polygamy in many human societies; it was certainly not necessary to generate this surplus only by puberty rituals.   Occasional succession of one of these males to "Old Man" status by conquest, or even employment of these gangs as soldiery, would lead to these cultural patterns (memes, p.8) invading tribal systems, perhaps becoming a (very alien, de-spised, feared) part of some tribal cultures.   Such a barbarian system can only have been passed on culturally, of course.   Sociobiologists could claim that rape may have transmitted the genetics of these young men, but this does not convince me.   The idea I am promoting here has its basis in cultural reproduction, in the male gangs impressing the rejected males of tribal communities.   It is an attractive idea that the tribal puberty-ceremony rejects were just the ones to reject authority, and could serve as a good substrate for barbarian ideals.   Tiger, and others, have almost suggested that.   However, Hollywood has made that story so much a part of our culture that we cannot criticise it.   Among Australian aboriginals, however, they are excluded, and have sometimes made social contacts with other, older outlaws when they have gone "walkabout" as part of their pubertal testing.  I know of no evidence that Australian "outlaws" made barbarian gangs that preyed on the stuffy old tribes. The trouble I have here, in constructing this model, is that like the wild dogs becoming Labradors, the out-back turns into Sherwood Forest!    I am continually conscious that we have all received these myths in the nursery, and must be on our guard against accepting them – or rejecting them – for that reason alone.

In "tribal" economics, each family works for itself and no surplus is generated.   There is usually parasitism of the families, however, perhaps as "tithes", by other tribal elements[23,24,25]. Food, woven goods, special plants, a proportion of agricultural produce, especially "service" to the general commu-nity, are taken from the family units for the support of these other tribal elements. These are usually unproductive necessities like warriors and – especially – priests. But the tribal system does not produce surplus; even in those cases, like the North-western American Indian tribes which lived off the seasonal salmon runs, smoking and storage gave maintenance and a little for trade – no surplus, no accumulation of capital (apart from cultural capital). Morgan[12] pointed to the tribes, Ojibwas around the outlet of Lake Superior and those in the valley of the Columbia, which lived off the salmon and showed "the gradual development of a surplus population"; he showed that they had budded off many other tribes, still closely related by language and patterns of totems. He further argued that this multiplication had begun in prehistoric times and continued into his times, down the Western coast, so that "an original family, commencing its spread from the valley of the Columbia, and migrating under the influence of physical causes, would reach Patagonia sooner than they would Florida." Indeed he believed this fertile area to have been the original "seed land of the Ganowanian family" from which America was colonised by the American Indian tribes. His documentation of the ways of life, the languages, the totems – as the labels of the gentes – of so many of these tribes makes a fascinating story of continent (in both senses) migration – and it was moderately reliable too, according to my anthropological friends. It is a model of tribal cultural reproduction, in groups of hundreds or, at most, thousands of people.

Barbarians also do not accumulate capital (except for cultural capital – usually "sagas"). They have occasional immense surpluses, gluts, but little storage – they blow it all on great feasts, great conspicuous wastages, great showings-off. Between the gluts there are often very hard times – no self-respecting barbarian child would accept "charity", of course, and it would be demeaned by the taking of stored food! Both Kipling, in *Kim* and Heinlein, in his imitation *Citizen of the Galaxy*, showed very beautifully that these barbarian honour systems had status-regulation which forbade the receipt of charity – not gifts – unless it was part of an honourable barbarian strategy like begging! Begging is alright, because there *is* no accumulation of capital wealth. The mark of the barbarian in our midst is the disregard of material wealth, the high valuation of honour, reputation, distinction.

Campbell's tribal and barbarian forms of human culture can be very successful, but even more successful is a culture with interaction of tribal and barbarian elements, his *civic* culture. Barbarians raid and loot agricultural tribes, and sometimes become established as "rulers" of a tribal peasantry. Examples of this, from the foundations of ancient Egypt, through Homer's Greeks to Viking domination of much of northern England, are well documented in history and fable. Campbell, and indeed Morgan, saw the heterogeneity of modern (Western... ) societies as having its roots in this association; artisans, priests and especially warriors appear among the barbarians, while the peasantry specialise towards different agricultures, as shepherds or farmers, as hunters of (non-honourable) prey such as fish. Routine, indeed ritual, matters are dealt with by the tribal system, while the "important" roles are taken over by the barbarian system. Our division of our mental menagerie into "Beasts of the Chase", "Game" beasts, and especially "Honourable" creatures like swans surely descends from such a categorisation of the people who dealt with them. Merlin's explanation of it to the young King Arthur, in T. H. White's *Sword in the Stone*[29], reflects this beautifully (I do not distinguish fictional from anthropological sources, because I am exposing persuasiveness of models, not "Truth"!). With the success of this division of labour in economic terms, more privilege is generated and a true urban state is born. The urban state has economic surplus as a characteristic or, to restate this in terms of its cultural reproduction, each generation of offspring is more privileged than its predecessor. Not only cultural capital of diverse kinds, but real actual wealth, accumulates as the generations pass. Civic cultures, producing urban economies, can be recognised by the accumulating food-stores, machinery, land, transport (initially oxen or horses, or human slaves in South America[30]).

Within the urban community the adoption of multiple role (status-sets) by an important segment of the population forces a new use of intelligence. The true citizen of the Morgan/Campbell pattern, unlike the tribesman or the barbarian (many of whom, of course, live in all towns and cities) must *decide* whether ritual, tradition, submission *or* honour, machismo, leadership are appropriate for today's role. Even for such "true" citizens nearly all of their lives are tribal, governed by ritual and ruled by custom. Very few of the day-to-day conversations and other inter-personal interactions break new ground; urban traditions are mostly tribal (ask any barmaid).

Versatility is required sometimes, however, and a reversion to juvenile barbarian codes gives this. The adult citizen has usually been a barbarian in his youth, for all juveniles in cities grow up through a succession of different societies. Family, mostly maternal, care is succeeded by toddler small-group associations, dominated by one or a group of mothers. Myths, legends, "fairy-stories" are inherited as a set of general-purpose rules. The mental menagerie of wolves, foxes, chickens (pp 58-60) – or monkeys, bears, fish and dragons further East, salmon, owl, beaver further West – is developed into princesses, witches, knights – or commissars, revisionists and Party Members. Religious or "historical" fables in their turn, descended from prescriptive myths or sagas, give common social values to the various tribal and barbarian behaviours later to be expected of adults in civic societies (the London East End adolescent has probably never heard of Beowulf, but many of his drinking rituals are descended from that culture!). Peer-group gangs, clubs, "pavement groups" engage the pre-pubertal children, and puberty is always associated with rituals and tests in these groups. These are usually not specifically associated with biological puberty, but are a specific set of ordeals, especially for males (but some female ordeals[2,26] can be excruciating for the participants).

Later adolescent groups, with their honour systems and leaders, have a perfect barbarian structure; they retain their versions of the songs, rounds, stories and games[31] learnt when they were younger. But as they reach adult status, they superimpose specific, adult-world, honour values. Status is always paramount, and ideals of purity (by group criteria), bravery, machismo differ from group to group (but not, of course, as much as the participants think they do). Many of the outer signs of such gangs, and the adults who result from them, are specifically designed to label. How to wear a hat, how the hair is cut or worn, label allegiances for all of us. Erstwhile Mods or Rockers, present Rastafarians with their "dreadlocks" (a beautifully barbarian term!) signal their honour systems to the rest of us, while the red sports car or the Porsche label similarly. Just as the cartoonist has knowledge of our basic face-recognition circuits, so the good advertising executive has a feel for our status symbols – and exploits them. Such must be explained by evolutionary models, too, for them to feel "right".

A usual urban requirement is subjection to an adult ordeal system before full adult status is granted. This may be a Bar Mitzvah, a Chinese public examination, or simply a "going for a drink with the boys". Acquiring a fishing boat, a horse or an apprentice signal adult status in different civic societies. Hereditary differences in privilege are usually great, the "best" teachers and peer associations being restricted to the children of the elite, who are often the cultural, if not the genetic, heirs of barbarian conquerors. In this way, as in others familiar to all of the readers of this book, the civic status-differences are retained through the generations, as in tribal and barbarian cultures. The cultural geography of the city is retained through the generations; the culture is reproduced.

In all human societies wars change fortunes, sexual liaisons warp social strictures, and new leaders arise from unexpected quarters. Citizens, unlike tribesmen or barbarians in our usage here, have versatility of individual response, and economic "room to move", so that cities are reproductively more stable than less heterogeneous associations. Systematic strategies and rituals are invented, evolved, to defuse the major strains in city life, which arise both from male/male interaction (friendship/competition/status) and the strong and continuous human sexual drive. The routine segregation of sexes in adolescence, the marshalling of juvenile boys through a military system, chaperonage and the duelling code are all examples of such systematic avoidance of problems. All these strategies are too wasteful of familial time for tribal use (though some *are* used, sparingly, in tribal systems) and involve too much loss of individual freedom for barbarians. Barbarian systems which have *not* yet evolved such defusing mechanisms as part of the social structure, but have evolved or inherited high-technology cities (as in many African states) always try to use the Army to keep civil order. This represents the most obvious social mistake, as any English bobby on the beat will explain. Flagrant abuse of the populace (especially sexual abuse, if my African friends inform me aright) must arise from confrontation of barbarian, honour-system soldiery with tribal peasantry or with different-culture barbarians. Only in the evolved, developed city can time and labour be devoted, and peoples' lives be committed, to a *police force* in whatever guise. This characteristically uses male/male social ploys to enforce the commonly-agreed reward/punishment system of the society, when the minor defusing strategies listed above have failed. Its "bones" are exposed in the Western film, when explicitly tribal and barbarian elements must be controlled by the Sheriff or Marshal using male status ploys; this may be why Westerns are so popular in cities all over the world. They are not popular in the newer African States, I understand – although there are of course many other reasons for that!

It is the existence of the real common capital, accumulating across the generations, which permits such apparent luxuries, parasites, as a police force. This same economic "room to move" permits the most pernicious of the cities' strategies, schools.

Schools, in all the senses of the word (see the digression about Illich[32], below), only appear in cities. Tribal children are educated within their family circle[26], as they help with the chores; this is followed by peer-group practices which cultivate, often enforce, the interpersonal, especially sexual, standards and customs. How much "personal space", how much touching is allowed, which pronouns and which euphemisms to use with which people, are all acquired out of the family, but within a juvenile system whose sanctions are usually more ready, but much less severe, than those of adults. Barbarian children are more usually reared by female groups until "gangs", often of mixed ages but rarely of (effectively) mixed sexes, take them into the status-hierarchy of the maturing juveniles. Barbarian "education" is a series of "trials", ordeals, ventures, often competitive in the early stages but progressively lonely as the special heroism is practised.

The education of the varied inhabitants of *early* city-states was very different from what we see now, also. An initial period of familial care was usual, except for the children of soldiers (warriors), prostitutes and the very rich, who were brought up by unrelated women or older children. Later, apprenticeship, gang rituals, familial and priestly instruction were all brought into most juveniles' lives. No group had responsibility for all of the children's "educational needs", just as the administration of medicine and the sanctions of the law were then in diverse hands. As in tribal and barbarian society, each child's development was seen to reproduce the route taken previously by the adults he was to emulate, perhaps to replace. He learnt honourable behaviour in status confrontations in the gang of his peers, he learnt his customs and rituals during interactions with his parents and sibs[29], and he learnt his adult role, and the expectations surrounding it, by interactions with the very adults who had the role.

It is certainly not the case that tribal ritual is learned in security, without the pain of error, or that the barbarian ethos is passed in a wild excitement of blood-curdling screams and war-axes. But contrasts of this kind do occur commonly as we build ourselves into civilised people. The development of children in these post-Freudian times is often portrayed as a sequence of contrasts.

|  | *Security* | *Learning* |
|---|---|---|
| 1. Baby: | Milk/warmth/mother | Weaning/cold/strangers. |
| 2.Toddler: | Home/comfort/family | Play-group/discomfort/peers |
| 3.Adolescent: | School/gangs/peers | Job/own residence/ adult confrontations |

This is easily, and usefully, seen as an accommodation to each new situation by a widening of horizons, a true enlargement of the self. The tribal/barbarian contrast may be seen in the above scenario as a set of choices: rules *or* adventures, formalities *or* challenges, answers *or* new questions become the framework of each adult's personal and interactive life. Either security (tribalism in our context) or constant trial (our barbarism) can manifestly serve as the basis for successful human reproductive systems.

But in the complicating, enriching life of the cities a new force appeared: "education". The development of the teaching function, usually I guess as a side-issue of the tribal religious instruction of the young by the priests, caused a separation of juvenile aspirations from the adults' goals for them. To a very large extent, this separation was inevitable in a more complex society than the tribal. Priests, who contacted all strata and professions, have always apparently been in the best position to reproduce the entire web for, and in, each child's education. However, it was unfortunate that the priestly view was not the most useful carrier of all the variety of privilege in each culture, because it *was* the most effective method for teaching children. It had descended in an unbroken authoritarian tradition from the old puberty-rituals – which we've all been selected to respond to. So, having been *initiated* by the priests, we were conditioned to give up the teaching function to the priests.

How did civic humankind, the Privileged Ape, set up this strange experiment in the passage of the most precious, accumulated wealth any species on this planet had achieved? It was a new cultural biology of reproduction, held in the grip of the priesthood at least initially; each child was to receive a broad culture from a low-status specialist in culture who was, however, uninvolved in any of the productivity of the culture. Contrast this, for a moment only, with the situation in simpler societies, indeed with the multi-male savannah baboon troupe and, probably, our own ancestors of some 6-3 million years ago: access to all society's roles is available to all juveniles *via* the high-status adults they interact with, at the fount of privilege at society's apex (pp. 43-5). In great contrast, the cultural capital of the Privileged Ape was transmitted *via* the lowest-status members of the society! Leacock[33], in his lampoon of the lot of the schoolmaster in fin-de-siècle America, shows how low in society's pyramid were the transmitters of our culture – below hairdressers, even below actors, both of whom would get teaching jobs to pay for their training! It was not only Christian culture which devalued its priests, whose priests took themselves from the mundane workings of society into the temples; Taoist, Buddhist, even to some extent Islamic priests/teachers were always seen to be unworldly. Rabbis, too, in their tribal cultures in the ghettos, withdrew into Talmudic study. (As they are the keepers of the social heredity, we should not be surprised to see this withdrawal; it parallels the retreat of the eukaryote DNA into the nucleus, the segregation of the germ cells in metazoans, the restriction of reproductive function to a few, uninvolved, bees or coelenterate polyps, wolves or baboons. I am not going to try to explain this here, but must draw, and emphasise, the parallel because it is close to the centre of my thesis.)

What of the children and their parents? Why did they accept that priests were the "proper" vehicle of the child's development? In England, before the reformation, the child was valued very much as an (innocent) immortal soul, and we must recall that only about a third made it to adulthood; it was most important that godliness was imparted – said the priests. After the Reformation, considerations of human dignity became paramount; with the development of new concepts of social justice, equality under the law, and of democratic government, the education of all citizens for adult responsibility became the major overt goal of the school system. This new reading of the old Greeks did not, I think, make us unique; it brought us closer to Islamic and Far Eastern school systems in philosophy, though not in content or method. From our point of view here, however, the apparent philosophical basis of this divorce of education from production is largely irrelevant. Its effect was that the dissemination of the most subtle and potent privilege won by effort of the parental generation was left to an uninvolved cadre. The problem has arisen because this cadre always sat on the treads of the staircase of an advancing society, it never was to be found on the risers. A new and special category of organism had been invented, a kind of middle-man of privilege, as special as the queen bee – or the drone: the teacher.

All citizens received part of their training from this special group, as a "basic", or general education ideally incorporating some literacy, some numeracy and much custom, usually as religious instruction. Laws, for example the Ten Commandments of Judaeo-Christian cultures or the Apho- risms of Confucius, were emphasised, so that each child was given a priest's- eye-view of his position in society. To such a view, education was a sequence of experiences, ideally showing to the child the previous treads of the staircase of its culture's rise to prominence; so Euclid, Pythagoras, Aristotle, Homer were far more "educative" than butter-making or metal-casting.

The most vocal exponents of the anti-educationalist philosophies have been the French school headed, I suppose by Marcuse and represented by Foucault (pp 121, 149). But at this point of my argument I must digress to the vital so- cial criticisms made by a most dynamic Mexican Catholic priest, Ivan Illich. He was perhaps the last man on earth you would suppose to produce a trenchant criticism of medical practice, of church practice, but especially of educator practice[32.] The burden of his message is in many ways the converse of Milgram's (p.76); Milgram showed that we are all liable to drop into "agentic mode" when we are an agent of somebody in Authority. Illich shows how we drop into "patient" mode when someone takes "doctor" status, but much more importantly he shows how we aggregate to form Authority structures in urban societies, which he calls "Schools". In *Medical Nemesis* he showed how the medical profession had progressively taken the freedom to act, the ordinary care of the body and mind, from the ordinary person and made it a "mystery", an arcane subject. People used to set their own bones, you know, and sew up skin wounds – now they have to go to the doctor to get an Elastoplast put on. As soon as you have seen how the School of Medicine has taken you over, you suddenly appreciate your other "patient" relationships: to your hairdresser, your tailor, your cobbler, your ski instructor.  Illich was not arguing against specialisation, or against expertise, at all.  He appreciated that medicine is an immensely complex art and science, and that his hairdresser could do a much better job than he could.  It was the abrogation of personal responsibility on the part of the patient, and the consequent closed-ranks, closed-shop philosophy of the professionals, which he saw as so unhealthy for both.  There is a desperately pathetic article in a Women's Liberation collection of articles about new reproductive technologies (I won't name it), which describes in detail how, with the aid of a mirror, women can help each other see inside themselves, actually see the mystery which till then had been kept from them in medical textbooks!  Vagina, even cervix can actually be seen!  On the other side my medically-qualified wife, who trains Family Planning doctors, was asked by a well-qualified (Asian) woman doctor she was instructing: "These condoms you tell them about ..... can they fit them themselves or must they be fitted by a doctor?"  True, honestly.

Just the same thing has happened, of course, with educators.  They have formed a School, and have taken the whole practice of Education to themselves.  Illich's book[32] is called *Deschooling Society* because it is mostly about educators, about the central issue of this book:  that the education of the next generation is taken from the real world, from the family and the workshop, and into the classroom.  I have heard many parents say "We mustn't teach our child to read, let's wait till she's at school where they'll do it properly!", haven't you?  Sex Education, even, has been taken into the schoolroom (though that is usually a cop-out), and P.A.L. is taught in my son's school: "Preparation for Adult Life ...".  What do the teachers at his school know about the adult life of our society?

So a paradox has now arisen in the reproductive biology of urban cultural inheritance.  The Ape's cultural privilege is now so extensive, and it is so secure on its base of real economic capital, yet it cannot be transmitted to its beneficiaries, the juveniles, *via* the designated reproductive route.  This paradox is, however, reproductively stable;  a "school" of educators reproduces its own arthritic culture in successive generations, adequate for most children to receive from their society but not adequate to build upon.  This is a peculiar and remarkable phenomenon of modern urban culture in all affluent countries, and will be examined in more detail, as a reproductive pathology like a venereal disease, in the next chapter.

# References

References in full are to be found from page 243 onwards. Below are listed names of authors and dates of publication.

1. Oldroyd (1980)
2. Fisher (1983)
3. Morris(1967)
4. Bigelow (1969)
5. Morgan (1972)
6. Morris (1969)
7. Tiger (1970)
8. Johanson and Edey (1982)
9. Foley (1987)
10. Dobell (1911)
11. Gilbert (1885)
12. Morgan(1958 [1877] & 1875)
13. Hardy (1960)
14. Morgan (1982)
15. Galton(1869)
16. Darlington (1969)
17. Rousseau (1941)
18. Ardrey(1969)
19. Darwin (1871)
20. Malinowski (1963)
21. Isaac (1981)
22. Campbell (1961a)
23. Sahlins (1976)
24. Langness(1977)
25. Turnbull (1961)
26. Mead (1971)
27. Campbell (1961b)
28. Milgram (1974)
29. White (1939)
30. Harris (1974)
31. Opie and Opie (1959 and 1969)
32. Illich (1973)
33. Leacock (1911)

# 7

# CULTURES, CADRES, THE "CLERISY" – AND THE RISE OF INCOMPETENCE

The Morgan/Campbell grades of human culture (tribal, barbarian and civic) place the transmission of privilege in our cultures in a naive, but I think workable context. Formal education in civic cultures was presented briefly as a perversion of the passage of human privilege in simpler cultures. Here I will choose examples, mostly from that context, to make the same case in a different way.

Before that, we should take a look at the way in which people change, from babies through adolescence to adulthood. What is *it*, we should ask, which is "educated"? This is an old problem of reproduction, of development, that most people have not met in these terms. There is a paradox that results from our calling the successive persons that each of us lives through by the same name, as if "we" are there inside all the time. In embryology this view was called "preformationism", and you have all probably seen the little man fitted into a sperm, drawn by Hartsoeker. We know, don't we, that it really isn't like that? The 16-year-old Jack Cohen was in no sense "inside" the three-year-old, and I am another person again. But we don't have easy language in which to talk about development; Pat Bateson, a Cambridge developmental psychologist, does it beautifully, however, and so does his erstwhile colleague Susan Oyama[1], in a book called, not wisely but well *The Ontogeny of Information*. How silly it is, she emphasises, to *distinguish* the genetic pattern from the environment. It is like asking of a machine "How much was contributed by the blueprint, how much by the mechanic, how much by the metal it is made of?" The primacy of the "blueprint" idea in our present thinking is, I'm sure, misleading. The answer is clearly "All of it!" to all three for the machine; similarly, the contribution of "genetics" and "environment", Nature and Nurture, must be 100% – each!

We can sometimes blame *differences* between two otherwise similar organisms on differences of genetics, or differences of feeding, but that is not the same issue. It is like saying that the machine doesn't work because of a mistake in the blueprint, an error in construction, or an absence of fuel. But there is a deep philosophical confusion here; we must not argue from differences to organisation, from defect to provenance. "Why not?", you may well ask, "Many geneticists do!" And that is true; geneticists find some flies with vestigial wings, say, and they locate the genetic difference, the difference in one gene (a mutant allele), that results in the different wing-formation. Flies with two copies of the mutant allele (from both parents), have vestigial wings, flies with (at least one copy of ) the normal allele have normal wings. "Here is a gene for making wings!", say some geneticists, falsely – what they have is a difference in genetic prescription that makes a difference to development. The difference to wings may be, usually is, at the end of a very long and complex causal chain; the "real", more basic difference made by the mutant allele could be a difference of threshold of response of *all* the cells to a common chemical, making small differences everywhere (it usually is more like this). When the wing is inflated, however, a tiny difference in the shape of the structure could result in collapse because of a little asymmetry. The wing *of these flies* is just most sensitive to the universal disturbance, and in other very similar flies the *same* genetic mutation could result in problems with legs, eyes or whatever else has a developmental process sensitive to that chemical difference. The mutation has *not* exposed a "gene for wings"; it has exposed a developmental sensitivity. Making an organism is much more like baking a cake than building a machine; perhaps if we were to think of the genome as "recipe" rather than "blueprint" we would have a better metaphor.

If we are to consider education, and especially if we are to consider it as part of the human reproductive process, we must be sensible about this. My way of doing this is to see education as that specifically human privilege required to complement the developing body and brain so that a person constructs herself, to become an acceptable and effective member of her culture. The new-born baby, as we've seen, is very far from being Locke's *tabula rasa*, a clean slate. Metaphors of buckets being filled with water just won't do. Nor will icing of cakes. Biological development changes the organism through and through; say to yourself: *there is no maggot in the fly, no caterpillar in the butterfly, no tadpole in the frog*! To make this point, let's start with a well-developed human being, nine-months developed, with the neural circuitry waiting for the new outside-world stimuli to respond to – not an empty bucket! As this creature feeds, sees, responds it changes itself so that it acquires new properties, new motives. This is true not only of the growing baby, of course, but of each one of us at all times; each action, each response changes us and engenders new motives.

Human actions can only rarely be assigned simple motives, and the sources of those motives are always complex (despite Agatha Christie). The set of motives of a human being at a given place and time seem to that person to define his "situation" then, to make him the very person he is – yet he knows they are ephemeral. We know that today's cares, taking up so much of "us", will be minimised next year but that we will consider ourselves the *same* "us". This apparent continuity, between the girl of six and the woman of forty, marks a continuing and characteristic interaction both with outside influence *and with what she sees herself as, at every moment.* Just as the DNA of an embryo provides an unchanging thread of information, referred to in each cell by an embryo complicating itself as it develops from egg to baby, so there seems to us to be a "real", continuing presence with which each event of our lives interacts, but which is itself matured further by each event (unlike DNA). This maturation of our identities differs enormously between human cultures, and indeed is understood differently at different times and places. Within any culture, as well as between cultures, there are consistent ways of bringing up children to make them peasants, princesses, or philosophers; sometimes special paths are segregated, more usually the children are given individual goals and share at least some of the instruction with others.

Sets of motives differ between cultures, and between ages, levels and roles in a single culture, in a consistent way which seems much more permanent to an observer "outside" the situation. Let us imagine one from a *very* different culture, let us say a Japanese geisha: when she sees French electricians solving a problem in a characteristically "French" way, very different from the "German" or the "Yoruba", she blames the French educational system; she knows that few human motives, or styles, have a "hard-wired" genetic basis, they are programmed in during development. To the actors, the electricians themselves, however, they seem to be motivated by aspirations, goals, desires whose possible solutions are infinite in scope and only constrained by the mechanical or economic strictures of the problem; *we cannot perceive our own style of living.* (Think of a blind swimmer in a river – there is no way for him to detect the flow, he is a part of it.) Yet these styles, so characteristic of different cultures (but so invisible from inside) are all produced using much the same human babies. A major property of human babies is programmability, and for this we need developmental stability to build on (pp 33-5). The interactive properties of babies (and their mothers) are the "givens" of the system. The societies they get plugged into are all "designed", evolved to latch on to these common properties to produce *people.* Geishas and electricians are examples but each of us is just such an example.

We all realise that aspirations, goals, desires do not spring fully-formed from "within" but are suggested by cultural cues *to* the imagination, which has itself been developed in particular ways *by* our culture. Some affect us deeply, are "character-forming", while others seem not to touch our essential selves. The belief that the "essential self" is biological, while the optional extras are cultural, is very pervasive but not well-founded; Susan Oyama[1] has done a lovely job of taking it apart.  Some events, some stimuli, react violently with our physiological "hunger" or "sex" circuits (frying onions, or "interested" eyes meeting across a room);  some resonate with neural programming about "Mother" or fear of heights;  but others only affect higher-level decisions relating to abstractions like chivalry or Marxism, or the prospects of hunger or pain in various plans we have.  Yet other desires may be truly whimsical, arising perhaps from deep chemical or physical perturbations in a few nerve cells;  some cultures constrain and edit whims, others value them, build upon them.  We are the results of interactions between what we were, and what happened to each different successive "what we were".  We call what happened to us, apparently by cultural intent during our juvenile phase, our education.  We judge cultural intent by the systematic occurrence of constraints (children *must* attend school ... ) and by sanctions against avoidance (truancy is punished).

The view that a culture "designs" its education primarily to train its members for their roles is general, at least naive and usually wrong.  Education in all societies is at many levels, and most of its structure is unrelated to any recent human decision.  Some of the levels are:  simple information presentation (drinks come in cups);  training in usual, or esoteric, techniques (taking buses, buying goods, making swords);  guidance in inter-personal skills (courtesies, argument, flirting);  guidance in learning the methods of learning (reading, writing, library skills, other meta-learning tactics);  training and assessment of professional and technical skills;  the formation of habits of self-assessment, and of personal standards for technical, intellectual and administrative expertise. T. H. White's book[2] *The Sword in the Stone*, dissects this beautifully, at the right level for adolescents to enjoy it, as Merlin instructs the young King Arthur.  Clearly, many technical and intellectual aspects of different adult roles *are* set upon a basis of things learnt at school.  But far more important for development of our "character", attitudes to games, to sex, to learning itself were acquired too, and these meta-attitudes have usually changed less than we think when we are adult.  Schools are, in many civic sub-cultures, little more than baby- or child-minding establishments, and in these circumstances the maternal teaching is followed by wider family connections, usually with older sibs, then into the competitive world of peer-associations and gangs.

In nearly all societies with civic pretensions, these peer groups are not simply reproduced by inheritance of a suite of peer practices but are sooner or later dominated by a designated class of adults.  These range from baby-minders, nursemaids, scoutmasters, curates, corporals to professors. Some information, and many attitudes, are culturally inherited *via* these adult/ adolescent relationships instead of *via* the more functional routes in the family or even the temple. So, for example, the cultural attitudes of the nursemaids and tutors of upper-class English society probably contributed more to the class attitudes of their wards than did their upper-class parents or the later, more professional teachers. This transmission of culture, like the earlier maternal/ juvenile relationship, depends upon reciprocal interaction between the parties, it is not simply a "giving"; complementary roles are generated, just as for the baby's smile and the mother's response. For example, those upper-class children developed a set of specific peer rituals ("naughtinesses") which elicited cultural sanctions ("bed without any supper") from the guardian. This complementation determines the rules of the cultural game for a long subsequent cultural history, even though the social counters used in the interaction may change over the generations, and be different in different strata of the society. The ways in which working-class children were naughty with mother or older sister was different from with father, different again from the upper-class child with the governess. Yet the upper-class, governess-type myth was told as nursery story to the lower-class child.

We should realise the irrelevance of some specific adult attitudes to the behaviour of children, which is determined far more by their perception of unexpressed, not explicit, demands and expectations of their peers and of other adults. Sometimes misunderstanding in this situation can generate a peculiar cultural legacy, a kind of short-circuit in the reciprocal relationships both sides should be fostering: I have heard a teacher in a class of rowdy nine-year-olds attempt to make her presence felt by screaming "Stop behaving like children!" at them! The naive expectations of Victorian nursemaids about the sexual habits of their charges (and perhaps the converse, in some cases!) doubtless contributed greatly to the characters of the products, and thereby to the laws which regulate sexuality in our society now. For example, sixteen and fourteen, as significant ages for legal sexuality have very little historical foundation, and their biological/endocrine basis has been changing greatly as puberty has come at an earlier age. Equally, the regulations which apply to the sale of "girlie" magazines must reflect attitudes acquired by our law-makers before they knew much law! They have changed considerably over the last twenty years. Extremely detailed, indeed demeaning, pictures of female genitalia, photographs of a variety of oral-genital contacts are now available moderately freely to the adolescent boy. Page three of many popular newspapers has a bare-breasted beauty for his father's breakfast delectation. Yet there are very few relaxations of our prohibitions about sexual *actions* ; we don't see photographs of people actively involved in sexuality. "Posing" is OK, but I have the feeling that "behaving in a beastly manner" isn't, at least at the *Penthouse* end of the market. Film and television have made some attempts to portray what people really do (as viewed through the eye of the director, at least) but the portrayal is very rarely a relaxed one. As a reproductive biologist interested in human sexuality, I get the feeling that what I'm permitted to see and buy is still being regulated by a slightly dirty-minded Edwardian governess and the adolescent boy "under her care"! The age-limits, especially, seem appropriate to educational changes-of-responsibility rather than biology. Few fourteen-year-olds were fertile in Chaucer's time, but many eleven year olds could be now. Yet the restrictions have got *older*, and the patterns of relaxation are those appropriate to Edwardian upper-classes. Young marriage, teen-age sexuality, children-in-the-same-bed-as-parents all react with our social prejudices, formed and set by our public myths, and mostly at odds with the patterns expressed in *Penthouse* and its ilk. In England now, the *News of the World* newspaper exposes the interactions of exposed events with changing public morality very clearly, and the influence of the governess is still there.

This kind of cultural mutation, the showing of deliberately arousing photographs of female genitalia in freely available forms, is a very real perversion of cultural transmission. These realities were nearly always discovered in *social* contexts in the past, and making them privately available will change the sexual attitudes of a whole generation of young men. I am *not* saying it's good or bad, just that it's a change which can tell us about education; the mutation is very unlikely to fit into the pattern of expectations set up by the rest of society's educational mechanisms. The thalidomide tragedy resulted in major part from our newly-publicised "genetic blueprint" models, coined in the euphoria which followed the DNA double-helix/genetic code discoveries in the '50s; they directed attention to genetic self-realisation, self-regulation, and away from environmental – including toxic – effects on human intra-uterine development. Modification of the young adult's sexual education by a change in the availability of photographs, in the interests of greater freedom of information, does not worry people who are committed to "blueprint", internal immutable "I", preformationist models. Nor does explicit violence in the media. This lack of concern about consistency of cultural input results from misunderstanding of its central role in making people, and can result in strange new traditions. This is exactly the comparison between "deformed" and "deprived" set up on pp 110. The mind-set we had after the Watson/Crick

DNA elucidation made us blind to outside effects, and resulted in deformed children (the effect of thalidomide is so early that I can consider it pre-privilege in this context). The changes in developmental influence on our children *via* photos of female anatomy, or television violence, could result in deprivation – because some of our cultural wisdom is not now available to them. New kinds of people will almost certainly be made.

Let me take another, very different and equally speculative example, but in a less delicate area. The Bowdlerisation of nursery rhymes by the brothers Grimm, and by Anderson, cannot have left their messages unchanged[3], and the wholesale adoption of the new versions in the last hundred years must have upset a vast continuing pattern which moulded Western children through the generations. The meaning of animal models, too, like the Three Bears, Fox and Geese, Red Riding Hood's Wolf in the granny-suit, has been trivialised almost out of existence. What has been done to the stories is even more radical, however[4]. Jack's Beanstalk, Red Riding Hood, especially Cinderella have been turned into twee little kiddie-stories, from the darker morality plays they (probably) were for so long (it was a *fur* slipper, not a glass slipper, for example). The odd "vestigial organ", reminding me of the unnecessary buttons on men's jacket-sleeves, may remain: Rumpelstiltskin, after the new queen has broken her side of the straw-into-gold/baby bargain, stamps his "foot" through the floor and cannot pull it free. This is absolutely gratuitous in the modern version, but like the jacket-buttons suggests that there was a quite different denouement in the original (analyse his name ... )! I simply don't know if we are now different as a result of this meddling; how could I? How can we know how, or whether, writing these things down has made different kinds of children, different kinds of adults? *Learning* the biblical stories, actually being able to repeat all of the Bible, before the orally-transmitted version was written down, must have been totally different from reading it – or from having it read to you, week by week, in a foreign language! Education changes as culture changes, and the two are part of the same process.

Let us now contrast such unconscious inculcation during development with technical induction into a cultural role, by those who are capable in that role – apprenticeship. Both of these more classical educational modes are very different, of course, from urban public education by incompetents who are supposedly expert at the task of culture-transmission, the teachers in officially sanctioned schools.

Small societies, or civic sub-groups, usually use apprentice-systems for the technical or professional induction to a cultural role. An African lake fisherman with his "boy", and a Victorian cobbler with his "lad", both assume that much culture has already been acquired; the youngster is expected to "find his way about", to cook (usually for master, too) to seek sexual liaisons, to earn outside the trade, often by begging, and to be loyal both to master and trade. Once this last is established, the apprentice may expect to graduate from menial tasks to the more rewarding rituals, practice and eventual expertise. In this situation, complementation of roles is succeeded by relative symmetry, and much of the information passage is explicit.

Contrast this with more formal, "educational" teaching, where complementary roles are maintained (student:tutor) and the explicit information transfer is constrained by the tutor to *his* syllabus. This always cloaks a moulding of attitudes to learning, to courtesy and to intellectual confidence. Usually this is not apparent to either involved party, but it may be plain to an observer of their interaction[5,6]. This implicit relationship, the deepest part of the "hidden curriculum", has been called "pedagogic action" and interpreted as "symbolic violence" by the radical French education theorists (e.g. Bourdieu[5], whose English translation of his *Reproduction*, about this very subject, came out just when my own *Reproduction*[7] came out in 1977!).

Apparently similar learning exercises may cover the acquisition of very different skills and attitudes, and similar skills may be attained by very different routes. Contrast the learning of writing as a skill, by ghetto Jews (for advancement in religious learning), by English farm labourers (for political, social confidence, or ritual motives), or Indian traders in Polynesia (for economic advancement and self-organisation). Then contrast all these with contemporary English schoolchildren whose position in society is to be governed in some still-to-be-imagined future by their literacy. The contrasting position and attitudes of the schoolchildren can be explained in several ways: they are much younger when they learn to write, and they are immersed totally in an educational system shared by family and school, within a society nearly all of whose overt status symbols are educational (but not, now, literate). These English children's motivations are insulated from the realities of literacy in real social life by two layers of woolly symbolism – but they are directly subject to the teacher's social philosophy! Parents are right to be more concerned about the political and sexual messages of the "hidden curriculum" than of the literary content of the overt teaching!

All of us can feel some empathy with the well-motivated learning-to-write of near-adults immediately disadvantaged by its lack and surrounded by competent literates; indeed, the great success of the BBC's literacy campaign was mostly due to the involvement of many people wishing to help in such an enterprise. Few can expect such motivation in schoolchildren whose immediate rewards and punishments are not related to literacy, and most of whose contacts are rarely *seen* to read or write. Such lack of immediacy in juvenile motivation is surely characteristic of "educational" transmission of culture in all advanced human societies. Television is *much* more exciting – and transmits a new set of myths, and of mores. (As I write this, my children are watching a re-run of the Judy Garland *Wizard of Oz* – don't *you* remember the Wicked Witch of the West?) The familial and apprenticeship routes become progressively taken over by the professional educator – and the entertainer – as civic societies become more complex. Lack of immediacy for school pupils, and consequent poor juvenile motivation, is surely characteristic of the trans- mission of "official" culture in all "advanced" societies. Our teachers really do have a very difficult job – and this is shown by the observation that they do it badly, on the whole. Television doesn't help with this problem, it competes with *serious* learning. But in my last chapter, I show how its new myths really can complement, and contribute to the whole – but new – kind of person.

However, legal sanctions in cities usually force compulsory state-approved "education" on all juveniles, so a new situation arises. There are no longer approved alternatives to schooling. So both the child's family and his mentors, experts (either artisan or scholar) with whom he may be acquainted, relinquish their roles as culture-transmitters. Reading skills, and "sex education", and – progressively – everything else, are *left* to the teacher to "do properly"! The child then learns social skills and information from only two major sources: peer groups with their ancient but charismatic "barbarian" codes, and the school system staffed mostly by commonplace, dreary "tribal" incompetents and with a massive and inappropriate ritual through which information is filtered. The child's peer group usually has criteria for success (related to honour, machismo and its female equivalents[6]) which are at least irrelevant to, and indeed usually contradict, the overt criteria advertised by the (tribal) pedagogue. That is to say, the child gets overt rewards, in honour and status, from peers by doing the reverse of what his stuffy old teacher wants. The teacher's demands include diligence, respect for authority, and skilled per- formance of routine tasks, all of which are scorned, derided by the child's peer value-systems.

In civic societies which have reached this state, many children develop two faces, two languages and often have a third for family interactions. Switching between these becomes a major skill which lays the foundation for the skilled role-playing citizen. So far, so good. But the educators may, and usually do, set their own criteria, their own "hidden syllabus", after the parents and experts have relinquished control to them. These criteria then spread into society with the products of this indoctrination. The educators advance their cause, usually honestly in the short-term, by building their special set of educational-advancement rituals to reward those who "pass". The reward is given younger in some systems than others, and different proportions fail. Nearly all children receive the stamp of approval by "graduating from high schools" in the USA[6]; this system is a little further down the slope than in the UK, where "graduation" *was* reserved for those leaving universities with their first degrees. Conformity is rewarded by diplomas, degrees, guaranteeing such ritual the support of worthy and powerful citizens (who, if they have not "earned" them, are awarded Honorary Degrees in powerful ritual ceremonies, so that they come to value them highly!). There are continuing pressures, as we shall see and as Illich clearly identified, for the educators to drop their standards, to reward lower attainments. But it is always a majority who "fail", by their standards – nearly everyone, indeed, out in the real society! There are some times and places, like the U.S.A. now, where everyone *seems* to pass, to "graduate". But if the failures attempt to cash in their "graduation" the reality of the hidden curriculum[5,8,9] prevents further success. This hidden set of criteria discriminates against those who failed the real tests, even if they graduated with honours. (This cryptic, "unfair" testing may well be an integral part of our growing up in society[9], not restricted to formal education.)

Much the same is now happening in British universities too; at the beginning of this century it was the Honours degree that meant "pass", educational approbation - the Pass degree meant "fairly-honourable Fail, but we know you're in the club so we'll help you out ...". Since the Fifties the line has been drawn higher; very few get Pass or Ordinary degrees unless they've come up by a not-approved route, for example without school approbation. Now the line is between 1st Class or 2i Honours and 2ii or 3rd Class Honours degree; the latter two grades mean "failed the real standards of this Institution".

Whatever the system, the hidden curriculum's demands and the real pass/ fail border are apparent to most of the students. From then onwards the "failed" majority of of juveniles cease to identify their motives, or rewards, with those of the educators and find more reward – and more true education, indeed – in the barbarian peer group. Motivation for formal education has, then, been lost by most juveniles; but other educational sources have been lost too, in the earlier history of the civic culture. So fewer juveniles can receive a real initiation into the fullness of the culture, because family and expert are alike out of reach, and the peer group has divergent, essentially barbarian ideals. The desire for self-education may still be present, especially in relative poverty, and many schools in poor areas have a few, human, teachers who each have a large caucus of dependent adolescents *wanting* their educational due but feeling that they've lost out – as indeed they have. So have we all, for these kids represent a mass of talent, of human resource, that has lost the privilege which it could have enjoyed, because the educational packaging excluded them. Desire for self-education is usually not enough, in affluent societies, because there are too many peer models which are more attractive to adolescents, and the "educational failures" rarely have access to the strength of will which permits choice. There is hope, however, as we shall see in chapter 15.

The educational system reproduces itself in the civic society *via* its "successes"; but nearly all of its diploma-ed products (on both sides of the podium) are failures by the criteria of the larger society (except insofar as that society has been persuaded to apply academic standards, of course!). This is not to deny that academics have material, attitudes, information that is worth teaching; on the contrary, they have sequestered nearly all of the vital knowledge stores of our society in their "nucleus". They *are* our society's "germ cells". But they have succeeded in persuading the rest of society that all that counts, from school-time on, is the approval of the academic community, while that community itself (for apparently the most Universal and un-blameworthy reasons) has been withdrawing from involvement in the real civic world.

Cities, and people in cities, can still function despite the abrogation of more and more of the privilege to the parasitic educator cadre, even when that cadre withdraws into ivory towers. This is because, even though much of the transmission of the city's reproductive wealth fails in each generation, the city-system is itself so effective that it can carry the load. Even when so many of its children become barbarians, vandals, breaking up the city's artefacts in search of honours, adventure, thrills, and when so many others become totally ritual-dependent "tribesmen", the few entrepreneurs, the administrators, the factory and distributive organisations can still produce privilege. This is produced both as capital and as income, especially as "standard of living" in excess of that to be found in simpler social systems (Dickens made this explicit for Victorian London). Only the educators, the charity administrators, the social workers and – progressively and unfortunately – the police can find fulfilment in the maintenance of such a heavily-parasitised organism, however. So we should ask if there is a way back towards a more equitable, effective way of using the city's organisation to promote privilege for most of its Apes. There *are* ways, I think, and we're already taking them – in the last chapter I'll set some of them out.

I have been rather shamelessly using zoological, natural-selection kind of metaphors for city structures and for the reproduction of the culture of the cities, and I have identified a pathology, a parasite problem.   In real zoology, of course, parasites become adapted to their hosts, and the hosts evolve to tolerate the regular presence of the parasite.   We must ask how serious the problem is, bearing in mind that the urban organism *does* continue fairly effectively despite the perversion of its internal heredity and its wealth. Anecdotes about the proportion of the city budgets of Cairo, Delhi, Valparaiso, even Boston which go to prop up the welfare, police, clean-up services are legion in the cities themselves.   10-50% of the tithing or rating income are figures suggested by university people I have talked to about these, their home cities.   Such re-direction, wastage of the wealth of the city can only occur, in every generation, because of the "black economy" in learning as well as in barter-systems which don't generate tax!  The perversion of cultural transmission by the educator cadre can only occur *successfully*, without killing the city in one generation, because people can and do learn by other routes than formal education.   The parasitised city is a great market for the gamin, the entrepreneur, the market trader, even the small shop-owner and the artisan.   All these *can* alternate the tribal and the barbaric, the ritual and the novel, to their advantage and that of their children.

I shall argue later that it is in exactly this decadence of the city that the *foreign*, reproductively-stable, sub-culture comes into its own, to the advantage of all of us.  For now, at this stage of my evolutionary scenario, I  leave our city-picture with a parasitic sub-group, Illich's School of Educators; they have taken over as culture-transmission "middle-men", claiming a role in cultural reproduction which very few of them can perform adequately.   The organisation of this sub-group effectively prevents even these few from acting as general purveyors of societal privilege, from training the new generations to *generate* wealth, privilege.   They can and do train them, not least by example, to *consume* it.   The major consequence of this block to the transmission of privilege in advanced civic societies is the appearance of a whole class of *deprived* citizens, different groups in different circumstances, often from different cultural "species" (pp 196-7).   These are denied access to educational, intellectual or technical privilege *via* family tradition, because they are forced to go to school and their parents have adopted "patient" attitudes to the Educators.   But they are also denied useful formal education *via* adult tuition (apprenticeship), because this practice has been discontinued in most artisan areas, having been replaced by ineffective schooling.   They are limited to peer (usually street-gang) practices which must always include justified denial of the relevance of formal schooling as an honourable access to ability.

In the next chapters I digress to examine this, and other, kinds of deprivation in various human reproductive systems before returning again, in Chapter 10, to examine the role of professional, but misled, educators in the spread of deprivation in affluent societies.

## References

References in full are to be found from page 243 onwards. Below are listed names of authors and dates of publication

1 Oyama (1984)
2. White (1939)
3. Opie and Opie (1974)
4. Luthi(1976)
5. Bourdieu (1977)
6. Lesko(1988)
7. Cohen(1977)
8. Rajchman (1985)
9. Foucault (1986)

# 8

# A DIGRESSION ABOUT DEPRIVATION – IN POVERTY AND IN AFFLUENCE

Deprivation is a common, but really rather difficult, concept frequently used as the basis of discussions about education, and especially about inequities. When we (and I include sociologists[1] here) talk of deprivation, this usually means failure to attain a qualitatively or quantitatively preferred condition (an "absolute"), but it may sometimes mean failure to attain a "norm", even an average; in this last case, half of a population may be called "deprived"! The children of starving mothers are said to be deprived, for example, because their intellect is impaired in comparison with the children of adequately-fed mothers. However, it is probable that nearly all of our female ancestors were, *by today's standards*, ill-fed; would we say they were "deprived"? Consider reproductive opportunity: in today's Western world infertility is seen as a great deprivation – of the "right" to breed – and most people do indeed breed. But in larger context, this has never been so. On average, in a stable population, two parents in this generation produce only two *parents* in the next generation; yet they always produce many more offspring than these two (again, on the average). So most of these offspring *don't* breed in their turn; reproduction is not a usual property of wild animals, indeed it is truer to say that nearly all sexually-produced animals fail to breed because they die first[2]. Reproduction does seem to us to be a "basic" opportunity – our ancestors had it, of course, but most of their brothers and sisters didn't – this seems to be a differential of the kind we might use "deprived" for, yet we don't use "deprived" in quite this context.

I am not trying here to be a Humpty-Dumpty, forcing my meaning on you. Nor am I trying to find the "true, hidden meaning" of the word "deprivation"; as with all words, there isn't one. What I'm attempting is to expose your usage of the word, to compare it with mine and (in this very one-sided kind of argument necessary in a book) to put it in context, with privilege, as a cultural reproductive term. Having done that, I hope to surprise you by showing how much more prevalent is cultural deprivation in affluence than in poverty, so that I can share with you a view of cultural transmission in affluence. For now, then, let's look at some more usages of "deprived".

In most human cultures, the enjoyment of very desirable but scarce resources (for example kidney machines, or Helen of Troy) is restricted to a few adults, and most people are deprived of these. Deprivation may thus be a matter of ratio (as in the "average" case above). But it may also have a temporal sense: medieval peasants were denied access to pharmaceutical antibiotics and to trade unions, and we are similarly restricted in our medical care to those methods developed before about 1990. Such restrictions were and are inevitable, so are easily borne even by the liberal conscience. It is only by comparison with an *attainable* cultural norm, matched for some social properties, that we discover deprivation in the usual usage[1.] Chronic starvation is associated with reduction in intellectual abilities, so the starved low-intellect Ethiopian baby is deprived *in comparison with* another baby born at the same time, in the same village. Or do we mean in comparison with an English or American baby, or to that mother if she had lived in England or America? We speak of deprived children, and adults, as if there were an absolute scale, but a little analysis shows the woolly comparative estimates that lie behind these judgements; there is rarely a useful "control" group, equivalent in all but the deprivation. A study comparing the I.Q.s of children born to Dutch mothers pre-, post- and during a period of national starvation showed no difference. Compared with heavily-parasitised "natural" African women, of course, these Dutch women were 250% healthy to start with! However, I am going to argue that there *is* an absolute usage of the word, comparable with my biological usage of the word "privileged".

That usage of "deprivation" which refers to inequitable sharing of goods or services is usually unnecessary, tautological, or both. Nevertheless, this is the usual usage, for deprivation in and by poverty. However, what is meant here is closer to the older word "privation"; that is to say "want of the comforts or necessities of life" (OED), although here again comforts differ from place to place and age to age. (The origin of these words is from Latin *privatus*, from *privo*, to bereave, strip or separate. "Deprived" was previously used as synonym of "degradation", for loss of "privileged" office by ministers or clerics. I will come back to the deprived/privileged antithesis in my argued, more biological usage.) To describe a contemporary Third World peasant as deprived, because he lives now exactly as a medieval English peasant *did*, suggests some general norm; presumably he is deprived in comparison with a modern English farm labourer, or even with a modern English university lecturer! Consider these two peasants, separated in space and time but living just the same life[1]. Can we speak of one being deprived, the other not? If it is only *contemporary* social or geographic contrast that is at issue, perhaps we should re-examine the medieval peasant without trade unions or antibiotics. When he lived, many other people had lives less wanting in comfort and necessaries, yet we do not in general compare him with them, comparing the peasant with his artisan friend or his feudal lord. Even if there had been a real Shangri-La, contemporary both with him and with us, with his lords and artisans as with ours, would that give a standard for deprivation, or indeed privation, against which we should all be measured? Such a judgement of the medieval peasant as deprived, I would argue, assumes a set of *universal* values for necessities, even for comforts – with most of which *he* would not agree.

A dreary shadow behind all such universalist usage, which I generally interpret as paternalist pretence, is the old, portentous call for "social justice": "Give them the same as I've got ... but without taking anything away from *me!*". This call, whether portrayed as socialism or justice, has always seemed to me to be a plea for the removal of guilt from the speaker, not of deprivation from the subject. Even if this political position were taken more seriously, it would suggest that the goods of a society, divided among its members, give a norm for social standards, below which is deprivation[1]; and then we're back to half of the population being deprived, and presumably the other half living in sinful affluence! Even a rule which defines the bottom 10% as below the poverty line, the top 10% then being seen as sinful, smacks of political expediency rather than insight. In many ways, a contemporary American pauper has a better, less deprived, life than America's Founding Fathers.

Sitting behind our popular, and some of our professional, use of the concept of deprivation is an even naughtier usage, which I must chase down before we can come back to a sensible, agreed but restricted usage for "deprivation", useful to compare times and places, cultures and roles within them. Our usage of the word "deprived" for the hardship associated with poverty, especially, implies a failure to reach *potential* heights of human ability and dignity. We might say that someone was deprived if their *potential* had not been realised, and this usage seems to work well for the peasant, the baby from the starved mother, and many other examples; this appeals to us as usage which is both subtle and apt. Potential is a potent word in education, too, and there does seem to be a general agreement what this means, at least among educators. However, the word "potential" has much more problem even than "deprivation" or "privation". To see why, we must go back to some very basic reproductive biology before coming forward to consider deprivation again.

It is commonly said that the genetic material, the DNA in the chromosomes of an organism, is a "blueprint" for the design of that organism; that is to say, the organism (the "phenotype") is built according to the instructions laid down, in coded form of course, in that blueprint, the "genotype" of a species or the "genome" of an individual. We are very familiar with this concept, because we are used to the mechanical instances of it: the machines we buy must come up to their specifications. We get our money back, under guarantee, if they don't. We are also happy with this kind of genotype/phenotype concept because we inherit the idealist philosophy. In our culture, it is usual to think of artefacts as good-better-best, with a "paradigm" heading the list, having all the required properties for perfection: the Rolls-Royce among cars, for example. We import this way of thinking, also, to our animal associates, but with much less success: the top dog at Cruft's is closest to an ideal – but such show dogs often pay a biological price for their close approach to that ideal. We even use this "paradigm" approach to people: film stars, pop idols, Nobelists, television scientists, publicans must all be conscious of the public image they must live up to. Sometimes, as with Marilyn Monroe, there is a biological price which people must pay, too, to be top dog. We are very ready to accept "blueprint" ideas, then: the list of attributes for a good Springer spaniel, Welsh Cob pony or Lyretail guppy shows that we see animals as attempts at an ideal, and the breeders try to pick puppies, foals or alevins with "potential".

This is just the sense in which your child's teacher will tell you that your little Alice "has potential", and in which you might use the word "deprived" if the potential was not realised. There is a fuzzy sense in which you see Alice's development as a person as being mapped out according to a blueprint inherited from you and your spouse. We all subscribe somewhat to this "essential you inside" model, to which things happen (p89 *et seq*). These uses of "potential" and "blueprint" seem to have the sanction of biology, at least as common usage, with recent elevation of DNA as the central core determining developmental potential. If this were indeed so, we could then, in principle, measure deprivation exactly; we could compare the blueprint with the finished article and list the differences. We can do exactly that with our washing machine or Rolls-Royce, and the show judges seem to be doing that when our dog or guppy gets a rosette for Third Place in the Annual Show.

However, the DNA is *not* a blueprint in any sense like this at all. It is not a description of *this* animal – even if all goes right with its development. Even in the simplest organisms, heredity doesn't work like this. The DNA information is in no sense a description, for sure. It is in some ways a *prescription*, needing a whole drug store for realisation. In some ways it is like a knitting pattern or a recipe, not like a description of a sweater or a cake. Even bacterial DNA depends on all the biological machinery inherited from the parent bacterium for reading the DNA messages. DNA, by itself, is only like a tape of a piece of music – or a better comparison, for some of you, is with a computer tape to turn out a component from an automatic lathe. It has no structure around it, and that makes it in the highest degree *ambiguous* as information. That is to say, we could read a length of DNA or tape "wrong" in a variety of ways: we could try the tape backwards, at the wrong speed, or read the wrong track, or even try the wrong face of the tape. It is the tape player, not the tape, which has special structure to ensure that we (nearly always) get these things "right". But that means that the tape doesn't have information which is *inevitably* translated into *Beethoven's Fifth Symphony* on it (nor does bacterial DNA have "*Escherichia coli*" on it). It has structure, information, which in the special case of being set up in a particular way, supplied with much outside structure and energy, nearly always results in that music being produced for you. You can make estimates of the potential fidelity of any particular playing, too – although you can't actually tell how good it could *ever* be, the utmost reach of its potential, as it were.

A computer disc file is in some ways a more useful example, especially if you have some experience of them, because there are thousands of ways of putting the "same" information on disc. If I were typing this on my Osborne, using Wordstar 2.26, the patterns of magnetic charge on the disc would be very different from what I'm producing using Wordstar 4 on my Amstrad; yet the words on the paper I'm copying, and on the screen, would be just the same. My Osborne can't read the Amstrad disc, nor can the Amstrad read the Osborne. I want to cheat for a moment here, to give us some practice at "information" and "coding" and so on, which we'll need to get "potential" and "deprivation" sorted out. Let's think of these *words* that I'm writing as the DNA code, and the different disc patterns they make as the organisms produced under different circumstances. I can, then, "develop" these words into a computer file in an Osborne world, and that can reproduce them for me using the rules of its circuitry, and the "animal" can then mutate, reproduce and evolve this information in that Osborne world (CP/M). The result can be a variety of Osborne animals coded by these words and by small edits of them. I can, of course, do the same in the Amstrad world (MS-DOS), and produce another little paddock of similar animals, but different from the CP/M ones (even if I've edited in exactly the same way).

The first, simple, illuminating question is "Are these words a blueprint for the Amstrad animals or the Osborne animals?". The answer I want is "Nei-ther.... they're not a blueprint if they make *two* different things." If the answer you give is "Both!", then imagine them being just a *little* different, enough that the sets of coding rules each give a defective organism, not just nonsense, in the other world. Would you still use the word "blueprint"? Now imagine all the ways in which this same set of words can be integrated, by many different sets of coding rules, into all the different kinds of computer disc files – yet come back as the same set of words. Do you still use the word "blueprint" if you can get a thousand different results? (Do see that I don't just mean that the *execution* differs each time the blueprint is given to a different factory; I mean that *in principle* the reading of the blueprint results in a different product.)

This example, I hope, will enable you to follow me into a much more recherché but dramatic illustration about the function of DNA in the development of animals. We have already (p.60) met Lewis Wolpert's attempt to discourage people from mapping organisms onto their DNA, and the converse, which is seeing the animal as its DNA code made manifest. To continue this further, I now want to answer a much more difficult question than the simple one above. "Could, in principle, the *very same sequence* of DNA serve as the nuclear heredity for two very different organisms?" You should see that if the answer to this is "Yes", there can in principle be no way that an organism's heredity can determine its potential anything! There is actually a natural set of examples I could use, the caterpillar and butterfly or the tadpole and its frog, but for later purposes I want to invent one (anyway, it *could* be that different bits of the DNA are used for specifying the different parts and functions of caterpillar and butterfly, which is a cop-out).

In Chapter 3 (p. 27) we saw that the early development of most metazoans starts *without* involving the genome of the new organism; it initially plays out a sequence of events determined by the structure that the egg acquired while it was developing in mother's ovary. This structure, and the sequence of biochemical events it causes in the early embryo, determines in what sequence, how much, and where in the embryo its own genes get turned on. That is to say, the egg structure acquired from mother's structure and physiology, mother's phenotype, behaves like the tape-recorder, or the Osborne or Amstrad computer, in the above examples. Which part of the embryo's own DNA is read, in each of its cells, is dependent upon pre-existing, surrounding structure, for the detail of its information production.

Now let us imagine two quite different animals, let us say a worm and a fish, that might be our two hypothetical organisms which have exactly the same DNA. Most of the DNA, anyway, is for cell "housekeeping" functions that would be pretty similar in the two animals, but what we're concerned with here is *what makes them different*. If they do have exactly the same DNA, can they in principle be as different as a worm and a fish? The answer, very surprisingly and only in principle, never of course in practice, is "Yes" and the clue is that an egg contains both tape and tape-recorder, both disc and computer. In the worm, let us imagine the worm mother's ovary has programmed the egg cytoplasm to read out the embryo genome as a,b,c,d,e,...towards z; this read-out, of course, produces a worm larva that in the course of a full and active life becomes an adult worm. If female, she has an ovary whose structure now makes eggs which will read out the DNA a,b,c,...z., and no other possibilities will ever appear without mutation, which is change of tape, then most likely of program too. In the (imaginary) fish ovary, on the other hand, the egg structure is made quite differently; the early development towards a young vertebrate reads the DNA in quite a different way, say z,y,x,w,......a; this read-out, of course, produces a young fish which, if it should become a sexually mature female, will have an ovary which makes eggs with the z,y,x,w,...a program again, and they would again become little vertebrates. There is no way in which they could suddenly start reading their DNA the other way round, and make a worm – they start in the wrong way, anyway, with a fish-type egg; even if a worm-order of DNA reading happened you'd get a third kind of creature, if you got anything viable at all.

In one way, all I'm saying is that the same tape can play two quite different tunes, if threaded differently into tape players. The imaginative effort is in seeing that the different messages can include the instructions which make them play differently. Either way is balanced, stable reproductively through the generations. If you have understood that this stability can be achieved in different ways in different organisms (but with the *same* sequence of signals on the DNA or tape), you will see that the DNA simply *cannot* be mapped on to the organism, the phenotype. The genotype and phenotype are associated by historical accident; only a very complex mapping of process-and-sequence, with information about which way it was done last time around and what effects are still "pending", can in principle predict the next structure.

That really was a steam-hammer example to crack the walnut of "potential". I cannot make this case too thoroughly, however. In contrast to a car, from whose "blueprint" a competent engineer ought to be able to tell you its top speed, miles-per-gallon and cornering ability, nothing can be said about the structure of an organism simply from the DNA sequence without context. We may well get to the state, in developmental biology, where a particular DNA sequence coding for a rodent myosin (a muscle protein) will tell us about that animal's muscular performance in some respect. We're nearly there now, for perhaps as many as a thousand different sequences (mostly those that relate to human disease, of course – the protein deficiency in Duchene muscular dystrophy has been located, and published this week in *Nature*). Even some rather general, apparently high-level common gene-arrangements, called *homeo-box systems*, have been found – but they do very different things in different organisms, just as in my worm/fish contrast above.    So I am convinced, partly because of the kind of thinking above, that it will never be possible to *argue* the animal from the DNA.   We can't locate genes for wings (p.90).   Life is not like that.

Because of this limitation of predictability, because life is not like that, we cannot in any single case say of a baby (or of any organism) what it *could* have been in ideal circumstances, what its "potential" was.   Even in the case where we might have 100,000 genetically identical mouse early embryos, frozen, all with egg structures produced by females with the same genotype and as near the same phenotype as we can achieve, we still couldn't tell what the *ideal* mouse from that genotype is;   mice are not cars.   Nor are people.   While we may be greatly disturbed by the spectacle of Ethiopian mothers, starving and producing babies whose intelligence is less than it might have been, it does not help them, or help us to help them, to use the language of potential, or of deprivation, sloppily.

There are simpler biological cases where this uselessness becomes clearer. Buy a packet of seeds, or tray of seedlings, even a single plant from your local nursery.   You may, in the interest of expressing *all* its "potential", choose to use potting compost, peat, fertiliser – you may use special lights,  on all 24 hours perhaps,  and you may make more growth still by supplementing the atmospheric carbon dioxide too.  What about the poor deprived plants, left there at the nursery, that didn't get your tender loving care?  That weren't forced? Are they deprived? Hang on a moment, though ... I happen to know that there's a new, rather different, plant hormone preparation that'll grow your plant to twice the height you thought possible ... and what about the new methods that'll be developed next year? Next century? Just what *is* possible to that poor plant? There's no way of limiting the possibilities, of course. *You can never know what the potential of any living thing is!*  You may think this plant example is a silly one, but just think of dogs, or goldfish, or cattle for a moment; they've shown possibilities never dreamt of at the start of their domestication, I'm sure. Many of them now *need* treatments which their progenitors were content to do without, and if deprived of them will not develop properly .....

Here is a usage of "deprived" that I think can be made useful.    It is, by no coincidence, symmetrical with "deformed", in a useful way.  If these domestic animals (or our nursery-bred plants) need further care in order to become like their parents (this is an indication – no more – of their "proper" selves) then this is close to my previous use of "privilege"[2].  Mammals need milk, care, warmth and instruction to become their proper specific selves; if they don't get these they fail, just as if their genetic program was deficient.  If the latter, we say they are deformed (we don't if it's a biochemical lesion, but the principle holds); if mammals don't get milk, let's call them "de-privileged" – deprived, for short. Because, the way I've told the story, human evolution has built up privilege to a whole cultural inheritance, then it is the lack of *that* which we can point to and say "deprived", de-privileged, in my special sense.

I think it's proper to say de-privileged here, rather than un-privileged, because the usual, natural, reproductively effective case to which the system has evolved *has* the privilege as part of its inheritance system – if this is missing, it has been *taken away*. This restricted usage works alright in the usual situations. My dictionary says "bereft, destitute, lacking, wanting", and this fits your plant, the goldfish, and the dogs moderately well but people much better. Something necessary has been omitted, as fertiliser for a plant, milk – or love – for a kitten. In the sociological usage, the developing human being has developed without something the sociologist regards as necessary, in context for time and place. Privilege is necessary for the normal Ape.

Sociologists use deprivation, like poverty, as a relative term[1]. I suggest, in contrast, that we can use it as we use deformation, as a threshold term distinguishing the abnormal, the pathological. The pathology, however, is in the cultural component rather than the more biological component of the person; people who fail to receive the normal quota of food, goods, services, information, tenderness can be called deprived. Note that this can be because of a genetic, or other more biological, disability which prevents their being able to use a "normal" route of receipt (e.g. genetic or infective blindness) or even because of other, culturally inherited problems (e.g. a minority language, or inculcated distrust of authority). Frequently it will be caused by inequities in the actual system of dispensing privilege; this is discrimination in the bad sense (I am not suggesting here that privilege should be *equal* – but that the dispensing system should be fair ... ). Nepotism frequently biases the distribution of privilege in a society, and this is usually the case with outside aid – despite the peculiarity of people that we will "take in" each others' children.

Poverty and the usual usage of deprivation go together in our minds; what of the new usage? Poverty is often, perhaps usually, recognised by the manifest inadequacy of that transferred material, energy or care which is necessary for normal development. It is the *children* of the poor that excite our compassion, and whose pathology is diagnostic of deprivation, but not uniquely so. We do speak of the old as being deprived, yet here again it is lack of care, attention, food, that same "privilege" which we transfer downwards through the generations, which is our yardstick. Some of the deprivations of poverty do cause "deficiency conditions" as characteristic as some genetic diseases, often from lack of vitamins or trace minerals. As with genetic disease, a "syndrome" is often recognised: parasite loads resulting from poor "nest hygiene", chronic malnutrition resulting from inadequate breast-feeding after starvation during late pregnancy, irremediable narrowing of horizons due to lack of teaching/ learning with siblings and parents, followed by inadequate competition in the older world of adolescence – these make a familiar group of symptoms. People that are made like this are not made properly, and much of the remedy is then beyond them as individuals and as groups, because so much of human ability can only be transferred *via* the privilege that these deprived folk did not receive, and now lack. Before I go on to consider the appropriateness of international aid programmes to this issue, let me contrast the real deficiencies listed above, real deprivation in my sense, with what has been called deprivation but is simply the removal of the comforts of life.

The classic case here, of course, is what happened in England during the Second World War. The amount of food was grossly down, fuel was expensive and required difficult treatment, there was much unfamiliar work, especially for women, and family structures were replaced by much more co-operative, collective relationships like the Land Army. But because the organisation of such privilege as there was became more effective ("morale" is perhaps what we feel when it is) the caring made up for the lack of comfort. Those of us who received care then actually *felt* privileged, in the old sense; you knew that what everybody was doing was for *you*. There was the same kind of feeling, too, in the New York sky-scrapers when NYC suddenly couldn't afford to pay garbage-men, and there was a real emergency. I was visiting a hospital department up in Harlem and found myself caught up in a great friendly co-operative game, re-organising the cars after the garbage had been dumped. Then we all, perhaps forty of us, sat chatting on the stoops planning tomorrow – blacks, whites, Spanish all brought together into a com-munal enterprise where all could see the immediate benefit. When comforts go, especially suddenly in a public kind of way, a snow-storm or a flood, the lines of responsibility become drawn more clearly, people really do become mutually supportive. We also have sets of behaviours geared to more extreme emergencies: "women and children first" is one such. When these systems work, there is no sense of deprivation even in extreme poverty or indeed privation. It is the chronic inability to *use* the interactive programs we have developed as part of our cultural mutual-help programs which deprives us – as indeed we say – of our humanity.

It is in the exploitative interactions between cultures that most deprivation occurs – in the aftermath of wars, of uprisings, of feuds and especially in slavery. When the net of international reporting brings this graphically to our attention, we all feel compassion, don't we? Yet this is a biologically odd response, even a culturally odd response. By all the mechanisms that we can imagine, culture A is going to profit if culture B's system, people, land is in trouble; we all *should*, in theory, have cultures which exploit others, do them down , joy in their undoing, their misery. But, far back in history, certainly in the Greek city-states we learn about from Homer, we show concern for the stranger. The Israelites in the Bible didn't think much of their neighbours' habits, but they seemed to respect them (when they weren't fighting them, and often when they were).

This biologically-strange compassion is exploited, today, by agencies of international aid[3]; these claim to enable co-ordination of effort to reduce human deprivation on a scale never seen before. They are attempting to raise the living standards of the starving fifth of humanity, shaming us into giving by comparing our life to theirs. The real misery and wretchedness of so many human beings eking out a meagre living on a poor agricultural base, tormented by disease and despair, forces us to give aid where we can. We can use this to illuminate what we mean by human deprivation in a variety of ways, by seeing what aid we want to give, what Oxfam gives, and what is useful in reducing deprivation. We may ask larger questions too, whether there has ever been a time when a fifth of humanity was *not* starving, and whether this is at all relevant, but the Oxfam response to deprivation can illuminate several paradoxes for us.

Firstly, there is the equality paradox. This results from portrayal of the recipients of aid as just like the donors, but starving: "That could be you in that Ethiopian village, and those could be your children.... ". There is, surely, no way in which any of the interesting, the admirable properties of recipient and donor can be equated – in many way it is just the complementarity of their ways of life, as well as their circumstances, which we value. Our concern to see others as our brothers and sisters, while useful *within* a culture, is actively misleading between cultures. It prevents us valuing differences, because if that Ethiopian woman *were* my sister, I'd get her sorted out in my social scene – which she'd hate.

The second paradox concerns the immediate need, short-term help versus longer-term strategies. The Oxfam workers are very conscious of this problem, but they know they can get money for *urgent* matters, but not so easily for more important, but longer term, reforms. This is exemplified by an Oxfam poster of the late sixties, with an obviously starved child holding out his hand

and a caption like: "I come from a village of 1000 starving people – please give money so we may have food!".    I can well believe that this jolted many consciences and channelled much money to such villages.   But when I first saw it, on my way to give a lecture on contraceptive methods, my immediate thought was: "Why do you come from a village of 1000 starving people? Why not 1200? Or 800?".   And I gave what seemed then, and seems now, a suitable answer within the frame of the question: "Because there's just enough food to keep 1000 people alive, but starving ... ".   Giving money then becomes an act which leads to more food and *therefore* to, say, 1200 starving people – not to an increase in the quality of life of those 1000!    Within the frame of the challenge on the poster (or even in the real world outside) 1200 starving people must be a worse situation than 1000 starving people; yet Oxfam seemed to be asking us to produce it.

The confusion, the paradox, here arises from the use of two overlapping uses of deprivation models.  Oxfam (or their copy-writer) asks us to help the "human situation", the people.  The biologist would want to help with the deprivation, to change the circumstances so that people weren't starving rather than simply giving food to a starving population.  Biologists are used to such paradoxes: the answer to the problem of not catching enough fish is only rarely to fish more effectively;  the discovery of insulin, as a palliative for diabetes, resulted in more diabetics in the population;  improving child survival by public health measures resulted, in many South American cities, in so many more adults that the public health system can't cope.  Solving the immediate imbalance *never* works in the longer-term.

Similar paradoxes, naive in basis but showing our confusions when we attempt to mix compassion, deprivation, aid and cultural differences, result from the Christian Aid  appeal: "We do not give a man fish," they claim, "we teach him to fish for himself!"  This sounds better, but how long before the local fish population is depleted by the new, more effective, fishing?  Many of the local lakes in West Africa, and even some of the large ones, have had their fish faunas completely upset, not only by this kind of overfishing but by putting in "better" fish, especially the large Nile-perch kind of predators.   In consequence, the lakes have become much *less* productive as a result of the "Teach him to fish ..." kind of meddling;  *more* people starve, just as in the Oxfam example. These "Oxfam paradox" examples abound in the "Aid to alleviate deprivation" literature[3];  we in the West should feel shame at the outcome of nearly all of our efforts.   The Sahel, south of the Sahara and at present very marginal country for nomads with cattle because of years'-long droughts, received much aid in the sixties and early seventies.  We especially promoted, and assisted with, small irrigation projects to use the oasis waters more effectively. Because, for these peoples, cattle are wealth, privilege, they multiplied their holdings. These extra cattle ate down even the extra grazing, and most of the rest of the plants too, especially the tree plantations which the locals did not value, but whose value was in the future encouragement of rainfall. There has, probably as a direct result of the depredation by extra people and cattle made possible by the aid, been the longest drought on record; again we have *more* starving people than we started with. Most[3] of the work done by international aid organisations is *not* like these horrible examples, actually, but is related to longer-term sensible projects – don't let me put you off giving to them!

The complex causality of human deprivations in poverty, the ways in which life-styles and standards, mechanisms and failures interact can be illuminated by two very different examples. The first is from the Third World, and is so good an example it had best be regarded as apocryphal (I heard it in the sixties at a contraceptives meeting at Birmingham Medical School). The second concerns a poorer, deprived sub-group within an affluent culture, and the formulae for comparing needs and abilities with the majority – it is real and continuing as a political paradox.

In the early sixties, an African fishing village was apparently discovered to have attained a balanced population structure without the high child mortality typical of the area. Few children, well-provided-for, were an anomaly; so a medical team was sent to investigate whether that village used a herbal contraceptive, abortifacient or other practice which could be used elsewhere. The team found a very interesting biological situation. The young men were usually apprenticed to older fishermen, who had their own nets and boats; they also often had their own carts for taking their catch to the local market town. When apprenticed, the young men would take wives and the first child would soon arrive. By then the wife had made or renovated a net, so that the husband had a catch of his own to take in to town on the master's cart. In town he would usually stay overnight, and the local prostitutes would ensure that he left some of the catch-money in the town – and took gonorrhoea back to his young wife. On average this sealed her oviducts at the required time for replacement offspring, but no surplus, to be born, so that he could devote his catch-money to procuring a boat and becoming a fisherman in his turn, bringing up his children on the proceeds. Antibiotics were brought in, the story continues, and now that village starves like its neighbours! The cultural reproductive system was stable; bringing in our system of standards and remedies unbalanced it. The motive may have been "to improve health care" or "to permit the wives more control of their reproduction". Our motives, our remedies, don't fit other cultures' needs. We are now all fashionably superior about the Christian missionaries going out to civilise the savages, but in reality we still have not learned that lesson; I suspect that Islam may teach us all a lesson in the comparative ethology of deprivation, before the third millennium of the Christian attempt.

Our second example, to illuminate and compare deprivation across cultures, concerns Arthur Jensen's studies[4] of the black and white child populations in the Californian school system. Jensen was apparently not concerned, in his original studies, with the mode of inheritance of educational disadvantage. He originally wished only to document its occurrence and the provision of special educational facilities to cope with "disadvantaged" children. He discovered, by examination of the school system records, that average black children achieved scores on the academic tests which were the same as those of average white children more than a year younger, and that the distribution of scores in the two populations was similar. The black children did not catch up at the end, but remained at a lower level of competence at the age at which most passed out of formal education. He has since shown[5] that the *order* of difficulty of the questions asked was similar for black or white children of the same sex, but very different for the two sexes in either group. This suggested strongly that language-usage-based differences did not account for the difference in scores, and pointed to a (culturally and/or genetically) inherited difference in the competence with which the children tackle these tests. (For a biased, but very interesting account of this, and other essays in the ranking of people see Gould[6].)

Jensen's publications produced much media coverage, and there was discussion of alternative political solutions to the educational problem of an identifiable, apparently deprived group. Firstly, what if under-achieving children were selected for special education *only* on their scores on these tests? Then there would have been a much higher proportion of black children in special schools, and in special low pupil-teacher ratio classes, than in the general population – and especially than in the white-collar segment of the population that sees itself, with some justice, as paying for education. There would have been complaints from egalitarians (a strong, culturally stable sub-group in California), concerned about the "social deprivations" in these "lower" schools and about discrimination against blacks at the higher, university end of the educational system. (Only Jensen, so far as I can tell, actually asked what would have happened if the extra tuition had *worked*, bringing up the academic level. I *think* he invented the term "positive discrimination", unlikely as that seems now that he's painted as a "fascist".) There would also have been complaints from the white taxpayers, concerned at the diversion of resources from the (cheaper) schooling of their children to cope with the problem.

On the other hand, children could have been selected for different educational privileges on a "corrected", percentile score in their racial group. Then the percentage of each racial group in each educational establishment would have reflected whole-population proportions; you may recall that "bussing" children to different schools was adopted in some States to attempt this. This would have resulted in equal proportions of the two groups being given apparently equal access to educational opportunity, equal privilege. However, three kinds of complaint could have been heard about that. Firstly, the parents of the low-ability black children – and the children themselves – could have complained that they were being deprived of privilege: they were denied special educational help when, if they had been white children with the same scores, they would have got it! The committees who determined entry standards to schools or colleges would have complained that they had been given an impossible task, dropping entry standards for a particular class of entrant. They would have needed to collude with examiners, tutors, all of the educational hierarchy to implement this – even minor incompetence in the implementation would have shown up as obvious injustice to an individual, and could not be rectified within the system. Thirdly, there would have been complaints by the graduates themselves, and their future employers, forced to deal with academic and employment records whose standards were different for different subgroups. There was, at the time, surprisingly little of the "If you give'm more attention early the problem will be solved for later....", and I recall a surprising diversity of proposals. In fact, there was actually a variety of actions taken, but the predominant impression I received (from teachers who were within the US system at all levels) was that the teachers were left to deal with it on a one-to-one basis, much as in the UK. The politics of cultural comparisons within a social system that pretends to be unitary are very difficult – while anti-discrimination laws may help, they cannot make clear which of the above solutions is anti-discriminatory!

Both of the above examples have an apparently "deprived" group, identified by disease in one case and educational discrimination on the other, and attempts being made to "cure" the situation within the "poverty/deprivation" framework. They are both seen as social problems by paternalist Western culture, which believes that medical intervention to cure identifiable (and especially *disgusting*) diseases like gonorrhoea is *always* right, just as spiritual

intervention by missionaries to cure "savage" sins like cannibalism or nudity
was always supported by public approbation – and money.  The education
system in the West, too, must be seen to embrace all the children equally heart-
ily – none (but especially not the *poor*, who deserve charity) should be seen to
escape the educational rod.

I am not denying that there are real deprivations, in my sense as well as the
older usages, associated with poverty, both in the poor nations and especially
in the poorer strata of the affluent nations.  Nevertheless the special human reproductive strategy which disseminates privileges within each society, from
rich nations to poor nations and across the poverty-line in the rich nations, has
raised the living standards of all peoples; at worst, *more* people now live in the
same indigence.  Evident inequities, selfishness and social injustice do not
detract greatly from the real human advance;  there is more privilege, seen as
a greater proportion of the human species now free of starvation, disease and
overt oppression than ever before.  Some cynical optimists might consider the
figure to be as high as 6-10% – this is still many more people than were alive
at the time of Jesus.  Those who are less cynical recognise that technological
advance really is spreading relative affluence in every society.  This has, for
most people, ameliorated that deprivation (new sense) which used to prevent
most children from growing-up.  More now breed, and the affluence has now
spread over the increased population of most countries.  This, as I will now try
to show, can lead to much more serious deprivations (new usage) which are
harsher, less remediable and more crippling for the individual than those of
poverty.

The affluent city-dweller does not, in general, see his crippled state as deprived; this is at least in part the fault of the educators, who often don't see the
difference between doing and knowing-about-doing, even reading-about-
doing.  In the next chapters I hope to show how privilege-corruption, by the
educational establishment in major part, has perverted the spread of human
dignity by spreading this misunderstanding.  The deprivations (both usages)
of affluence remove the *wish* for betterment, even the curiosity as to whether
better exists.  The poor and starving do strive for improvement of their lot, and
that of their children especially, until chronic starvation takes away even the
ability to seek food.  But watching professional football in the comfort of a
modern town-house prevents even the desire to visit the ground;  actually
*playing* football, in the rain for example, is inconceivable!  The car displaces
the bicycle, the TV-meal displaces even the fish-and-chip shop or bar society,
after the art of the omelette has become too onerous.  The Initial Teaching
Alphabet (I.T.A.), Readers' Digest Condensed Books, "Gems from the Shows",

all mark treads on the staircase down – all deprive the affluent of the *will* to improve.

Schools, not only of educators but of doctors, of farmers, or hairdressers close their ranks to outsiders, letting their original innovatory competence fossilise. Both professionals and their clients are then carried by affluence and lack of outside criticism back into the tribal "patient" state (Illich, p.85). This forms a substrate, as in the young city-states, for the barbarian who grows up from his street gang to find an amenable, affluent tribe he can conquer. But he can now be more powerful, more inescapable than ever before, whether he is a Mafia chief or an ad-man, a union organiser in a fossilised profession or a pop group agent.

Thus "ordinary" people have had their horizons irremediably narrowed by affluence at least as much as by poverty, and are surrounded by such luxury that their health suffers too, as in poverty. Joy becomes rare, and the newer affluent order made possible by the new technology becomes just as necessary as the previous necessities – central heating, or instant food, become necessities. The affluent "tribesman" uses his time and effort just like his indigent ancestor – the mandatory television replaces the mandatory totem-pole, and he struggles just as hard to maintain his "high standard of living" as his grandfather did for his "simpler" life style. As in all tribal life styles, his life becomes saturated with mandatory actions, to the point where decisions are unnecessary because his life resembles that of everybody else in his ambience. All the unemployed and some of the manual workers go to the pub, the sexually-bored young marrieds go to the video shop for their soft porn, the salesmen on the new estate *all* wash the car on Sunday mornings, as all used to go to church – and all can follow the general pattern without thought.

This insect-like, thoughtless activity was difficult to establish in a curious primate, and the next chapters seek to document this part of our biological history. It will, for many sectors of the human civic species, be a long, uneventful future history, for decision followed by thoughtful action will be needed to escape this full-time, empty life. There are few irks which can provoke this in most people now, and further technology is directed towards the removal even of these. Getting up from the armchair to change television or video channels is too much for some people already, it seems (see "Couch Potatoes", p157). The Ape wanted an easy life, and cultural transmission of the cities' riches has given it to him. I'll now try to show both how we got here, and how there are trends which hold the hope of escape.

# References

References in full are to be found from page 243 onwards. Below are listed names of authors and dates of publication.

1. Runciman (1966)
2. Cohen (1977)
3. Cassen *et al* (1986)
4. Jensen (1969)
5. Jensen (1978)
6. Gould (1981)

# 9

# EDUCATION ENCOURAGES THE APE'S INCOMPETENCE

This chapter is the fulcrum of the book, and it contains, at its centre, the event which persuaded me of the philosophy I am attempting to portray. This was the discovery, in the person of a very attractive and apparently well-motivated and successful student, of an intellectual and emotional deprivation which shocked me deeply. It forced me to re-examine all my educational assumptions.' We both came out of that tutoring exercise considerably wiser. She went on to get a good degree and to lead a much more satisfying life. I went back to Illich[1], to Foucault and Marcuse and the rest of the "student unrest" literature[2] of the late sixties. A synthesis of my reproductive biology of that time resulted in *Reproduction*[3] in 1977, whose last end-of-chapter question was "What passes between the generations to reproduce a bacterium, a trout, a cuckoo, a Frenchman?" Within months the English version of Bourdieu's *Reproduction*[4] appeared, in the tradition of Marcuse and Foucault, and showed me that the educational cadre had indeed perverted our cultural wealth, to produce deprivations in affluence which are much less remediable than the deprivations of poverty.

In this chapter I rehearse this picture twice, firstly as an "evolutionary" story, from animals through tribal and barbarian systems to urban affluence and its three kinds of deprivation, which result in a "consumer class" lacking much of human dignity. Then, after a brief account of the crucial tutoring experience, I take a biologist's look at the maturation, within urban society, of such a deprived person. I cannot use the word "education" for this process. I can then, in the next chapter, move into the larger aesthetic, sexual and generally artistic consequences of such a "consumer caste" for the organisation of our species as a city culture.

The deprivations associated with poverty are well-known, and a couple of examples were rehearsed in the last chapter; many in fact are privation, the lack of the necessities of life, rather than de-privilege, lack of the formative influences in the making of each baby into a person. It is the latter, however, which seems to me to be the key to many of the problems of technical urban affluence. Such affluence seems to result from the inordinately successful tactic, used in all human cultural reproduction, of disseminating privilege from all over the human group to each child. This results in major part from the "division of labour" adopted by even the most primitive human societies, and permits human children the longest privileged pre-adult life of any animal. There *are* animals (*Gyrodactylus*, a fish fluke, *Glossina,* the tse-tse fly) whose offspring are coddled right up to adulthood within the parent's body[3]. But only within human (and naked mole-rat and some insect) societies can a majority of the population lead whole lives, fertilisation-to-death, entirely cosseted by the food, goods, services accumulated as cultural capital by many organisms of previous generations. The technology of people (and ants) permits many entire lives to be privileged: "They toil not, neither do they spin" was not as true of the lilies of the field as it was of the drones of the hive – or the Levites of the Jews. The ants, unlike humans, have a genetic program which directs their neural circuitry into various kinds of pre-programmed behaviour, so that the privileged lives of soldier or male are nonetheless integrated into the web of their society. Mole-rats, which are like mammalian ants, have slightly more versatile behaviour but all members of the colony do labour. Human society, with privilege accumulating as goods and technology through the generations, has invented a new "caste", the *consumer*. But human castes are not programmed genetically to any extent; each kind results from cultural constraints and opportunities found by each individual[15].

Human industry, fuelled by agriculture or fossil fuel, is immensely efficient. The growth of technology could permit a robot-run society, with *all* humans freed from labour and relegated to consumer-caste. This was very nearly achieved in ancient Athens and some plantations of the Deep South; slaves, of course, were not considered to be of the same human group as their owners! Such efficiency is not unique. Dolphins, because of the rigorous selection for strength of bone and muscle, homoiothermy and intelligence, which moulded their terrestrial ancestors, are the most efficient marine predators; less than ten per cent of their time is spent getting food. Yet they don't have an accumulating privilege for they have not, as far as we know, any method (additional to milk) for passage of this privilege from many adults to each offspring. Each dolphin hunts for himself.

But a few humans may produce for a vast society and an infinite future. Towns are the means by which human privilege is usually accumulated and disseminated today, and even the poor of the towns are usually better off than the ordinary countryman. Even in modern Hong Kong, or Dickensian London, the society of the poor is preferred *by them* to that of the peasantry outside the towns. In towns even the poor have access to a variety, and standard, of experience sought in play and fantasy by all humans. This can only be made available when the manifest cultural capital of many people is concentrated in a small area – an Oriental bazaar is a good example. I have already exposed, in the last chapter, some aspects of the deprivations of poverty; in cities, there are compensations. Most town organisations have privileges which *only* the poor have access to: charities, mendicant (begging) rights, poor-houses. They also have opportunities for the poor to alleviate their relative deprivation by acquiring privilege illegally: picking pockets, prostitution, small-time blackmail are only possible in large affluent communities. Barbarian groups, often gangs of adolescents, can parasitise such an aggregation of poor *and* rich, but the social pathology of a Mafia probably requires a more permanent organisation which both supports and reduces poverty. So the urban poor obviously have less privilege than other urban groups, but more than they would have outside the cities.

There are three special kinds of deprivation in towns and cities, other than those associated with simple poverty, from the special viewpoint adopted here. Two are not serious, for there are compensations, but the third can be more debilitating, more dehumanising, than all but the most extreme poverty (and returns us to central issues, the failure of cultural transfer).

The first is the converse of that privilege extended to the poor. It is the tax, levy, tithe or donations demanded from the urban privileged, to accumulate as cultural and technological capital, as the city's wealth. Taking from the rich, or competent, or charitable-because-guilty, and investing in the future of the society, the "general good", by public works, educational grants, medical research and so on, is a major function of city government. The ancient Greek city states, and Plato's *Republic*, exemplify simple forms. The latter, too, shows how this necessity deprives the giver of authority over part of his wealth; medieval Florence was a good example too, with its system of supervised patronage. There is usually a complex recompense, in honour, *via* barbarian rituals which reward the noble. Such transactions involving privilege, profit and position are usual for competent citizens, and account for many of their satisfactions in urban life, especially for the males.

There is a second deprivation characteristic of urban affluence, and it affects most of the population. It is related partly to class structure, partly to the urban "division of labour", but derives mostly from that human cultural invention, the school[1]. Concepts like "alienation", the "ossification of bureaucracy", or "deschooling" are sociological or psychological labels for the side-effects of this simple biological perversion: the attempt to pass specialist culture across the generations by those withdrawn from the general culture. The specialisations characteristic of urban life foster subgroups, which initially engender or transmit different cultures, each trade or professional group forming a more-

or-less independent reproductive lineage *via* cultural inheritance. The early socialists, especially the Fabians, and the Webbs with their vision of political pluralism, the "multiculture", wanted to enfranchise each such cultural thread[6,] perhaps each with its own "parliament"; I take up a rather more radical multicultural model in the final chapters.

When we think of human beings in a society as doctors, teachers, workers – especially workers – we must avoid the error, associated with some naive sociobiologists and exposed clearly by Sahlins[5], which compares them with insect castes. Human beings are not insects. Among the termites the soldiers are programmed virtually entirely by their genetics, acquired directly from queens and kings, and progressive change through them is impossible. What human beings are, in contrast, is derived from contemporary social organisations, which can drastically change all the rules in one generation. For example, in human societies it has been common for a military group to evolve a philosophy differing from the authorised version and to rebel, setting up a new regime in which their cultural mode is dominant. Then many of the cultural patterns of heredity, including who does the teaching as well as what is taught, may be changed by the new regime. Sometimes new teachers are appointed, but it is often the old teachers who transmit the new philosophy. They are, after all, specialists in the passage of culture to the young – they declare. They can, and regularly do, serve the new masters with the same attention to their own privileged position as under the old regime. Under the new regime, however, they pull the same educational levers and strings to produce a changed outlook in the new generation – several recent South American countries, perhaps Argentina most dramatically, show this clearly; so, of course does Cuba. China has changed twice in thirty years, but I am much less ready with such a simplistic description.

This is the *origin* of this second area of deprivation in urban society, and Ivan Illich[1] has made much of it: professional educators (but also professional doctors, lawyers, and politicians) have closed ranks, formed 'schools'. They have each formed a cultural reproductive sub-system, with its own "patient" group dependent upon it, supplying it with societal privilege both material and status. Such sub-system formation is characteristic of different specialisms within the human urban system, but cannot happen in biological reproductive systems because there the specialisms (termite workers, or Portuguese Man-o-War stomach-animals) share the common genetic program and are re-created from it in every generation. Human sub-systems share some of the constraints and authority-pathways of the general society[5], but in some respects they acquire advantage by performing to society's disadvantage. For example, Illich has shown that it is to the immediate (short-term) advantage of both teacher and taught to ritualise the teaching function and to divorce it from any contact with social or physical reality tests. Then it is to the advantage of both teacher and taught to drop standards.

There are many other sub-groups (all called "schools" by Illich[1]) whose internal reproductive practices similarly work "against" the society of which they are a part: Trade Unions may deprive their members of the freedom to work, the medical profession fosters illness rather than health, and so on. Children, workers and patients are deprived of personal status in their interactions with these subgroups and become "numbers", alienated from what they consider to be their roles, their rights and their responsibilities even as "patients". Education becomes "keeping them happy", worker involvement in production becomes reduced to "strike leverage", and the patient finds queues rather than cures. Most people are then deprived of those kinds of privilege which have been sequestered by the sub-groups concerned. Of these, the most critical are certainly the special authority-routes of the educational sub-group, for it has taken to itself the task of reproducing the culture in each generation, and all its immediate advantages lie in failing to achieve this[1].

These two losses of privilege are serious in urban cultures, but the third deprivation is both more insidious and more damaging. It is the deprivation of the chance of attaining ability, of improving individual competence. Whereas the first two deprivations we have considered *remove* privilege (for example, by taxes) or make *access* to privilege difficult (because, for example, teachers have sequestered access to jobs behind educational rituals like examinations), the third deprivation reduces the ability of the deprived person to *accept* privilege, change himself thereby, and become more human – it destroys any wish for self-improvement. This deprivation is administered to some extent *via* the professions, especially the educators, but is most successfully transmitted by parents and then self-administered by most people in a technological urban society.

In order to put this most serious deprivation in context, we should recall the final links in the evolutionary series leading to man (Chapter 4). The case was made that, unlike gnu, guinea-pig or giraffe, the primates (and carnivores and some rodents) do not only *program* their offspring by developmental/physiological maturation in the uterus. They bear them into a nest while they are still helpless fetuses, so that the latter part of " fetal" life is spent secure, learning. These parents must set up two situations for these learning offspring, if reproduction of the species-specific qualities is to occur. The offspring must be made secure from environmental dangers like temperature change, parasites or

predators.  But they must also, unlike nestling birds, *be given the chance to fail.*
They learn by trial and *error*.  Even if reward is usual, for example milk for
finding a nipple, there is an element of tuition which can only result from sometimes *not* finding the nipple.  This situation, of insecurity-within-security, must
be established by behavioural responses of offspring to parents and from
parents to offspring, presumably programmed or developed in each organism
by interaction between this very behaviour and the developmental program.
(For example, when Harlow's baby monkeys were denied mother-interaction
themselves, they were unable to mother in their turn.)  For our kind of animal,
then, we should suppose that both security and pain-associated-with-error are
part of the offspring-learning process in our reproduction.

We have all at least read about human children who have lacked the security
apparently necessary in early childhood – many of them were orphans, or from
"broken homes", or the victims of the dislocations of war and its tragic sequels.
These children have been subject to many privations, and have often been
deprived of food or other necessities.    However, if there is no physical
pathology such children usually live full lives as far as their society permits;
indeed their own feeling is often that their hard early life was in some sense
"good" for them, "made them what they were".   These children, very
interestingly, are the heart-wringing examples used by the children's-aid
charities to get money from us.  (What they do with the money, however, is
usually admirable – I'm not criticising the philosophy of the work, just the effectiveness of the adverts, the location of our guilt!)   These children are *not*
deprived, in my third, urban, affluent sense (but of course they may have been
deprived in other aspects of their lives).   In order to describe this third deprivation clearly, I must relate the incident one of whose sequels is this book.

In Birmingham University Biology departments we ran a personal tutorial
system; tutors saw students for an hour each week, on a one-to-one basis, and
were assigned to a new tutor each year (the system has recently been "diluted"
to the point where it is barely, if at all, effective).  One of my second year tutees
was a very attractive girl with a fairly good academic record.   In our first tutorial I enquired, as I always did, about her other interests, reading habits, and
so on.  She read "historical novels".  "What was the last?"  She couldn't remember.  Author?  Plot?  No, it had left no mark.  Other books?  "No, apart
from biology texts."   Music?   "Yes, provided it isn't too classical or too
'pop'...."   Other hobbies? "No."  Games or sports? "No".  What turns you
on, if anything?  "Well, nothing *really* – except biology I suppose".   It turned
out that she had failed Maths at school, had got into university on other criteria

despite this, had avoided make-up Maths in her first year, and was due now to enter a fairly high-powered Statistics course. In discussion it slowly became clear that she had *never* found anything difficult. On any occasion when there was a possibility she might be stretched, someone (usually a man; she was and is attractive, and soon learnt the ways to ensure help) provided the wanted impetus, strength or information (except of course in the Maths at school – female teacher, unusually, I think!). She couldn't understand my immediate demand that she should pass a fairly high-standard Maths test in three weeks, or leave. I tried hard to explain to her that she needed the mathematical expertise, to even begin her Statistics – but that she needed the discipline which would result from accomplishing an almost-impossible-to-accomplish task, much more! I failed, again and again, to show her that there was virtue in trying hard, in surmounting difficulties. She passed the Maths test we set, after some evenings' coaching by a research student. Only later, when a demonstrator offered to do her lab experiment for her and I commented "Deprived again!", did she see the point – she said "No, let me do it!" – and changed her life. She got a good degree – with difficulty, I'm delighted to say – and is now doing a job she finds difficult – and doing it very well, I'm sure. I would like to go right back through her "education", finding all those who chose to give her security in exchange for her affection, rather than teaching her to find the joy of achievement – after failure informed her. They denied her so much joy, and much human dignity, by taking the easy short-term-reward path themselves. How many teachers do you know who do that? And how many who don't?

My initial failure with this girl made me think deeply about the system which produced her, and about what her teachers did, and about what I did and if I could get a general rule out of it. I don't like general rules, in this kind of interpersonal ethical relationship or any other important one. I believe it to be unethical to refuse to judge a case on its merits, or to decide, but simply to apply a previously-decided rule. I do this all the time, of course, for the unimportant things – we all do. Some of the art of finding general rules is that they can *genuinely* make important decisions routine – that is, make them quicker, sometimes make them unimportant! The generality of this student's case, however, started ramifying into all kinds of other things (as you can see from this book). Our society, I decided, had got its cultural reproduction wrong if we could mess up someone like that. Did other societies get it "right", then? Was there a good, reliable way of turning out able human beings?

The reproduction of abilities in tribal systems is only accomplished by apprenticeship-like relationships of (usually) family members; skills are practised by the young, who *fail and learn*, by correction, contributing to the family accomplishment. The very young *play* with adult tools and skills, developing them to usefulness through trial and *error*, practise reducing the error as it earns punishment or fails to earn rewards[7,8]. In barbarian systems, the passage of criteria across the generations is often by confrontation systems: bluff, rarely violence, ritual games, myths whose underlying systems instruct the juveniles as they *fail* to play them or pass them on correctly. That is to say, congruence in honour-based rituals is achieved by trial-and-error, as is competence in more mundane activities. In apprentice systems, both the honour systems *and* the competences are transmitted from the "master" by practice and occasional failure – so reproduction of the activity is achieved.

In civic systems, passage of cultural competence is delegated to a group not involved with either the honour system or the competence of each activity, the professional educators who follow on from affluent parents. Then, as Illich showed, standards necessarily fall. The juveniles receive no immediate punishment signals from their learning failures, and replace each learning task with the more general task of learning "school rules" which regulate interaction between teachers and pupils. The task changes from "learning to write words" to the new tasks of "learning to please teacher" and "learning to placate peers", often requiring a carefully balanced display of only moderate ability at writing. Failure in these tasks *is*, of course, immediately signalled, especially by peers, so the child can and does learn the *social* rules. But the child doesn't learn to write competently, or to like writing. The teacher, also, gets negative signals if he (more often she) moves the attention from the relationship with the children, where they do know the rules, to the task, where they more usually don't. The teacher's relationship to the child progressively relaxes, so that formal punishment becomes an impossible option, damaging to the only relationship which survives. So the requirements change. The teachers, then, must substitute the requirement that their products can engage in specific activities by the requirement that they can attain a threshold in a more general, testable competence. "Can he repair a cart?" is replaced by "Can he write about repairing carts?"; then "Can he score more than 50% by writing answers to questions on this formal syllabus about carts?" is replaced by "Can he write about *anything*?" to get a diploma allowing him to apply for a job repairing carts.

Some professions, notably the medical professions, have retained the apprenticeship system. Of surgical operations, registrars joke: "See one, do one, teach one ......"! But, even in medicine, there are increasing contributions by educators who insist on the acquisition of "general competence", e.g. in molecular biology, which is almost totally irrelevant to the *practice* of medicine – but has become necessary for qualifications in medicine. (Family planning practice, or counselling the bereaved, or understanding the mathematics of epidemic disease, are not generally taught as such.) This requirement, for publicly testable abilities in *lieu* of effective abilities, is only possible in affluent societies, for only in affluence can incompetence survive without pain.     Further, because the "security" of juveniles is more immediately rewarding to their mentors than is the "insecurity" of real learning situations, the educational process becomes progressively (*sic*) softer.   Even the public tests become mutually-confirming rituals between "teacher" and "taught", with "teacher" always reducing the effort required of his wards.

Children, like other young learning mammals, should use play to exercise their abilities, to improve their competence at living.  In pre-affluent societies they play at adult roles, and usually fail to attain adult goals, of course; but the juvenile goals, practice and learning, are achieved.   They also have their own well-defined tasks with their own successes and failures.   Only in affluent society is effort dedicated to the *removal* of difficulty in all the juvenile's tasks – as if they were to be given bicycles to train on the running track!  Examples of this deprivation of educational exercise are many.   The Initial Teaching Alphabet (ITA) was devised to make learning to read and write easier, by replacement of compound letter sounds like "sh" and "th" with single symbols. Not surprisingly, *fewer* children learnt; however, this was usually blamed, by progressive educationalists, on the further step needed to move to the "real" alphabet. "Understanding" is now usually a major goal of educational tasks, not the mere (and more difficult) acquisition of volumes of information. Learning of the "set" book, or "set" play, even of the "set" poem is no longer required in the literature class – but "The child should be acquainted with all the difficult words ... "!

"Projects" replace rote learning;  so cheap motivation replaces the self-discipline acquired by learning to force one's brain into unmotivated paths. Pocket-money is seen as a right instead of a reward, and this philosophy of "Make my way smooth, I am a Child" continues into later life as the university student grant system.   This takes intellectually able children smoothly from school to university, with no judgement or decision having to be made along the way. Do bear in mind that schools are judged by how many of their products get into university, and universities feel the draught if they seem to be picking up fewer students.  Both interests have been well served by the apparent lack of available employment at about the 16-year-old level in the U.K. in the eighties;  more children are staying on into the sixth form, and some more are doing the higher school-leaving certificate, A-level.  One result of this is that, because of the fractional system used by Examination Boards to apportion *A*s, *B*s.....*F*s and *G*s, *more* students are getting the upper grades.  It seems to many of us that students who, ten years ago, were getting *C*s are now getting *B*s and *A*s.  We do understand that there is no immutable standard, and that we are getting older.  But more children, in real numbers, *are* getting *A*s and you will find it hard to find an authority who would claim that the teaching is better! Certainly our biology entrants know less biology, although perhaps they do know more biochemistry.   In many universities and colleges considerable employment has been created, too, by the provision of accessory, supplementary or "make-up" courses.    The alternative was to have the first year at university duplicate nearly all of the last year's work at school; three university biology courses I knew well adopted this approach.   That saved considerable effort on both sides, too.  This "knowledge without pain" philosophy continues into adult life, of course, and accounts for the "rights" of all UK citizens to the understanding of important issues.

All of the above can be argued as a good tactic, of course. The university student certainly is spared anxiety, and is given much more time for his studies, by his grant.    My strong impression, however, is that the high motivation shown by most of those who "put themselves through college" is very rarely seen in those who get education "free", as a "right" (I have had one major exception in each direction).

The adult equivalents, too, are usually seen as labour-saving, anxiety-removing, happiness-promoting:  TV meals, newspapers with no long words or more than one side to a story, radio programmes which are all "pop" music and "pop" news, girlie magazines ("soft porn") which provide sanitized sexual stimulation with none of the intimate risks of the real interaction, spectator sports with vicarious success as well as vicarious failure.    Because our biological nature requires real challenge in order to grow, and to learn, the real standard of living is reduced by such as these.   They contrast with washing machines, polythene, paperback books, special systems of national insurance (Social Security) and some Public Housing systems; all these use the resources of society to spread the investment of privilege more widely, and they usually are distributed in the UK in ways which enable competence rather than negating it.   But these systems, however well run, however available, cannot help the trained-to-be-indolent;  the book must be lifted from the shelf, and opened. I am reminded that "You can lead a horticulture, but you cannot make her think..... " (Dorothy Parker.)   Mmm.

So, I have suggested that progressive softening of requirements for juveniles is a necessary consequence of relegation of the inter-generational transmission of expertise to the schools. Also, I say that softening of requirements for adults is a necessary consequence of the success and complexity of increasing technology, and the development of exclusive technocracies. Neither of these points is new or dramatic but I hope to show that the biological view, showing this failing transmission of privilege, illuminates such failure to reproduce competent people, and gives both warning and remedies. Both genetics and privilege are required to make a human being; distortion of either gives deformation or deprivation and the latter is, perhaps surprisingly, a necessary result of our kind of distributed affluence.

Most people, I imagine, have looked around them, seen what a weedy lot we are, and blamed "modern conveniences". I'm doing more than that, in blaming education – about, and using, modern conveniences! Isn't it rather strange, you may feel, to demand "survival skills" of twentieth-century man? Am I not harking back to Rousseau's Noble Savage, or to the polymath Renaissance man? I would be among the first to agree that competence in Greek translation should not be required of all children, nor the ability to wire a house of all men. But the desire for a comparable competence in a variety of areas should be there. I agree with Heinlein[9]: "A human being should be able to change a diaper, plan an invasion, butcher a hog ... design a building, write a sonnet, balance accounts, build a wall, set a bone .... take orders, give orders, program a computer, cook a tasty meal .... specialisation is for insects.". This is all very high-minded, you may retort, and a worthy aim; but we have *never* attained this ideal in any past society, and the suggestion that we are dropping standards now is the reverse of the truth. Children, you may say with justice, now learn more, about more, to a higher level .... and I would still agree that this is true, but *irrelevant. What* they learn now covers more ground; but in order to show that it fails to contribute to the whole urban man, we should compare the process, the product, and the sequence and choice of learned material in our society with others. For I believe that our society is now failing to reproduce its nature, is not maintaining itself. Even our simple-minded Campbell/Morgan model lets us see that other societies – however we classify them – succeed where we fail. They are, to the eye of the reproductive biologist, reproductively stable: generation $N+1$ is like generation $N$, or better. Our reproduction of our culture is grossly faulty in the general society (but subcultures like Irish Catholics, all over the world, may be doing a good job – see p208 !).

A criticism of this "reproductive stability" failure model, made by a student in one of my classes, is interesting but, I think, mistaken. She said: "Of course the savages, the tribesmen are reproductively stable! You've chosen them as examples for just that reason! And of course they contrast with our progressive attitude, where every generation has more *leisure*, more affluence, more foreign holidays than the previous .... you have chosen the stagnant, ecological balanced but *primitive* societies because, like the *Amoeba*, they've survived by just existing!" As a reproductive biologist, yes, I have chosen them for existing through time, reproducing their cultures; but I still judge that we are *not* reproducing our culture, *although we say that we want to*.

There is, too, a detailed consideration of standard of adult performance to be considered; we, much more than any previous – or most contemporary – cultures are protected by our technology all our lives. We have made enormously effective nests and we live in them. We would each *like* to be able to do that Heinlein list above, wouldn't we? I agree that tribesmen, bye and large, can't and that barbarians only *boast* that they can! But we are progressively becoming *less* able to ... and that is contrary to our expressed desires (see any James Bond film), and to our philosophy of natural progress. This is why I chose the simplest anthropological model which was congruent with my prejudices. Please pick up any anthropology text and work this bit out for yourselves. Here is the simple-minded view. I like simple theories, they are easier to disprove – if wrong.

In Tribal life, the adolescent routes to adulthood ensure standards of performances in customary adult roles. Children are tested as warriors, as cooks, as potters, as builders, as fishermen in apprentice-type roles[8]. There is usually an explicit hierarchy by inheritance (e.g. of warriors, witch doctors, or wives[7]), related to *competence*, sometimes with ritual competition for place and "face". In Barbarian society, gangs support leaders, and position is maintained by rituals related to honour instead of custom. Individual development proceeds by a series of emulations related to 'face', honour, bravery, loot, machismo. Training in this society results in many real losses, and the trained barbarian is a strong character, like the trained warrior tribesman (but very different). Early Civil organisation often showed customary routes for rise in status, by emulation (e.g. apprentice, midshipman) as well as the reward of *some* individual honour systems with high status (generals, Greek philosophers). A multi-dimensional customary hierarchy involved most citizens; each could be high (honoured, obeyed) in some regards but obedient or even servile in others, especially within an aristocracy.

With the advent of both "democracy" and affluence, however, honour loses its hold, and customs fade as they become inappropriate to the technology (e.g. duelling, Harvest Suppers, ploughing competitions). As we have seen, motivation for education then fails except insofar as the educators can force their (usually socially irrelevant) strictures onto juveniles and parents. "Models" for competence replace individual aspirations. Such models may appeal to tribal culture, as to-be-emulated – for example, British news-readers on television – or to barbarian "hero-worship" (Elvis Presley). This failure to model *general competence*, but only specific aspects chosen for emulation, can have serious consequences for the maintenance of urban culture by reproduction of expertise. We seek models to follow, but we lack the criteria (usually painful) that tell us when we have not done so successfully. They were, and are, necessary in simpler societies, but they don't sell well in ours.

There is a *new* maintenance problem in a technologically affluent urban society, very different from the maintenance problems of tribal or barbarian life. Custom, alone, will maintain the tribe; if contagious disease, war or affluence rocks the system the tribe will either fall or continue in the old mode. Many of the Arab States on the Gulf have tribes, Bedouin to the un-initiate like me, some of which have suffered each of the above – and survived. Similarly, a barbarian system is always diverse, as individuals confront, retire, follow new leaders or fail; *its* maintenance depends upon a constant reward of high status. This can be a supply of loot, rapine, extortion, or in general a source of honourable activities with an overall economic profit. When this fails, as in confrontation of some American Indian groups with white settlers (*both* sides had tribal, barbarian and citizen modes, in different places), that honour system loses its hold and that barbarian system collapses. Some Western films have just this cowboys/Indians plot, and we therefore recognise it. We don't want to believe it's a real story, because we've had it presented as myth. Hollywood Indian culture is based, I feel sure, on old Morgan's book *Ancient Society*, which was so full of American Indian stereotypes in beautiful, boring detail with all their wampum and totems, and extended complex families. For us, this has been transmogrified through *Hiawatha* for the most part. However, because so many mythic threads in our Western (*sic*) culture go back to these views of the "savage", and because Hollywood has portrayed it so often through the prejudices of the producer, I doubt my ability – and yours – to judge cowboy/Indian confrontations wisely. The Hollywood Indian Chief, the Hollywood Mongol, and the Hollywood Gangster usually fit my barbarian model well. But I don't think that, because Hollywood believes them, they are necessarily untrue..... When a barbarian culture loses face to an outside culture, it dies.

Urban systems, however, have heterogeneity in space, and change with time as part of their successful structure. Artisans develop or learn techniques, and bring them in to the towns, where the technique may soon become essential to the advanced culture. The practitioners then form a guild, for their own protection and advancement. Some of these were formed locally (in Bromsgrove, Worcestershire) as late as 1907; others were medieval or earlier, and have considerably changed their function (e.g. the Freemasons). In guilds, the traditions or customs soon become rules. They then bind the guild artisans as rigidly as tribal custom, and the guild or trade union descends to tribal level: every action is either mandatory or forbidden. This is assisted by the "quality-control" regulations within the guild, which give more status to each member by demanding high standards from all; in such as the Goldsmith's, Royal Assent and patronage further rigidified the practice. "Secret" techniques, even common expertise which required experience and practice, also prevented innovation. Meanwhile, new technology had been incorporated into the way of life of a new citizen group, which soon became another urban elite (e.g. Ironmasters), then an institution, then it in turn degenerated into tribalism.

So, historically, urban organisation rests on a broad foundation of culture which is basically tribal. Only the cadres familiar with the newer, still-restricted, technologies and experimental innovations have decision-making powers. Past technologies pass into the education of most juveniles, but *only* after they have been ritualised to the point where even the technologically inexpert teacher can transmit them. For example, writing and reading can now be taught and learnt by those who add naught to literature, and the geometry of Euclid could pass from teacher to child with neither expected to do more than the ritual exercises. Dead languages, too, can form a very useful part of the educational ritual because they are complicated, public, transmissable mechanically and can later serve adult ritual purposes.

Foreign language teaching is very different; it is the last degeneration of colonialism, of the broad supernational culture of the Empire. Teachers are rare who can transmit a wide culture, and the foreign language forms the last transmissable remnant. In the same way teachers will only be able to teach computing when little expertise is needed, only "rules of thumb". All our local High (13-18) Schools have bought computers, with Government-granted money, but none teaches even the lowest-level course. Anyone who *can* work with a computer is, of course, doing so – at higher pay than teachers get; only the unable can be found to teach a new technology. The same has happened with biotechnology; those teachers who can comprehend the techniques have been employed by industry. How does the next generation learn new technologies? It doesn't, in affluent Western society. Nor does it in the socialist countries, for interestingly different reasons; new technology is always suspiciously radical, and socialists are the most conservative of teachers! Japan and Mexico *are* teaching new technology, Japan because it isn't *their* newest technology and Mexico because even technologists make more money from (oil-)rich families by tutoring their children – and gain status thereby (in Illich's own country, too!).

The education system in an affluent society collects those rituals, themselves the fossils of earlier living technologies, to form its substance. These remnants are *not* inherently useless, however. They could in principle provide a vehicle to teach a child to learn. But their irrelevance to major life is a major difficulty with the motivation of the child. For nearly all those children growing up in a television age, reading seems irrelevant as an expertise to acquire, a fossilising pastime of the previous generation. Calculators soon become an easy alternative to "arduous" calculation, just as the supermarket shelf becomes an easy alternative to adult work in the garden or kitchen. The softening of educational disciplines, an obvious route once it is seen to serve the immediate interests of both educator and juvenile, ritualises even these remnants until the fossil is useless. The old abilities, such as a knowledge of the classical literature, or some Shakespeare, or the multiplication tables, or spelling accuracy, have been lost, too.

Their earlier use was only superficially the acquisition of the ritual knowledge. The deeper reproductive function was the conditioning of the child by the joys and pains of intellectual exercise, so that as an adult it would put enthusiastic effort into its intellectual role. Literacy and numeracy are acquired *attitudes*, not primarily *abilities*. They are measured as abilities, of course; but a truer measure would be the light in the eye when a new book is started or a long and interesting calculation is being checked! My point here is that the Ape cannot learn the attitude without a foundation of effortful ability; brains require that effort be made for enjoyment to ensue, and for attitude (habit) to appear. This is our heritage from the trial-and-error learning in the nest, if I'm right about the origins of intelligent culture. This is not, I believe, a Puritan position, although it may help explain the attraction of Puritan pleasure-through-pain or the I-know-I'm-working-hard-because-it-hurts attitudes. Effort need not hurt, and doesn't if it is habitual – but few can learn that lesson in affluence! Very few learn it in school. My deprived student taught me that.

Once the old ritual tribal content in education has been seen to be irrelevant to living, "projects" are invented so that little effort may produce recognisable success. The parents, who vote or whose support is needed for the school in other ways, and the juvenile herself have the illusion of immediacy. Language teaching loses the literacy, and becomes the "real world" of everyday conversation in French, or German, because this seems to be more relevant to life – *and* the teacher can more easily be seen to be teaching conversation than style. However, the major point of the education has been lost; the *Black Paper 1975*[10] had many articles relevant to the contentions of this chapter, indeed of this book. Bantock[11], for example, countered the "Teach them to *speak* French ... at least that will be useful if they go there on holiday." approach, with "...there was no virtue simply in teaching them to speak French – there were fifty million Frenchmen who do that but few of them had anything to say worth listening to; the emphasis must be on language at its best – i.e. the literature of the country".

Because of these failing motivations in all involved in affluent education, the pursuit of excellence cannot be maintained. Adequacy for the majority is sought instead, and the attempt to replace falling standards is seen as "'elitism" and supposed to be powered by divisive motives. "Discrimination" becomes a bad word in education; "competent" comes to mean "adequate", and "special education" comes to refer only to the bottom end of the ability spectrum.

"Compensatory egalitarianism" becomes a useful philosophy to excuse failure in any area: "If she's no good at Maths, she's probably good at languages ... No? Then she must be good at sports ... No? Then, because she has failed at so many things she must have a beautiful soul, great *motivation* .... this is how she has not failed in our education system. We have *not* failed her, we have recognised her gift!". This whole "compensatory" philosophy of human competence must be dismissed as an educator's myth, useful only to excuse persistent incompetence in front of an egalitarian teacher. Surely, the contrary is more like the truth: the competent seem more so because they can *avoid* areas in which they are weak, while the incompetent cannot avoid being shown up. This exaggerates original differences very unfairly, and much educational technology is devoted to the search for areas in which the "potential" of otherwise less competent children can be "realised". We have already seen (pp106-9) that "potential" does not have the quantitative value which is assumed in these "educational" exercises. Because of the high emotional value of intellectual attainment or failure, compared with variation in physical abilities (deprivation as compared with deformation) strange, indeed paradoxical values emerge. An example is the ritual admiration of sporting success in children, especially in competitive activities. Comparable training, extra-curricular practice, and variation in ability would not be tolerated in intellectual or emotional pursuits. Can you imagine a school Open Day in which children would do mathematical or stylistic exercises, in open competitions? Would you send your child to such a school? In the education of which most of us approve, teachers may be paid to coach football outside regular school hours but rarely, if ever, French or fractions (I dare not continue this prohibited list, but see Aldous Huxley's *Island*, and p 149 ).

The excitement and joy of discovery, even the simple satisfactions of rote learning of poetry or multiplication tables, have been replaced by the teacher's approval of ritual acts, easily attained – and leaving the teacher popular. Exceptional performance is no longer rewarded, either by commonly-agreed rewards like status or money, or by the unique attainment of new thrills. Comparable thrills to those achieved by a rewarding performance are available in surrogate form, as the delights of film, drugs, food, holidays on semi-tropic isles – more than any old-style emperor could attain, and all for less than a month's average wage. These are now an expected part of all affluent children's lives, not requiring more effort than the tolerance of parents' company.

A "Pop" attitude then supersedes effortful appreciation of the arts. Enjoyment which requires training or effort is "not worth it" in competition with easier satisfactions. Immediacy takes over from subtlety as a standard for the syllabus, and cursory examination of a list of "pop" subjects (Baudelaire's love life, or predators in the jungle) replaces learning about a subject in depth in the *hope* that this will excite a professional and critical appraisal. The attitude of "B.Sc. in 3 years, for that is the time I have my grant for" pushes both British student and university department to produce an educational "package", a syllabus comprehensible to the lowliest student, and resembling a TV meal in its avoidance of any flavour which might put anyone off.

In biology, for example, dissection is replaced by examination of plastic replicas, all beautifully labelled, and students copy the explanatory drawings of microscopic specimens into their "practical books" before (sometimes) giving a cursory glance at the actual specimens. The specimens are less relevant than the theories, the physiology, the more apparently modern approach. It is as if biology, for them, has lost its connection with the outside, real world of structures and organisms, of birds, bees and lamb chops. Their biology has become a dead science, a body of lecture notes about contemporary theories of process, to be maintained until the examinations and then pushed back to the examiners. Additions to the weight of this body, extra facts or theories, are resented rather than welcomed because the system is so obviously artificial and controlled by the "educators". No purpose can be seen to be served by the extra information except to take time from the student, which could be spent more enjoyably in other pursuits.

Because people *can* learn after school or college, there are many posts for graduates which are tailored to the 21-year-old who has not yet learned to learn effectively. Those who do well in the academic system are mostly retained in it and not exported into such posts, so they in turn pass on the system. In contrast, the exported mediocre have to learn to learn in their first job – they are generally not good at it, for the educational system has failed them. They have mostly not even taken the first step in self-discipline: "Become able to make yourself do what you don't like doing, and do it effectively at *your* convenience – don't wait to be pushed; then you can get to what you *do* like!". Still fewer get to the second step: "Make yourself *like* doing what you have to do anyway, you'll enjoy life more, do everything more effectively, and become able to take and give orders". They have not had to train themselves, because nothing unpopular or difficult was permitted for *children*, during what was called their *education*. So most didn't learn the Great Academic Truth, that there are no uninteresting subjects, only incompetent teachers. *All* their intellectual fodder was bland, boring, unstimulating, and most of their physical training, too, was designed never to hurt, or to excite. It is no wonder that sex, violence (both usually vicarious) and drugs seemed the immediate route to the heightening of experience. "Pop" art of all kinds has become a major commercial sector, specialising in a consumer caste whose juvenile background has prepared them only for this.

There are many viewpoints which oppose the above declaration that each succeeding generation of Western affluent urban life is less competent than the last, for new reasons. Some historical viewpoints show that such degeneration is not special; Athens, Rome, Florence, Constantinople all degenerated in affluence (see Chapter 12). Other, contrasting and optimistic viewpoints of our own English society point to sectors which show more energy, like do-it-yourself hobbies, pet keeping and showing, and perhaps especially "messing about in boats". These fractions of our culture are, perhaps, growing points and do, I agree, form a platform for optimism. But I would argue that this is precisely because their culture is passed on *without* the involvement of the professional educator.

A hobby which I know well, tropical fish-keeping, thrives because it is *not* involved with the academic world except in a fringe, showing-off way (in both directions). Another group of which I am a part, science fiction fandom, is quickly losing its character as science fiction courses appear in schools and colleges as part of the "immediacy" trend. Shakespeare, even Eliot, are lost to Heinlein and Asimov, who are more immediate, relevant, exciting – and shallow. It may indeed be that more people now read more, because of paperbacks, and that more people now enjoy the classical stories *via* television. Many people *do* still apply great effort in hobbies, becoming familiar with *all* the matches played by the home team since 1900 or all of Mauritius' stamps or all the Lake Malawi cichlids or all Larry Niven's (excellent science fiction) stories – and some know all the Bible, still. But most people have lost this involvement with the major intellectual part of their culture. As with Shakespeare, they were "put off it at school". So the great classical and intellectual wealth of our culture has failed in transmission. Equally, I believe, we now fail to transmit our human techniques of emotional control, of enjoyment, of interaction with others in joyous ways, because our cultural transmission has been perverted. That is another story, considered in the next chapter.

# References

References in full are to be found from page 243 onwards. Below are listed names of authors and dates of publication.

1. Illich (1973)
2. Smith (1977)
3. Cohen (1977)
4. Bourdieu (1977)
5. Sahlins (1977)
6. Hsiao (1927)
7. Mead (1971)
8. Turnbull (1961)
9. Heinlein (1974)
10. Cox and Boyson (1975)
11. Bantock (1975)

# 10

# THE SELF-SATISFIED
# APE – CULTURAL CAPITAL FOSTERS
# INDOLENCE

Nearly all animals have more than simple nervous circuits which determine reflex behaviour, and most have more than the complicated nervous circuits which produce instinctive and conditioned behaviour. Animals often produce different responses to what is apparently the same external stimulus, and these can be connected with internal factors such as satiation, different reproductive states, or the more subtle variations we call *emotions* or *moods*. Some of these differences may indeed be based on subtle neural circuits modulating activity levels of different parts of the nervous system, affecting feeding activities, courting behaviour, aggression or sleep. Some may actually reflect random-ising behaviour, "whims". In the vertebrates (as well as in other kinds of animals, of course), there are also endocrine variations, which are called into being by, and may themselves promote, these kinds of activity. We can identify these with our own emotional states when we observe them in other vertebrates. In our close relatives the mammals, we can probably quite usefully compare our moods and their activities. Even some very alien crea-tures, like octopi[1], show surprisingly understandable moods too; I kept a small tropical octopus for about nine months in my room in the Zoology Department, and it got to "know" the regular visitors quite quickly. Strangers would frighten it into its cave, but one of my research students would bring small crabs and it would almost climb out of the tank for him! We do find it much easier, however, to identify with close relatives. Dogs, cats, and especially our cousins the great apes, show behaviour which we find it impossible to believe does *not* indicate passions such as rage, jealousy, terror, lust.

Such behaviour is integrated into their normal lives (at least in those few cases which have been investigated) by a complex response system which seems ritual but is actually at a lower, instinctive or automatic, level. The wolf or baboon which, when threatened by an animal of higher status, bares its throat momentarily to turn off the frank aggression, is exhibiting part of a rich automatic interplay. The "confusion" shown by dogs and cats in response to each others' tail-signals, and the difficulty they have in overriding this, shows the automatic nature of many of these signals – and the responses to them –

even in these versatile and intelligent animals.

Human beings clearly also have a large repertoire of these "automatic" signals, many of which may be monitored consciously, so that we may exaggerate or depress them at will. Examples are smiling, eye-meeting, whether we carry our shoulders hunched or braced back and so on. Parts of this language are reflected in phrases like "open-handed", and our greeting and appeasement rituals. A large proportion of our participation in this language, however, is not available to our subjective analyses, and certainly affects our impressions of, and responses to, people we meet[2]. Much of our human social action is therefore unintentional, at least in the sense of conscious intention. "Postural congruence" is a good example: when two people are intimate, or even have just resolved a difference or come to an agreement, they often take up the same posture. Then, *they* simply don't realise that both have left-leg-crossed-over-right and that both are fingering their chin with the left hand, but it is obvious (if only as un-analysed recognition of friendliness) to an onlooker.

Much, too, of our response in more complex social interaction is unintentional in the sense of rational, intellectual responses. The "passions" of Spinoza[3] – rage, jealousy, terror, lust – are usually regrettable and rarely further our desires; nevertheless few of us can control their occurrence totally. We do this much better as adults than we did as children, and our passage from infancy into childhood shows progressively better control of our tempers. This is in part the rational, Spinozan, progression from frustration to control by finding the rules. Initially the child kicks the chair in fury when it impedes his passage; later, realising that it is in the nature of the chair not to make room, the child walks around it. As more of the rules become built into customary action, passions are aroused less frequently. This is the adolescent developing intellectual control of the external world; control of passions permits goals to be attained more regularly, which progressively promotes planning. Spinoza called the ultimate personal goal "peace of mind", congruence with the Will and Order of God, but even those of us who are not Spinozan will recognise the pattern.

This, one hopes, is the internally programmed, internally monitored, internally reflexive part of growing up. However, for most of us much of the feedback comes from outside, from parents, from peers and from the environment. The major part of our developing self-control, therefore, surely comes from unpleasant internal responses to external events: the frustrated "lump in the throat", the punishment for tantrums, and all the other unpleasant responses of parents and peers. We have learned to control our "internal" moods, largely because we have been conditioned by unpleasant events when we didn't. Most of us, too, have learned to control our "public" expressions of mood or passion in social situations. We learned this, generally, in peer interactions when words like "bully", "coward", "tell-tale", "cry-baby", "clever-dick" were emphasised by argument, example and shame-provoking rituals. In the development of human beings by interaction of biological and cultural (and accidental) developmental factors, such social constraints on our emotions must surely be one of the most potent forces. It is involved in all learning above the simplest level, and in all the interactions with other children, with adults and with any performance of tasks. It surely represents the mainspring for our later motivations. Extension of this metaphor leads to visions of successive frustrations tightening the spring – the pent-up energy can then be released constructively *or* as passions, and we are constantly rewarded for the former and punished for the latter. So we come to some measure of self-control, to some ability to be self-directed, to use our dissatisfactions to power the springs of desirable action.

In our "tribal" societies, primitive (e.g. "Forest People"[4]) and sophisticated (e.g. ghetto Jewish[5]) such "correction" of children in the family situation is frequent, usually corporal, and apparently effective. Later constraining of individual passions is often by tabu, mystical threats or more realistic demands by the priesthood in the form of ritual sacrifices or other fines. The attainment of adult tribal status required the ability to avoid, or at least submerge or repress, aversive passions (terror) at the rituals involved in the rite of passage. So if there is a case to be made that we have selected ourselves as *Homo sapiens* by these rituals (p 75), we have selected for breeding those of previous generations who were good at repressing, or more usefully restraining – or retraining – our emotions. Adult tribesmen repress mood, emotion in the service of their ritual desires and actions.

Barbarians, in the sense we have used the term, control their passions rather than repressing them, and use them in personal and interpersonal trials and challenges. Such control, the ability to tap the emotional energy of the passions while keeping a tight rein on their expression, is exactly the prized ability of the successful barbarian. The hero uses this control to maintain his position, never mere strength of arm, but strength of will. The appeal of the Wild West story, the Saint stories, James Bond, even Biggles was just this control. We reward it in many of our society's rituals, from the courtroom drama to the poker-table.

In towns, the barbarian rituals of juvenile peer groups and of apprentice-gangs have been well documented. Dickens told us of Victorian London, Willmott[6] of early sixties London adolescents. There may be four or five, there may be fifteen in the gang; games of street football, knock-and-run and "chicken" (daring to run in front of cars) are followed by petty pilfering from big stores and barrows. Sexual elements enter the showing-off in the later teens, with motor-bikes, alcohol, drugs in different gangs. However, as schools take over more control of the adolescent's life, his interaction with teacher replaces such barbarian tests, and he is moulded to conform to external constraints rather than internal frustrations. The television soap opera takes over many of the old heredities of the gangs. In Victorian London the street fight scores, the honour systems and challenges of the gangs were passed from child to child as they were accepted into the gang structure. Today, leading on from the film-star culture of the Thirties into television, rock and especially pop-group fashions and values, the adolescent receives promoted values rather than the "native" set. There has been such a set for the more academic child for many centuries, and its more modern representatives are the comics heroes and anti-heroes, perhaps C.S.Lewis' *The Lion, the Witch and the Wardrobe* series for the more mystical, followed by Tolkien, Saint, James Bond and other popular adventure fiction; these, and especially television series, have replaced the oral sagas as moulds for the developing barbarian in urban culture.

As Tom Brown's Schooldays are replaced by thirty day-boys watching a television play, so the abrasive self-honing – monitored by peers – is replaced by different societal moulding. A gentler personality emerges, but it is weaker and less interesting too. "Self-realisation" becomes the aim of education; this can only mean allowing the plastic character to flow into the societal mould, and to harden with as few flaws, bubbles – or other differences – as possible. I think it was Shaw who wondered about the child psychologists and their attribution of adult problems to juvenile trauma, their desire to have children lead stress-free lives; we might find a severe shortage of great mathematicians, violinists, and playwrights, he warned.

"Repression", as a concept inherited from a psychoanalytical view of human nature, is regarded as dangerous by the general wisdom of the modern educational establishment, leading to neurosis rather than freedom. It seems *anti*-educative to them because it appears to reduce the options for the repressed person, allowing less "satisfaction". Concepts which relate lack of passions to success, or self-control to ability, are unpopular in this anti-repressive educational philosophy, for they have the Puritan taint of salvation-through-pain. Affluent urban education promotes ease, painlessness – if it is painful to learn, your teacher cannot be doing his job properly. We collect and invent techniques for making *all* learning easy .... and educational technology replaces the effort of the child by tricks which require less of both teacher and child, yet inculcate an echo of the subject. Because the child has exerted less effort, it loses a sense of achievement and replaces need for self-discipline with a search for "pop" attractions.

The intellectual consequences of this replacement of learning effort by "pop" subjects have already been considered in the last chapter. The emotional and artistic consequences are, if possible, even more serious. I will take my examples from the four areas of human spiritual development, of aesthetic activity: the *arts*, especially music, have become "pop"-centred for nearly all of the urban population; the *law* has lost both respectability and coherence as it applies to anti-social action; *religions*, as philosophies, have lost backbone, and have been replaced by much more plastic cults; human sexuality, in both *love* and *lust*, has lost its ties to religion, to aesthetics and even to joy.

As we saw above in the educational spheres, the new "pop" aesthetics of music and the visual arts lead to "discipline" becoming a bad word, "self-expression" an admired activity. Disciplined approaches to the artist/audience interface are discouraged from both sides, just as both teacher and taught co-operate to reduce effort in education. Effort on the part of the responder, audience, is discouraged by competition between "artists" for instant appeal; effort which shows "relaxation" is socially acceptable, but effort in enjoyment is progressively lost. Paradoxically, much effort is put into television and film productions to make them *look* informal, relaxed; the technological exertions are frequently more strenuous than in the old, disciplined days! But these older productions now look stilted, formal, uncommunicative. Emotionally-potent sex, violence, socially-challenging plots – but all "relaxed" in performance – have replaced formation dancing, parades of military precision, exquisite ballet or operatic art as the public's appreciation of its culture, for most people in the West. The "Pop Concert" is the paradigm art form for most people, the "Disco" is the limit of their artistic self-expression!

The educators' new ideals of "self-expression" ("self-control" and "self-made man" are rarely heard) are reflected in social patterns. Then these patterns mould laws, which recognise personal liberties (often expressed as personal "rights") which can be socially inconvenient – but which make laxity legal. Such laws relax sanctions on personal irresponsibility. For example, children of "single-parent families" now have inheritance rights, and rights to public welfare funds, and such "families" come high on the lists of those requiring mandated public support. "Squatters", appropriating other people's houses or apartments, have complex legal protection in a manner unthinkable to an earlier urban legist. Abortion, as a voluntary act initiated by the mother, is legalised. Sexual crimes and minor thefts are taken less seriously than in the recent historical past, whose verbal usages are still with us (few people are hanged today, for a sheep *or* a lamb).  Incest or intercourse with minors are rarely taken to the courts (perhaps they were not in the past, either;  but then, social disapproval usually resulted in immediate physical or shaming action!). Instead, an infrastructure of the social services is set up to deal with such "embarrassing incidents", as part of the increasing control by bureaucracy which is needed, and appears (p 165-7), as people make less decisions for themselves. Decisions require self-confidence, and judgements require knowledge, found less and less in the "patient" as they are sequestered in the professions.

The relation of the law, and especially of solicitors and the police force, to the trivia of people's lives illuminates the problem.  They are quite often used to oppose the inevitable action of natural law! I have in mind the readiness of consumers to sue the suppliers of consumables, especially medical preparations.  Perhaps thalidomide *was* inadequately tested by today's standards, but *no* responsibility was taken by mothers or general medical practitioners for the awful consequences.     There is a similar, very illustrative full circle in American medicine at the moment;   the Dalkon Shield, an intra-uterine contraceptive device (IUCD or "coil") caused rather more than the average number of septic abortions, infertilities due to pelvic inflammatory disease, and other problems.  The manufacturers, A.H. Robbins, were sued by lawyers representing associations of women who had suffered these problems.  They were made bankrupt, they and their insurers having paid out hundreds of millions of dollars.  No responsibility is apparently assumed by the *patient* in these matters;  it is the Evil Organisation which must carry all the blame.  As an immediate and obvious consequence, all other manufacturers of IUCDs have withdrawn them from the American market, at least.  American women can now not have *any* "coil" fitted.  The profit on one coil is about a dollar; the risk is a population-fraction of about $10,000, the average settlement.   Some American women I know are seriously contesting this loss of their "freedom", of the "right" to have a coil fitted!   They want, I think, the companies to be forced to supply them ...  This is exactly the kind of situation children cannot understand, but adults – who have met real difficulties – can.  The "patients" who have been "done to" cannot behave as adults in their circumstances;  they *need* the lawyers to get the doctors to tell the other lawyers how much the Multi-National Company should pay them ....

When most people have not met any difficult tasks, or any deeply-disturbing emotions, most of them only rarely decide anything for themselves, and the system becomes like the erstwhile control of children by adults.   The difference is that *these* children will never have to accept adult responsibility for most of their actions.   They live all of their lives within an environment made of other people's activities.   They *depend* upon the police, upon all the professionals who surround them;   only a minority of them are professionals for other people, of course, and most of those perform only routine tasks within their traditional system.

Most people growing up in affluent urban society remain in the nest, then, but without learning the lessons of the nest.   Urban life, with its people encouraged to be self-indulgent by its educators and its artists, has let itself down – decadent seems an appropriate word (but see Chapter 12).   Even the barbarian belief, that control of one's own activity and desires by a self-made set of rules chosen to fit person, place and the rights of others is the only honourable human freedom – dignity – is better than this real decadence.   Urban police usually prefer to deal with such "barbarian" criminals rather than "citizens" – self-respect makes communication easier.

The attitudes of the older religions to this undisciplined, self-indulgent decadence is interesting.   Those Christian groups who have retained some Augustinian philosophical basis, like the more liberal Jewish forms, see this self-expression as sin, just as did the earliest Puritans.   They view such proscribed acts (they differ on *which* acts) as wrong because they diminish the future choice of the actor.   Whether or not Hades awaits the sinner, they see the immediate punishment as dreadful:   the ineluctable slide from what one *could* have been.   Each sin makes the next easier, hence the "slippery path", the fall from grace.   Islam has, to my mind, a more "barbarian" concept which sees these acts as affronts to human dignity: we should all feel shame, that some people do them.

Modern religions differ, and indeed vary, in their attitudes.   Much current English "Christianity" seems to take the "It's alright if you think it is, or if you can't help it" attitude to personal failure of this kind.   Some Catholicisms, and some orthodox Judaisms, use confessional or atonement mechanisms as a repeated attempt at facing the issue, but in most people this probably relieves the guilt rather than re-living it, truly atoning.

Other modern faiths, which serve as religions for their members, differ in their acceptance of the reduced capacity for personal responsibility of most of their ("consumer caste") communicants. Communism makes any apparently-personal decisions only the result of Society's constraints on the individual, and so relieves him of any personal responsibility – only the bureaucrat carries responsibility, and then only for the wholesale decisions he passes on or interprets.   Scientology, on the other hand, like many other recent philosophies such as Theosophy, Reichian orgone-energy, Rosicrucianism, proclaims the organising power of those in and around the central organisation, and then uses this to advertise the system to which communicants aspire. Their mystical promises for spiritual growth (telepathy, astral wandering) are such as to give *more* scope for the old sins, not the opportunities for spiritual exercise (exorcise?) sought by the older religions. These new spiritual systems, no less than those of the past, are adapted to their communicants, but these are now of the new consumer caste – these modern systems need, and cater for, self-indulgent and especially undisciplined minds. The "soft" explanations which they offer for the personal life-failures of their communicants are very interesting in this context. They are often "conspiracy theory" variants, totally unconvincing to those of us who have tried to align a bureaucracy to *any* task, malign or benificent! So poorly developed spiritually are most of their customers, however, that they genuinely do help many of them to find a new dignity, self-awareness, which was denied to them as they failed to grow up.

These new "religions", adapted to the deprived, decadent urban innocent are enormously seductive; many of my tutorial students, over the years, have succumbed (but perhaps less than those with less philosophical tutors ... ). These new religions ("cults" to the unbelievers) are very good at pulling in the undisciplined mind, but not as good as the old ones; they compensate for less refinement over the ages, less evolved subtlety, by more advertising gimmickry. They *are* adapted to the consumer, so few of these new spiritual solutions demand much from participants. Even the new, successful versions of the old religions are "pop", instant soul-renewal for consumers. It really *is* very easy to be "born again" today. Few of the applicants have had any trauma at their first birth (usually, indeed, sedation spill-over from mother!) or during growing up. Even the minor rituals demanded of the initiates only fulfil the desire for a "meaningful experience", which so few have had. They have never learnt that "meaning" is entirely in the mind of the beholder – more mind, more meaning! (Transcendental Meditation may be an honourable exception to my generalisations above – I have seen several people re-make themselves within its discipline.)

Sexual practices and their social and individual integration show changes closely related to, and probably derived from, this "pop" attitude. The demands of sexuality are seen as an important part of individual freedom in an affluent society, pinned to female emancipation and the desirability of satisfying "natural" urges. Sexual "satisfaction" becomes a "right". Note the choice of words: "satisfaction", not "joy" or "fulfilment" or "play" or even "excitement". "Excitement" is threatening without the promise of satisfaction, and "right" soon becomes "rite". This reduction even of sexuality to expected norms, to "everybody's biological urges dealt with", has two consequences of immediate relevance.

The first consequence of this "acceptance of personal sexuality" is that because most people know they have a functional set of sex organs, they have been taught to expect gratification from them. They either use other people to further these desires, or turn to the less threatening erotica of magazines or films. These often assist the special "self-satisfaction" of masturbation – the most individual of pleasures, but one doesn't increase one's circle of friends that way! Using other people selfishly is the opposite of loving, too, and this doesn't help personal growth or competence. The second consequence of sexual "satisfaction" becoming a rite, in conjunction with the devaluation of aesthetic values generally, is a decline in the practice of the sexual arts. The few sexual artists are mostly in special minorities, are homosexuals or "bondage" experts, and most people never come across them (*sic*).

In many tribal societies, in contrast, sexual arts were and are highly developed, at least in myth and legend; so that sexual norms are continually exposed for emulation. The *Kama Sutra*[7] is a codification of such a tribal formulation. On the other hand, barbarian sexuality is associated with machismo, male superiority, female mystique (Helen of Troy launching her ships) and technique (Cleopatra), and especially with the virtues of self-control and purity, seen as chastity. The *Perfumed Garden*[8] exhibits just such a panorama, and contrasts with the ritual exercises and courtesies in the *Kama Sutra*. Early urban societies all had specialists in the sexual arts (hetaerae, tribades, courtesans). Some, at least had difficult exercises for boys and girls in the control of sexual function[9], and this was a mandatory adolescent activity; Foucault[9] is most concerned with the power-relations and customs which were associated with disciplined or libertarian attitudes, and makes very sophisticated comparisons with our own times. Of course, most human societies have doubtless also had much unthinking engagement of the sexes at all ages and at all levels. Probably all societies have had the "Are you feeling better now, George?", the "tits and bums" or the "Don Juan" kinds of relationships too, and all the varieties of sexual blackmail and extortion. Aldous Huxley's very interesting and utopian *Island* was shocking in the Fifties, because in this Utopia teachers taught children the *artistry* of sex! Just as if it was cooking!

In our society, sexuality has lost much of its personal, technical and communicating artistry, but of course its more subtle social face is used by the advertising industry. Personal sexuality becomes "dirty", messy, exploitative and clumsy because of ignorance and unwillingness in both physiology and aesthetics. But the shame and desire-provoking aspects of all the sexual neural circuits are exploited by many sub-groups, from advertisers to industrial spies, from "Pop Groups" to *haute couture.*

The affluent urban society has several niches for sex-as-profession, and these have interesting parallels with cooking-as-profession. Both functions are female responsibilities in nearly all pre-literate societies[10], geared to provide males with satisfaction at least, and a scale of delight ranging upwards through aesthetic superlatives. In tribal society, there is regulation of sexuality within marriage, within the constraints of ritual purity; and there is usually a separate system of out-of-marriage liaisons, frequently homosexual (for example in ancient Greek and modern Arab societies) but often involving concubinage.   Occasionally men are involved as central figures in sexual rituals, but mostly they have ambisexual or trans-sexual roles ("berdaches" in some American Indian tribes[10]). The comparisons with chefs is intriguing.

In barbarian society woman's roles range from commodity to command, from child-bearing to human sacrifice (at either end of the knife).  The urban equivalents have barbarian resonances with sexuality exposed as its extreme, chastity (Joan-of-Arc, Florence Nightingale) or as power-via-art (Nell Gwynne, Madame de Pompadour).  In early urban life sexual prostitution was common and rewards could be high for competence;  the profession continued at least into middle-age, and there were many niches for experienced women (and men) in the organisation and entertainment of custom[11].  Both tribal and barbarian cultures had (and have) their versions of the mundane end of the profession, and these continued through the Industrial Revolution and into and through Victorian  England, for example, without much change.

Equally, the upper end of the profession has found its market in the aesthetics of the  highest level of urban "barbarian" activity: newspaper "exposures" of the courtesans associated with politicians, big businessmen and even senior churchmen  have  become  commonplace. This is usually portrayed as decadence, but surely the routine sexuality, and all the "pop" attitudes which fail to  support most effortful aesthetics, is the more decadent.    Creative explorations in sexuality have been maintained by a few (Sir Richard Burton[7,8,12], Dr. Alex Comfort[13]), both of whom merit "charismatic" and other "barbarian"-style adjectives for their life-styles.  In contrast, most public exposure of this urban sexual activity has a clinical sameness (Masters and Johnson[14]) or a weary ineptitude. This latter is exactly matched by the expressions on the faces of the participants in many "blue" films and video-tapes, where the actors so often seem to have been told "We'll do a re-take on that last scene, where you're ... " three or four times!).   There is hope, I'm told, in the "massage parlours", of some resurgence of sexual arts;  these form a new legal route, long lacking, from the exploited bottom end of the market to the upper echelons of the profession. It is worth noting that the professional educators are not involved in this success, at least in their professional capacities! Perhaps Aldous Huxley's attempt to involve them, in *Island*, would in reality have been a grave mistake, because they would have made that joyful area of life dull and boring too!

The contemporary "relaxed attitude" to sexuality in Western society parades as tolerance. I suggest that, just as in engineering practice, tolerance can become sloppiness. Emotional control is normally gained as part of learning to conform to external strictures, or internal constraints, as they pinch one's desires. As technology removes the strictures, and the need for some of these constraints, and communication becomes more ritual, so emotions are less involved in the day-to-day living in an affluent society. The commitment to another person becomes less serious as divorce becomes easier, and there are fewer legal sanctions on the informal pairing up. This is indeed encouraged in many Welfare situations. Emotions are less involved, pairings are more casual, and the sexual element of the relationship so often becomes dreary, demand and satisfaction. So sexuality becomes ritual in the casual as well as the committed pairings, associated with the removal of fears of pregnancy, disease or even discovery, in technical affluence.

In poverty, the control of emotions is a succession of triumphs, which mould the personality and make it capable of greater things. The "soft" life of the affluent society leaves the emotions, like the intellect and indeed the body, flabby from lack of exercise. The inactivity of the decadent contrasts with real calm ("cool") and results from lack of internal or external conflict. It is not a "controlled" calm, Spinoza's "peace of mind"[3]; it is a maximum entropy state of satisfied desires. This leaves no emotional energy, no drives, and is "unnatural" for any animal. The Privileged Ape is no exception.

# References

References in full are to be found from page 243 onwards. Below are listed names of authors and dates of publication

1. Nixon and Messenger (1977)
2. Morris (1985)
3. Hampshire (1956)
4. Turnbull (1961)
5. Singer (1963)
6. Willmott (1969)
7. Vatsayana (1963)
8. Nefzawi (1967)
9. Foucault (1978 and 1986)
10. Ford and Beach (1965)
11. De Vries and Fryer (1967)
12. Burton, R. (1985[1890])
13. Comfort, A (1973)
14. Masters and Johnson (1966)

# 11

# THE APE THAT GOT WHAT IT WANTED – CITIES AND CIVILISATION

We can now look at the changing needs and desires of people as more and yet more privilege passes between the generations. The affluent animal, civilised man, has arrived. What new elements entered the picture to make the important differences, to give the Privileged Ape dominion over land, sea and air?

The cultural reproduction of pre-literate tribal man was not, and is not, different in kind from some of our primate cousins, or indeed wolves. There is transmission of privilege within a very restricting set of cultural rules, predominantly within families. This tribal privilege is partly material, but mostly a set of rules applying successfully to most problems. The barbarian transmission, in contrast, is of cultural values and expertise rather than material privilege or rules. If there are rules, they are unstated, implicit. Such transmission may only be possible to an organism self-selected for dominance of imagination over more mundane biological needs. In the barbarian society of perpetual rivalry and changing allegiance, desires are never satisfied – except, one presumes, temporarily for the hero or chieftain. Their human physiological needs are satisfied, but only periodically, in a life whose essence is intermittent adventure productive of loot, alternating with periods of boredom and intra-group rivalry.

For the barbarian, there are several routes to more permanent, rather than transient, increase of loot and decrease of privation. His biological needs can be satisfied by exploiting more productive human cultures, in various ways. Some of these involve taking prisoners and lead to slave societies. Many medieval Arab societies, indeed up to the seventeenth and eighteenth century, were of this kind. The routes toward civic affluence from this kind of society are well depicted in Sir Richard Burton's *1001 Nights*[1]. Other routes involved staying as overlords of the tribal productive groups, but this required an elaborate set of "courtly" restrictions to remain effective. One example of this cultural restraint was "chivalry" in medieval Europe; another was the khan code of the Mongols, which prohibited all but the most ritual of exchanges with *hoi polloi*.

None of these routes seems to lead to simple reproductive stability, because they are so successful materially – they generate affluence[3]. Both the ancient

Greek and the Turkish cultures, based upon this barbarian aristocracy held up
by an agrarian base, lurched from flowering to decline to resurgence without
ever becoming as stable, say, as ancient (or modern) Egypt. China's stability,
I believe, has been due to her immense size, her inertia as a political system
(although recent events, with modern transport and communications, have
seen immense changes *within* that stability). Paradoxically, one of the most
stable, yet successful, systems was the combination of white colonists with
black slaves (acquired from the Arabs, who already used and sold them) in the
Southern United States. The plantations were essentially a carry-over from
Europe of a peasant (feudal) agricultural pattern, and the Africans (of very
different cultures) had no common culture which could fit a feudal level. So
they became a kind of superior domestic animal, as far as the white colonists
were concerned, and lost whatever culture the first generation had brought.
Subsequent generations were perhaps the most deprived large human group in
recent history. This feudal system could perhaps have achieved stability,
permanence at that economic and cultural level, were it not for the "meddling"
Yankees, who shared our beliefs about the evils of slavery. Yet such is Man's
versatility that the descendants of these slaves have produced a variety of
cultures rooted in precisely this deprivation, some of them very rich; they have
produced art forms and philosophies which have added greatly to all of Man's
cultures. In contrast, another potentially stable barbarian/tribal system, the
British rule in India, did not seriously change any of its cultures, except towards
technicality and affluence. It almost did achieve a kind of permanence.
(Perhaps this is because the Civil Service, that peculiarly British invention,
stood between the rulers and the ruled, and provided a buffer.)

Most of the barbarian/tribal symbioses were not even that stable, however,
and either failed quickly or settled into an early urban pattern. Such aggregates,
whether they were stockaded desert forts, castled villages (see White's *The
Sword in the Stone*) or fishing/raiding villages, provided a local surplus of *both*
food and excitement. They were an attraction to local artisans, and soon
formed a common pattern of human habitation, familiar to us from the *Arabian
Nights Entertainments*[2] (Andrew Lang's children's version of the *1001 Nights*),
and from all the films made around its themes. Towns were made up of sectors,
often clustering around a castle or, later, a market. Each of the various sectors
contained predominantly one kind of folk. So, a Street of the Silversmiths, or
of Leather-workers, may have abutted a district devoted to the amusement of
visitors, with many taverns and bordellos. Many groups of people were not
geographically isolated, but plied their trades wherever status or material gain
could be found. Such skills as those of interpreter, scribe, fortune-teller

flourished in this way, and these various itinerant skills would often have been drawn into the orbit of the priesthood. That the description fits both middle Eastern (old Baghdad) and Occidental (ancient York) townships cannot be accident, and similar patterns occur in Japanese and Mayan history. My friends who have visited them tell me that modern North African townships, in Morocco and Tunisia, have just this flavour.

It is not my intention here to imagine origins of priestly groups, or indeed of the religions. Human beings certainly require, or can be made to require, theological counsel and an ordered structure for their lives, to relate to agricultural and astronomical cycles. The benefits are manifested as integration of society for larger works like bridges or irrigation systems, or indeed cathedrals or mosques, and a collective sense which is larger than family, trade or even town. Such integration permits warehouses, docks, caravans and a sense of security as these are guarded by representatives of the local aristocracy. The populace sees the security of its social capital, visible as full warehouses, as variety on the market-stalls. The historical sensitivities of both the ruling class and the priesthood are always longer-term than that of the peasants, so more ambitious projects are undertaken. For peasants, every day is like every other day – monotony rules; for barbarians – and priests – life was investment of discomfort, and reward in the long term. The reward was, of course, in the currency of honour – only peasants (tribesmen) valued recompense in coin! Celebration in a story was an honour paid to the priest, as prophet, and to the ruler, as king – the Old Testament provides excellent examples. Not only pyramids and temples, but also amphitheatres, sculpture, coinage result from the longer-term view. Warehouses lead to larger ships as surely as metal-working leads to specialisation among soldiers.

Whatever the multitude of reasons, urban man, both tribal and barbarian, prospered. Probably, in general terms, the stability of the ritualised, enduring pattern of the agricultural tribesman accrued sufficient capital, and this permitted the barbarian his long shots at high odds. Occasionally these paid off in material wealth, or procured slaves with new techniques, new technologies, new crops or domestic animals. The traveller, the trader, the entrepreneur were barbarian, long on honour but without much capital; the agriculturalist had the accumulating capital, but no new things to do with it. However, as technology grew, and the arts too were passed across the generations, so whole new areas of desire became possible. Great buildings, new art forms, new foods, or better transport or domestic animals, all opened new horizons for the tribal peasant (as far as this was possible) and gave new status-symbols for the barbarians. In towns, the juveniles even of the most tribal enclaves are to some extent barbarian, and the new technological ambience could often enter the tribal strongholds in this way.   Modern tribesmen see the old stories on new televisions, and some play the old games on electronic computers.

We have seen, in the last few chapters, that this progressive affluence has unfortunately been reflected into a deprivation of both intellect and dignity by the educational system, paradoxically just as more vistas are opened and more material and imaginative privilege (cultural capital) is generated.   The extent to which any class in the growing town, or any individual juvenile, is affected by this educator-fostered intellectual flabbiness must vary in every way.   The whole pathology of deprivation, like that of deformation (its developmental equivalent), is very complex;  but a useful distinction must be brought forward from Chapter 8, again in this context of the growing town, between the deprivations of poverty and of affluence.

Many of the deprivations of poverty cause biological deformations, pathology of form or function of the body by infectious disease, other parasites, chronic malnutrition or irremediable neurological defects.   But some poverty consists only in *relative* lack of goods and services considered the norm in that society.   This can produce motivation, and thereby competence.   Most of the newly-able in any growing town are probably those who retain the barbarian skills, and often status, of their adolescent gang.   A healthy contempt for the parental poverty, both of privilege and of ambition, drives many young men to "seek their fortune", as we say in the lessons for our young.    "Dick Whittington" stories, myths of all the princes who started as beggar-boys, shoe-blacks who became President, even "Ugly Duckling" paradigms, encourage the young to seek status beyond the parental level.   Some Chinese stories show the unwisdom of rising beyond one's station, but few do in the Western European traditions.   All the social encouragement is to rise, and this can produce anomalies.   The just-qualified teacher in our society, for example, often feels unjustly poor by comparison with those of his peers who left school early and got jobs in industry, and who have achieved ownership of washing machines and colour televisions while the young teacher is failing to get his first mortgage.   So he may earn by "do-it-yourself" jobs for friends.   The poorly-paid student nurse is still living very well compared with her equivalent in, for example, twelfth-century Spain or even Victorian London, but her poverty is still real to her, and can fuel social action.   We compare our situation with that of others on the same step of the staircase of progress, of standard of living.   Sometimes we feel only "unworthy passions" like envy, jealousy, rage, or despair;  however, constructive feelings can often incite us to improvement *via* ambition, revolution, even – occasionally – co-operation.    Lack of affluence in an affluent society can motivate betterment, often violently; it can sometimes provide the energy for an increase in human dignity within all of that society. Or it may destroy that society, whose territory, artefacts and even language may be taken over by neighbours; they will build the historic failure into a moral story for *their* children, and may be less likely to repeat it......

Deprivations in and by affluence (the "third deprivation" of Chapter 9), however, remove the *wish* for betterment, even the curiosity as to whether "better" exists. The paradigm of the deprivations of affluence in our society might be the fat man, in a centrally-heated apartment, watching professional football on a colour television while eating a "TV meal". The existence of the easy TV meal precludes his own cooking, of course; central heating makes going out much less attractive; going to the ground, and especially *playing* football just don't happen to him any more. (There are now, indeed, clubs of "Couch Potatoes" all over the United States; they watch several televisions without stirring from their sofas, send out for meals, talk to each other by 'phone. Most are out-of-work, living on relatives or savings, and are grotesquely fat even for Americans!) So the car displaces the bicycle; the TV meal displaces even the fish-and-chip shop, after the art of the omelette has become too onerous – and tinned food requires washing-up .... Readers Digest condensed books, "gems from the shows" all deprive the affluent of the will to improve. The ambitious may be generated from among the indigent, as we saw above; but only very rarely will they arise among the affluent.

The extent of both kinds of deprivation will vary, and in all urban cultures there will be those who for various reasons put effort and ability into life. Some are "barbarians" in our model: great athletes, some politicians or criminals, many lawyers, most entrepreneurs. Because so much of the city's social struc- ture is determined by the status-conflicts of these barbarian elements, much bluff and counter-bluff is required of the ambitious. The sanction of "loss of face" to a barbarian is the worst punishment. So maintenance of "face"[4], the ritual "face-work" involved in all human interaction, from simple conversation to sexual intercourse or industrial competition, will drive many to enormous competence. For this kind of person, however, life at the top is not secure, stable. Even if there are no outside pressures – perhaps especially *if* there are no outside pressures – high status itself drives us to risk. The rewards of high position, Goffman believed, must always be compensated by a self-generated risk of self-destruction: there must be constant "testing" of one's place, one's honour. In his essay *Where the action is*[4] he documented the sins of the wealthy, the powerful, the noble as driven by just this desire to test status. Even the highest-status barbarian, then, still is driven to find more. Again, fairy-stories are full of such people; they are not content with the Tinder-box, they must have the kingdom *and* the princess; not content with the Genie of the Lamp, they must have ..... the Kingdom and the Princess, of course!

So, this self-advancement (or avoidance of "face-loss") motive in industrial competition does still provoke enhancement of privilege. This may come about through a general improvement, an accretion of capital resources through competitive trade, or by innovation in affluent technical societies. Even some of the lower-status citizens may innovate, because of profit motives or even simple diligence in invention. Sometimes, as with polythene, nuclear power, integrated electronic circuits, antibiotics, more is really possible as a result of such innovation. Technical innovation increases both cultural and material capital much more effectively than the slow accretion characteristic of agriculture or even trade.

Of great interest for our concern is the way this is promoted. Stories ("myths") about such invention always come loaded with a message: the inventor was apparently motivated by the spur of poverty, deprivation. We emphasise the "barbarian", honourable nature of innovation by using for our myths the "painter-starving-in-a-garrett" model. We don't re-tell the story of nylon, or nuclear power, or sulphonamides, which were the result of capital investment in industrial research. We do tell the stories of rayon (cellulose acetate), steam engines, and penicillin which were more "romantic". Here is the story of Watt, given in a 1920s Children's Encyclopaedia[5]: "....unfortunately his father lost most of his money, and James had to find employment.", "....young Jamie found that the long hours and the poor food were telling on his health", "For many years, Watt had to struggle against discouragement, failure and occasional despair." And beneath a picture of Edison, in the same work: "This is the famous inventor, Thomas Alva Edison, looking very tired indeed. And no wonder! For he has just worked five days and nights with scarcely a break on the contrivance you see before him. And he has made it work at last. He has invented the phonograph, which will some day bring music to countless people." You will never see the ordinary business of improving everyone's lives by trade celebrated like that!

Innovation is encouraged by honour, therefore, and we are led not to expect much financial reward. Unlike some of my socialist friends, who see this as evidence of a capitalist conspiracy to squeeze the intellectual cheaply, I see it as congruent with the Morgan/Campbell barbarian philosophy. Naive though it is, this view of reproduction and advancement in urban society does match the observation that barbarian pursuits are encouraged, but not financially. Even the financiers themselves, and especially most of the young ones (the financial "yuppies"), seem to value the "barbarian" labels (classically the Porsche....) rather than the simple riches. It is these barbarians who supply the yeast in the urban mix, causing the rise in privilege as the generations pass.

Within any urban society, of course, there is great variation in privilege; this is part of the definition of an urban society[6]. The raising of the general level by importation of spices or slaves, reliable water supplies or sewers, new road-making techniques or new methods of transport affects everybody. So do Edison's phonograph, and rayon and penicillin. As a result of the increasing comfort, however, an ever smaller proportion of the affluent society is driven towards, or finds itself in, the discomfort which engenders such advance. To return to my earlier "staircase" image, a progressively smaller group of innovators carries a larger, replete majority up each successive stair.

Advertising, in our society, might be the visible part of the social circuit which drives the consumer to prod his boss (or his Trade Union) for more and more exciting goods. The tribal "*Everyone* has a ...... be sure to get yours!" contrasts with the barbarian "Only the very special man has ........ and has *this* kind of woman!". Both work, it is clear, but populist demand of this kind is self-limiting. Consumer demand does *not* provide innovation, but can only limit its application to the familiar. This is very clear if one compares the television shows which return "by popular demand" and for which the advertising rates are highest; they are limited to non-thought-provoking well-worn recipes. This applies, also, to advertisements for mass-circulation "labour-saving" products like vacuum cleaners, electric drills and televisions (thinking *is* labour, to most people!). The style of the advertisements always emphasises the routine use of the product, and only occasionally its effectiveness. Even the "scientific" approval of "new" technical gadgets or panaceas, with the "scientist" actor always removing his glasses to gaze earnestly at the viewer (why?), is a status-stamp by the current priesthood, not an encouragement to the consumer to innovate. Of interest here is the word "NEW!"; in advertisements it *always* means "the old product you know and love, in a new packet, or with a *touch* of difference you won't notice unless we tell you."! So advertisement, the visible feedback system of what-the-consumer-gets in our society, is carefully tailored so that involvement in innovation is *not* required of the buyer. This is even true of new products, CD players for the Porsche for example, which attract the barbarian.

The self-limiting nature of consumer demand can be seen in several ways; some authors would quote conservation-groups, back-to-Nature movements and the "consumer backlash" which has resulted in "organic" farming and "health food shops". Such examples are obvious, at least in some of their aspects. I will use less obvious examples of consumer limits, so that the *way* in which the replete majority contrives to suppress most innovation which will *really* change lives can be demonstrated. I am not concerned to discuss Rifkin[7] problems here, the real questions of whether nuclear or fossil fuel production is safer[8], or whether DDT kills more people than mosquitoes/malaria. I want to discuss manifestly unrealistic safety demands, in several industries, which effectively prevent innovation. In my own field of contraception[9,10], there are several dramatic examples. We have already seen (p 146) that the demand for complete safety of IUCDs (coils), evinced by courts allowing large demands from the manufacturers by injured women, has resulted in *no* IUCDs being fitted at present in the USA. A similar situation applies to the contraceptive pill; because we now have enormous quantities of information about its effects on healthy (but unphysiological, menstruating) women, any newly developed oral contraceptive must be tested on a tremendous population to see whether its, perhaps tiny, incidence of side-effects make it preferable to present ones. The cost of developing and trying out a new contraceptive pill runs into hundreds of millions of pounds[9]; even trying a new formulation of old and tested ingredients costs between £20M and £60M. Non-steroidal drugs for rheumatoid arthritis, of which the classic is Opren, have already been involved in so much litigation that I know of three companies who have decided not to enter this field. While I must concede that testing of these pharmaceuticals is necessary, their development for a market which regards *any* side-effect as actionable is both economically and ethically impossible. So, since thalidomide, drug companies are now hobbled by impossible testing procedures.

A comparable example is nuclear power development[8]. Nuclear power kills and maims very few people compared with fossil fuels, and is slowly being forced by longer-sighted politicians onto an unwilling public, who resist by making the safety procedures impossibly costly. Because there can be no accurate quantitation of the damage done by the burning of fossil fuels (in direct medical effects on people, without considering secondary issues like "acid rain"), whereas radioactivity can be accurately measured down to trivial levels, the latter is considered more dangerous! Even in the year of the Chernobyl nuclear accident, I am sure that more coal miners, oil drillers, natural-gas pipe-fitters were killed and maimed than were damaged by Chernobyl. The mutational damage in other countries, too, is very slight, judging by work on children born in Hiroshima and Nagasaki (though there was a high level of infertility there); it is comparable with the mutations caused by radon in draught-proofed homes.

These examples have been used to show "democratic" action by the consumer, but this is not so.    In ancient Greece, in fabled Baghdad, in Elizabethan London, new public utilities were comparably resisted by the majority for "health and safety" reasons (I could imagine that it was well known that water didn't do you any good if it didn't *taste* ... ). Most people in towns are tribal and resist change.  In our present Western circumstances, more people probably feel themselves to be involved in these decisions than ever before (except, just possibly, in ancient Athens).    Nevertheless, effective discussion of new drugs, or nuclear power, actually involves very few people, so cannot be innovation promoted by democratic means.  We are told, usually by someone well qualified by the educators, that  these subjects, these decisions, are "too complex for ordinary people to understand".  So they are usually  given to a sort of barbarian trial of strength, the champions being *experts*, *pro* and *contra*, who advance their powers thereby but do not increase the general level of understanding of the problem.    Nor should they, for the "common folk", like the fat man at his television, *want* no freedom to choose – only figure-heads to blame.  They blame the explainer for their own failure to understand and thereby to judge the issue.  This has become very clear in the apparently "public" discussion of the effects of the contraceptive pill, and in the case for and against various sweeteners. These are useful examples to show the interaction of an apparently responsible "democratic" political decision with contending "schools", cadres of experts in the generation of a public decision.

There is a low level of risk of circulatory problems for some women on the pill. This is much less than the risk of the same kind of problem in a pregnancy (especially in a fat or smoking woman). But risk *is* measurable on a large population.  This large population does not have the "natural" human reproductive cycle anyway: "First-World" women alternate menstruation with sexuality instead of the more natural alternation of pregnancy and lactation, with continuous sexuality.  The very low incidence of thrombo-embolic problems with "the Pill" is the small price paid for very convenient maintenance of this less physiologically apt, but socially desirable, menstrual cycle.  Women who develop pathologies attributable to "the Pill", however, sometimes (but not usually) attempt to sue the drug company.    There is clamour for the development of a "risk-free" contraceptive method – but of course the barrier methods (condom or diaphragm) *are* virtually risk-free, except that the increased risk of pregnancy itself carries risks.  Consider the spectrum of methods available, with publicly-available levels of risk, aesthetics, difficulty and reliability[10,11].  This freedom to choose is *not* wanted; what *is* wanted is the explanation which tells you which method is *best*! The explanation should also tell you who to blame, and who to sue, if things go wrong. Explanations which don't do that have little following.

On the other hand, where governments make decisions for people, that also calls blame upon the decision, and upon the autocracy of such government. People are happy to confess their ignorance of a subject, *but want to be able to decide just the same*! This is pandered to, in Western democracies, by "electing" (appointing, in effect) public watch-dog committees which apparently act "for" the people. Leaving aside for the moment the old questions of the suitability of cane sugar (sucrose) in human diets, and the current question of the possible very low carcinogenic effect of saccharine, recall the furore about cyclamates. Cyclamates were used as sweeteners in diabetic, diet and other proprietary foods, and especially in soft drinks. Tested in relatively high dose (apparently mixed with saccharine, for no good reason) they caused some increase in breast cancers of beagle bitches. Acting on this basis, the American F.D.A. (Food and Drug Authority) outlawed cyclamates, and the UK followed suit. In order to administer comparable doses to people, at least 30 bottles of soft drink would have had to be consumed per day. Nevertheless, the F.D.A. basic assumption of interconvertibility between dose and incidence (i.e. that 1/100 dose gives something related to 1/100 the incidence) required that the substance be removed from the public-health arena. Because saccharine is the only sugar-substitute still acceptable to such interconvertibility assumptions, and because this is *not* acceptable (because it tastes bitter as well as sweet) to some people, one must presume more sugar to have been consumed since cyclamates were banned. The extent of the resultant obesity-associated disease increase *cannot* be estimated, just as we cannot estimate respiratory disease caused by power production from coal as an alternative to nuclear fuels. The cyclamate decision was a bad one, made for very good reasons. Most people affected by it are happy for it to have been taken, as with fluoridation of those public water supplies which are naturally low in fluorides. I disagree with the cyclamates decision, agree with fluoridation, but that's not the point. Thousands of such decisions affect urban dwellers all the time, and part of living in town is the acceptance of non-involvement in most decisions.

The educational elasticity which must arise from non-involvement of teachers in real life, and this necessary non-involvement of most citizens in decisions made for them by experts, together remove power (= choice) from most affluent citizens. Their affluence comes to them by routes they have no control over, and although they may deplore "pollution" or "waste" or "exploitation of workers" there is no ready-made political route for change. Technical and political decisions and judgements which affect life-style, culture, privilege of all citizens are made by a set of élites, usually mutually exclusive although their effects may merge in unpredictable ways in citizens' lives. Institutionalisation of the elderly, for example, changes the pattern of young parents' evenings and removes a source of cultural continuity for the young, who are then baby-sat by their own parents' generation. Together with the lack of elderly teachers in schools, this insulates the young from all but contiguous generations. This is a very strange new reproductive isolation in our culture, which could result in a general lack of historical sense. The time of nuclear power will just arrive, and so might Big Brother, not because "They" wish it or have planned it, but because of apparently necessary fragmentation of expertise and because human beings in a human culture are conditioned by it, *whatever* it is.

There was a decision taken in China in the late 70s which decreed that one-child families would be approved; this has resulted in much female infanticide, and in a growing generation consisting mostly of "only" children. These are usually spoiled by all their extended family, and I cannot believe that any single judgement was made about the desirability of that political decision, which included that outcome: ten million spoiled brats. Perhaps it looked different in 70s China, but it certainly worries many Chinese now. How did we arrive at this strange urban culture, where nearly all our decisions seem to be made for us by face-less "experts"? These experts are usually promoted by vocal (but often irresponsible) minorities with a particular axe to grind, the majority having no major concern in the area. The expert decision, however, whether it be "No to cyclamates!", "Yes to dumping nuclear waste in salt mines...", "No 'streaming' in schools!", "Yes to any woman's Right to an abortion!" does affect everyone in the majority too. They suddenly find their lives changed, and the issue becomes one of backlash and progress, consent and freedom. Paradoxically perhaps, it is in the so-called democracies that the rule of vocal minorities over the replete majority is most effective, most flagrant, and that causes the most – ineffective – frustration.

There is an emotional "argument", sometimes given biological trappings, which sees such a global decision-making process in society as mediated by a "higher" organisation. This is perhaps our Western version of the old Animist view of Nature: the Great Mother knows what she's doing and will look after us. This kind of "argument" depends upon the "Everone knows that ... " kind of biology which compares your arm to the horse's, and the whale's flipper, and calls them the "same" thing (p 59); the comparison is much easier in the mind than in the real world. One version of this was Adam Smith's "Invisible Hand"[12] which arranges that the selfish actions of individuals combine to make market forces which act for greater good, and greater freedom for all. Another version is that the killing of the weaker deer by the wolves, or the dying of sickly human babies, "improves the species". Dawkins[13] has shown the errors in this argument for the biological cases, and although I don't have chapter and verse for the Adam Smith, I'd bet that the same criticisms apply. Note that I'm not saying that market forces *don't* give us freedom, or that sickly children dying doesn't give us stronger adult populations in some senses. I'm sure that attributing these results to action of a "higher" rule, at a "higher", *unknowable* level is not good explanatory tactics, that's all. There may well be emergent laws at high level – I'm actually sure there are. But this formulation is just a sloppy, hand-waving kind of way to talk of the kind of things which geneticists have now formulated in "inclusive fitness" or Evolutionary Stable Strategy[13] terms. To speak, then, of "market forces" being the major arbiter of decisions in our Western societies, and implying thereby that there is some magical higher-level law which contrives that these decisions shall always be "just" for the majority, seems to me poppycock. I would sooner a panel of experts got it wrong for me, because of good old-fashioned honest and dishonest mistakes, than rely on the lowest common denominator of my cultural population to choose the flavour of my hamburger or my tomato soup. At one time all these market forces thought the world was flat; even now, they seem to act as if "Space", with its truly infinite prospects for our species, was just a thin skin around the atmosphere with the stars and Moon hung on the back-cloth. Nearly all our replete citizens, because they don't understand arithmetic, have combined into a market force which declines space travel, for "public" reasons which I know to be false-to-the-future, just as in Spain of Columbus' time. I would sooner trust the cadres of innovators, however small and unrepresentative and however "barbarian", than presume the existence of people-in-the-mass laws which will get it right for my future. I advise you to do the same. People and cultures are so *different*!

Human beings are very versatile, able to express a great range of emotional relationships within the strictures of a variety of cultures, from hunter-gatherer to jet-setting atomic-energy engineers, and at levels of discomfort from chronic starvation to gross over-nutrition. Each person learns and adapts to the expectations of his peers, acquaintances, parents, and rivals, and enjoys or suffers life to different extents. Most of his/her personal success and failure relates to these interactions, and long-established human society has many complex routes to emotional satisfaction for its participants, and many modes of frustration, charm and the joys of intimacy.

In complex tribal systems (e.g. Yoruba, or Orthodox Jewish ghetto culture) each participant's humanity is fostered by the existence of many roles with expected behaviour from the incumbents, and with permitted deviations (e.g. many Yiddish stories – or some Irish jokes). In barbarian cultures emotions are greatly exercised in the honour-rituals and competitions for status, often by "facework"[4] and usually by some violent confrontations too; sex is usually a major counter in this life of encounter, "thud and blunder", pride and slavery.

The full urban life of the *citizen* includes both of these kinds of fitting-in with others; some of his positions are ritual-customary (tribal) while others are honour-related and personal-status-determining (e.g. Agamemnon, Harold Wilson, Richard Nixon). However, technical affluence permits successive levels of expertise (masons/geometers, colonisers/polyglots, scientists/ polymaths) to move from charismatic to ritual *via* the educator. This series of declining status-values for each subject, until it has declined far enough to be comprehended by the teacher, is argued in Chapter 9. So the Western pupil citizen-in-the-making is bored in successive centuries by Euclidean geometry, a foreign language, and science, all "taught" by those who cannot practice any of the expertises sufficiently well to live by them. The irrelevance of these exercises is abundantly clear to any observing adult, and with any societal analysis comes disillusion, and then a more liberal educational ethic based on "understanding" rather than "rote" learning. However much we believe we see through the educators now, even when they turn our prized aesthetics from "ir- relevant" into "liberal" then "liberating", we all take serious notice of them. They have taken over all the "attention structures" of our present civic society. They have us by the emotional short-hairs, as well as by our intellectual necks! This Educational Authority had a real function in pre-affluence: it served to imprint cultural mores on each generation, so that each child could see the rules by which it would be judged, and awarded a niche, a role. It still awards niches, and these still relate to pre-affluent days, but they now constrain much more than they train.

In our affluent society (e.g. UK, USA, USSR urban, even modern China) there seem to be three kinds of people, products of the educationalists' versions of our cultural-reproductive process in these societies.

(a) Most people, most of the time, are "tribal"; custom rules, and most of the complexity of an urban society passes them by. The technology, the law and the politics are responded to as "pop" issues; any emotion is "instant", even sexuality is routine. These people express their position in terms of "rights", not of responsibility, and their values are traditional.

(b) There is leaven of "barbarian" in several subcultures. Not only the race- course gangs, protection racketeers and exploiters of prostitutes, but also the highly successful accountants and especially lawyers show status and honour confrontations. Within this group too, are some "intellectuals", artisans, some artists (especially those at the "top" of opera and "pop" scenes), courtesans, gigolos and especially sports people and their exploiters. These people play on their emotions, live with their hearts on their sleeves. We value them, and they profess value, according to a romantic code.

(c) There is a cadre of a few citizens who enjoy the rights, responsibilities and privileges of the society's affluence. It includes technological innovators and especially developers, entrepreneurs who work *within* the law, directors of large companies; it is that political and technological *establishment* which is integrated into the decision-making process. Many of those in university departments have allegiance to this group, or are part of it. Most of the time even these people live and act "tribally", by custom and especially by complex rituals often involving clothes: the dinner-jacket, the dirty blue jeans of the sociology lecturer, the wonderfully subtle badges of the high-class courtesan; sometimes they compete honourably, or dishonourably, for status. This group contains those who, rarely, make responsive *decisions* affecting the lives of us all.

Coleridge's "clerisy" most nearly describes this latter group. He used the word[14] to describe those who passed on the great ideas of the culture: "... the clerisy, I say, or national church, in its primary acceptation and original intention comprehended the learned of all denominations: the sages and professors of law and jurisprudence; of medicine and physiology; of music; of military and civil architecture; of the physical sciences; with the mathematical as the common *organ* of the preceding; in short, all the so-called liberal arts and sciences, the possession and application of which constitute the civilisation of a country, as well as the Theological."

Another small diversion here about the word "*decision*" above. I need to make quite clear that I do not use "judgement" and "decision" in the more usual, overlapping sense but distinguish them carefully and usefully. *Judgements* are made by tribesmen or barbarians, weighing the issues and using traditional or honourable criteria to judge between balance-pans of historical issues. The balance-pan metaphor works very well – you put the items to weigh up on the two pans, plus and minus, according to what you know at the time, what history has told you. You bias all the issues, even giving different weights to the same item on plus and minus pans – we are all very expert at this, we do it every time we cross a road with traffic. Dogs, cats and octopi do it, and even *amoebae* do it in a very simple way; all animals must balance issues, must judge. *Decision*-making is the very opposite of such mechanical, if preju-

diced, judgement.  It is *the* entirely human process, deciding the future when
the issues are judged even, when the balance-pans are equal.  It is done best,
according to the values of each human society, by the emotional adult in that
society.  It is, in its essence, not historical;  history has failed us, the balance
pans stubbornly refuse to tilt.  So we must decide for our future, commit ourselves to an unknown, unpredictable future, but with a complete emotional
conviction.  The adult will never say "I wish I had decided the other way ....."
or "If only .... ";  self-discipline retains the coherence of the decided path.

Few of our "tribal" types are involved with this distinction.  Tradition lies
heavy upon one pan of the balance, always;  every act is mandatory or forbidden.  Equally, the "barbarian" cannot commit his future to a past decision, cannot be true to his own past self because new opportunities, new excitements re-
value old emotions.  Only the human being who can transcend both the "must"
and the "must not" of emotional immaturity can take decisions for the rest of
us.  The immature is recognisable by insistence on minutiae of judgement, so
that history will prove the judgement to have been accurate: "The left pan *was*
a touch heavier, and I photographed it in case you challenged me with questions
later ... ".  Unlike judgements, decisions cannot be *wrong*;  but they are often
unwise, unsatisfying, frustrating, even destructive to the people they affect.

These decisions are usually considered wise by that majority of tribal or
barbarian kind (which is therefore out of touch with the civil mechanisms of
urban society) if they give more security, more affluence, more comfort.  Such
a so-called "wise" decision too often renders their decision-making needless,
and so quenches their human competence.  In a democratic society those who
would give more power (less security), more trials (less comfort) to the
majority soon lose elective power themselves.  This lesson has been learnt very
painfully by the English socialists in the 1980s;  Maggie Thatcher may be hated
by the majority (I don't think she is) but she *decides* for them!  There seems to
be no way back to a fulfilled life for most Apes, once affluence has given the
Ape what he wants and others, like Maggie Thatcher, make all the important
decisions for them.

This relates right back to Illich's diagnosis of the "patient" relationship that
most people achieve with the professionals with whom they interact (p.85).
Most people now don't want, don't have any confidence in, a doctor who says
"Well, what do you think we should do?";  they need the reassurance of his
authority – it removes their necessity to think!  That must be why so many
medical consultants are so dogmatic, even rude to patients.  By doing that, they
stop patients thinking, which is a relief for the patient.  But they then find all
patients stupid, malleable, with no ideas – and don't recognise this as the direct

consequence of their own authority. The apocryphal joke about the ideal middle-class marriage points this way too: he makes all the *big* decisions, like "Should America have a strike force in the Middle-East?" "Should the Government drop interest rates?" or "Should Arsenal go for a defensive play on Saturday?". She makes the *small* decisions, like "Which school for the children?", "How big a mortgage?" Indeed, in our society the women, especially the housewives, are much more emotionally mature, much more able to make these important decisions that will commit the family future, than are their menfolk. This is why that joke is, or is not, funny or tragic; marriage guidance counsellors say that that is half of the problem. (The other half also relates to emotion, I guess; it is epitomised by a cartoon with the couple glaring at each other and holding up flags. His says "No love if no sex!", hers says "No sex if no love!". Culture and basic biology are not separable.)

Even though we now have what we want, our affluent society, this is not stable either. In the next chapter we look further at the decadence, the rot at the heart of getting what you want, of leaving the decisions to others. There are, however, forces at work in the cities which may bring the Privileged Ape's culture to a new organisation with a new set of possibilities. These are the subjects of the next chapters.

# References

References in full are to be found from page 243 onwards. Below are listed names of authors and dates of publication.

1. Burton (1985[1890])
2. Lang (1898)
3. Darlington (1969)
4. Goffman (1972)
5. Ogan (c.1925)
6. Mumford (1961)
7. Rifkin (1985)
8. Fremlin (1985)
9. Djerrassi (1979)
10. Cohen (1984)
11. Guillebaud (1985)
12. Smith (1776)
13. Dawkins (1986)
14. Coleridge (1830)

# 12

# DECADENCE AND DECLINE IN THE AFFLUENT CITY

If you have read as far as this, you cannot have avoided the message that, after a promising start around the times of Ancient Egypt and Classical Greece, mankind has put its wealth in the hands of educational consultants and is now going to Hell in a hand-basket! This has been such a regular emission, as often as not from those who have retired from the educational establishment, that you have every right to ask whether I differ from previous doom-sayers in my forecasts. You might be forgiven for imagining that, like all previous doom-callers, I am going to tell you that the young, having been so badly brought up, cannot possibly keep civilisation on the rails. This certainly was the feeling of many famous Greek and Roman philosophers, and it wouldn't be very surprising to find an early *Homo sapiens neanderthalensis* camp-site with, scratched in pictographs on the rock-wall: "Young ones no good! No time spent on flaking flint, all time spent messing with bendy wood! No good will come of this.....!"

Of course, the Neanderthal writer would have been right, and for a deep re-productive reason that has not yet been made explicit here. The older generation would *not* have been helped by the development of bows-and-arrows, indeed. Progress! Slowly, for the most part, human culture has been changing, and the human species has been expanding, over the last half-million or so years. This is unlike nearly all of the species with which reproductive biology has been concerned, with the major exception of some domestic species like pigeons or cattle. In these species, however, the progressive change has been tied almost entirely to the genotype; in our species the changes in the genotypes have been almost trivial compared with the progressive changes in our cultural inheritance. Our reproduction philosophies are good at dealing with re-production, with replication, with $n$ parents in generation $t$ producing a similar spectrum of $n$ parents in generation $t+1$ or $t+x$. Changing through the generations, slowly from dependence on gathering to early farming, or rapidly from flint axes to bows or boomerangs, is not the kind of process reproductive biologists study. But equally, evolutionary biologists are much happier with genes, with longer time-spans, and with real fossilised bits rather than the saga of human cultural history (but the geneticist Darlington did two marvellous jobs[1,2] on the latter!). In the next chapter I discuss the utility of

169

thinking of us as a divergent family of cultural species. Here I need to look at some of the historical divergences, and expose my arguments that some are decadent, leading to the extinction of the cultural species which adopt them. As in organic evolution, roads to extinction are a part of the great tableau. They do not, however, lead me to feel pessimistic, even though I am in my fifties!

To the contrary, I am very optimistic about the future; I am confident that mankind will spread out to the other bits of real estate in our solar system, and will produce a great variety of cultures, perhaps even on other star-systems altogether. I doubt these people will be the direct descendants, cultural or genetic, of our Western culture, that's all. They won't speak English, American, or Spanish or even Russian; Chinese quite possibly, more likely Japanese. If they are spawned from American culture they'll be from such an aberrant part that they'll be disowned! As a reproductive biologist who sees a pattern in our evolution so far, I am observing that most urban individuals today, and most of our cultural systems, don't seem to me to be able to carry the wealth they've generated. They are frittering it away, supporting the vast majority of their populations in indolence. Any part of any wealthy human culture that does manage to pick up this torch and run with it will carry the future of mankind; I'm only suggesting that it won't be us.

In the last chapter I tell you who I think does have the future, who will take over this experiment in primate culture which raised reproduction to a new level on this planet; for now, let me reiterate the steps of the argument so far.

Chemical reproduction (Chapter 2) was followed by chemical-system reproduction; then, one part of the system, the nucleic acids (self-catalytic RNA first, followed by DNA, probably), segregated as the heredity. With that step the prokaryote appeared, with its reproduction separate from the everyday workings of the physiology. Then a system of different prokaryotes got together to make a eukaryote cell, and soon segregated much of the system's heredity into the nucleus (a little was retained by some of the symbionts, as in the mitochondria). Then systems of such cells (metazoans) were formed, probably by specialising parts of the original, protistan, organisation rather than by aggregation of different cells; but in any event the system's heredity was soon sequestered in the germ cells of these metazoa, the body having as little future as a bacterium's membranes and enzymes. Metazoa of diverse kinds were very successful, but many of these kinds were not successful as individuals; they evolved as groups. Systems of metazoa as different as coelenterate colonies like the Portuguese Man-o-War, groups of cleaning symbionts like the wrasses on coral reefs, mounds of termites, and packs of wolves, swarms of bees, all constitute groups which relegate breeding to a few individuals. Mammalian examples of such systems invented ways of passing privilege from the non-reproductives to the colony's offspring, ways more subtle than simple passage of food material, and that cultural heredity became a major strength of these communal mammals. Man capitalised on this passage of privilege, and the cultural heredity diversified to the point where one might almost regard it as a separate reproductive system, using the families of mankind as a substrate for its own reproduction. It possibly used the (verbal) children as its "sexual" recombination mechanism. It enabled larger groups of men to share their way of life, and to distribute privilege in a new kind of system of cultural communality. Not surprisingly, the cultural heredity, like each previous heredity, was soon segregated into a smaller group (medicine-men and other priests, initially). As this successful way of life took over the surface of our planet, differences of social "style" appeared, which I've naively labelled as "tribal" and "barbarian"; in several places and styles, systems of barbarian/tribal aggregates formed civic reproductive systems.

Such cities had much longer lives than the individual human lives, even than the tribal or barbarian systems within them. As well as organising the human geography around them, they segregated their cultural heredity into a nucleus, the educators (as, earlier, the hereditary wealth of the villages and small towns was segregated in markets and trading areas). This germ-plasm of the cultural wealth of the cities has, however, faltered in its function. It is most probable, I suppose, that the first RNA or DNA, the first eukaryote attempt at a nucleus, the first metazoan germ cells, the first queen bees were not successful. The ones we have today may be the descendants of the tenth attempt, or the millionth; the variety of attempts at each of these evolutionary innovations was supported by the strength of their highly-evolved support structures. But the support system around our new cultural nucleus is not a healthy one, depending as it does upon transmission of so much of its culture through the educators.

If there is a biological lesson here, it is that the nucleus must divorce its reproductive and system-maintenance functions. Mammalian germ-cells have endocrine functions, they make hormones as well as eggs or sperms. Similarly, queen bees organise the hive chemically (with pheromones) as well as laying eggs; they have a control as well as a hereditary function. But in both these examples, these different functions use *different* properties. However, our educators do both badly, both the retention/replication/advance of knowledge and the passage of the knowledge to those who must use it. Universities and research institutes, as distinct from the teachers in schools, might seem to have initiated such a split in educational functions, resembling germ-cell or queen-bee divergent functions; but I'm sure that is carrying my metaphor too

far.  Perhaps if I knew *why* heredity is repeatedly centralised, what the immediate one-generation benefits are, I could push the metaphor further.  I can of
course see many advantages of *having done so*, I can't easily see the *immediate*
advantage of doing it, or any real generalisation of how it's done!

Many previous cultures have become decadent;  is there any future in
digging over this ground again?  A *Decline and Fall of Western Civilisation*,
based as I've suggested on a *trahison des clercs*, certainly would not go down
well, dependent as it must be on adoption and promotion of the book by the very
people whose role I criticise.  What we should seek is a meta-theory of
decadence: not "Why are we becoming decadent?" but "Why do all our
cultures seem to get senile, decadent?"

I could certainly list a comprehensive set of *our* decadent practices, match-
ing that of any previous cultures.  I would employ the rule that all decadence
would, of course, have to be judged by the ethics of the immediately previous
"healthy" parent culture.   Ours would not be appropriate to judge others by,
just as you wouldn't get Cleopatra to judge ours – apart from anything else, if
we *are* decadent, that must affect our judgement in these matters!  We should,
to do the job and put our own decadence in perspective, judge late Inca
practices by early Inca standards[3] – ours are certainly not appropriate;  we
should judge post-Roman Egypt by the standards of Pharaonic Egypt, Nero's
Rome by Julius'.   We should also be prepared to learn from great cultural
traditions that have apparently suffered revolutions but seem not to have
changed in some basic characters thereafter, like the several Chinese changes
of political path, and perhaps England pre- and post-Cromwell.

I am not a historian, I am a biologist;  I doubt my ability – I doubt anyone's
– to go a-cultural and to judge this matter.  If people really *are*, as I have argued,
made of the culture in which they grow up, such a meta-principle of cultural
decadence can't be perceived by us, because we're the atoms of the system.  If,
of course, people are *not* made by the culture in which they grow up (but are,
for example, genetically determined in their social development as they do *not*
seem to be in their biological), then all I have said so far is nonsense and there
is simply no point in us using decadence or anything else to further it.  This form
of negative argument, about the validity of kinds of investigation, does not
apply to most small-universe scientific investigations, like those on maternal
effects in development or the inheritance of albinism or even IQ.  It does apply
to the relating of results, from an inheritance of IQ investigation for example,
to political action, or even to relating maternal control of development to the
models people should use for deciding about education[4]. I take this argument
to mean that all systematic abstractions about culture, like Marxism, Maoism

and this guess I'm attempting here, cannot in any sense be scientific proposals which are disprovable. However, they may still be usefully explanatory, possibly predictive, and are usually prescriptive or they wouldn't be written for others to read. They may also be *interesting* in the special, useful sense of "potentially able to change people's minds".

Bearing in mind, then, that we're looking for facets of our culture that would have seemed to our pre-decadence ancestor decadent, and that we really can't be rigorous about this, what do we find? We have recently legalised abortion; is this decadent? It seems only to have been *illegal* for a couple of hundred years; much will depend if our judge lived before or after that! Homosexuality is rampant in our society, just as it was in Greece and Rome in their decline..... Yes, but it was also rampant at their peak, and is rampant in some Islamic societies today which no one (so far as I know) has criticised for being decadent. We have gone soft on capital punishment, we don't kill offenders any more but imprison them in a way which demotes their dignity below the human and certainly doesn't, on average, reform. Well, perhaps, but who do you choose to judge us on that? Our music, and indeed much of our art, has become fragmented, incomprehensible to the majority, and often seems only a dull sanctification of the commonplace. We're told, by artists, that this has always been said of the avante-garde, that it was said of Beethoven, of Wagner, certainly of Stravinsky. Don't you think that your decadence judge, of say 100 years ago, could match our artistic affectations, even shams, with those of his own time?

Let me suggest that, in the special context of looking for failures in the true transmission of culture, and distinguishing these from real advances in civilisation, we need a yardstick that stands outside our local prejudices of the kind I've aired above. We need to be able to quantify, to particularise, changes that show where, perhaps how, culture has failed in passage. I will present five examples, additional to those elsewhere in this book, which signal to me decay of the organisation of our society. I will state the general case, then give some criticism of it and some other examples. The examples I have chosen are deliberately heterogeneous. I want you to find similarities between the attitudes which label children as dyslexic and televisions as irreparable, foster DIY and fast food, promote easy abortion and poor care of pets, sanctify Animal Liberation and vegetarianism (and innumeracy about them), provide instant gratification of whims and throw-away manufactured goods.

Firstly, we do not now insist on standards in the education of children, *or* (its complement) in the performance of teachers. If a child cannot now learn to read, we do not hold this to be the responsibility of either child or teacher, but "dyslexia". Perhaps there is some organic basis to a few cases, but this condition seems to have spread through the population at just the same time as new ideas for making reading easy.    This is not restricted to educational practice; responsibility for the outcome of many tasks has passed from the practitioners and is diffused more widely.    Your car mechanic, or television shop, will be reluctant to mend, rather than replace, because they then carry the burden of obligation to you; they are happier to pass it up the line to the manufacturer of the bits. I could explain this by mass-manufacture of complex items, usually not reparable; but I choose to emphasise the willingness to be the "middle-man", not the executive, the actor (both words which have changed their meaning in exact concordance with my message).

Secondly, there is a general willingness to receive, rather than to acquire or, especially, to make or repair.    Despite the apparent multiplication of Do-It-Yourself (in America, Fix-It) shops and products, few people do other than patch their problems with these goods. Advertisement for the goods *always* emphasises ease of use, very rarely quality of finished product.    The finished goods sold in these shops, too, are noted for their temporary adequacy, not for their promotion of quality of life.    Equally, fast food chains emphasise adequacy, their claims for excellence being (perhaps unfairly) discounted by the large segment of the population which uses them; they seem to care little for quality, even for taste (perhaps the fish-and-chip shop promotes this same apathy, but on p 215 I give reasons why not).    Again, as in my first example, the middle-man has come in: the odd-job-man very often gets his plumbing or electrical parts for your job from the DIY store.   In consequence, the professional outlets are finding it increasingly difficult to compete.   So are professional plumbers and electricians, who must charge more for a workmanlike job (another old word which repays study in this context).

Thirdly, there is less responsibility for other people's lives.   Sexuality has become cheaper, in many senses, but so has the responsibility of starting a new life.   In the UK now, it is common (again, an interesting word) for girls of around the legal age of consent to become pregnant, avowedly "only" to get out of the family home (usually a council, publicly-provided dwelling in these cases).   They are then provided with a small, independent apartment on public funds.  I contrast this with the shame such an act would have occasioned, had it become public, only fifty years ago – shame was then used, with public rigour, to force "responsibility" on the young.  This social pressure has not retained its force over the generations, it has decayed.  I do not think there is more licence in our society now; there is no sanction for the licence (again an interesting change of usage, of both words) to flout.  There may well be more sexual promiscuity, but this is not, I think, relevant to the decadence argument (it may be regrettable on other grounds, of course). This, I think, could result from the awareness of advances in medicine, particularly availability of contraception (even if not used, its public availability changes attitudes), publicly-advertised cure of venereal disease, and publicly-approved abortion services. The existence of these social cushions certainly blunts the fear of consequence, and permits more "freedom of action". Also relevant to the diminished responsibility for other lives, I think, is the casual attitude to pets. Animal welfare organisations are overloaded with cats, dogs, rabbits bought as a plaything for a few weeks and then discarded, and their reports declare this to be an increasing problem.

Fourthly, and in apparent direct contrast to the addendum to the above, there is the tremendous public following of the Animal Liberation story. From the general reluctance of most people to be involved with the butchery of food animals, abhorrence has spread both ways. Intensive production of agricultural animals, contrasted with the pastoral scene of egg and milk production (in theory, not reality!), is held up as inhumane. Production of mink for furs, laboratory animals for experiment, even dissection of dead animals in biology classes, are all regarded with disgust. So-called activists have bombed butchers' vans, vandalised research laboratories, released mink and other exploited animals into the countryside, to "give them their freedom". This is an inconsistent gesture, for released fur-breed mink die slowly of starvation and parasites, usually. At least, the "freed" laboratory rabbits are usually killed quickly by foxes, feral dogs or, of course, feral mink bred from the odd survivors (or previous escapees); while the mice die from cold, owls, weasels, before wild lice, mites, fleas and the diseases these insects carry from wild rodents can kill them!

More people are becoming vegetarian, even vegan; I worry about the ethical consistency of putting more land to nuts and soya beans, taking land that could be used by wild, or even domestic, animals! To most of the readers of this book, my attitude will seem callous in the extreme – but I want to emphasise how "soft" I am by the standards of a century ago. The animals were simply for the use of mankind, then, and were handled effectively (therefore, bye and large, humanely) by farmer and butcher; the same is true in most of the Pacific countries, now, and in most "primitive" peoples. Western peoples, perhaps encouraged by Disney, perhaps by David Attenborough's TV programmes, seem to see other *mammals* as babies, our babies. Most of us (perhaps especially the most rabid liberationist groups) don't care much about nearly all of the animals we share the planet with. Mayr has been quoted as

"To a close approximation, all animals are insects!"; a parasitologist friend of mine is fond of showing that there must be many more species of parasites than of hosts! Animal liberators don't bomb insecticide manufacturers, or the makers of tapeworm tablets; they don't release tse-tse flies from laboratories, even fishermen are usually not subjected to abuse. Spiders and snakes, frogs and toads, even birds have their coteries of people who are interested in them, and want to see them conserved in the wild – but it is never the ornithologist (or the herpetologist) who releases the broiler chicks to pneumonia in the outside world. For the Animal Liberation lot, "animal" equals the nursery cuddlies – something in the mind, not in the world.

The real effect of most Animal Liberation activity has been to increase security costs, and so to make *our* producers less cost-effective; so the supermarkets now buy foreign meat – just as many animals are treated cruelly, but they are further away from the "activists". There is a great reluctance to use arithmetic among these "soft" liberal minds; they seem to believe that animals in the wild live for ever, that the "death of one laboratory mouse is too much to pay for a cure for cancer", that "women should have the freedom to do what they will with their own bodies" but (another group) that no embryo should fail to be born to a loving home. I agree with Garrett Hardin[5] that too many people are caught in a web of words without numbers; he quotes a Catholic priest, Austin O'Malley: "An innocent fetus an hour old may not be directly killed to save the lives of all the mothers in the world." It is difficult to imagine the situation to which this, or my mouse example, could apply – but they sound ever so good, don't they? They have instant appeal – to the soft, innumerate liberal at least. He sets the "scientist" up as an evil genius, who uses hard figures (interesting words again) to prove "scientifically" cruel, weapon-producing theories; in contrast, the liberal sees himself as kindly, but bereft of argument in the "hard" world.

Fifthly, credit cards, and especially "Instant Credit" in shops make it possible to acquire goods *quickly*, when you need or want them. The alternative, having to wait for them until you've earned enough credit, or until you've earned the money to buy them outright, is avoided by most consumers. The "never-never" has taken hold like never before, and present practice is not in line with its more responsible origins. Perhaps it started with the mortgage arrangements for houses; I guess the previous business arrangements by which banks supported businesses (see any Western film) were copied by the Friendly Societies. Capital in one organisation enabled prompt action by the dependent person, family or organisation. This was good business for the banks, and the "patient" relationship (Illich, see p 85) was soon set up. I have it on reliable evidence (a friend who worked in one) that more than 10% of loans in Mid-Western small-town banks were *expected* to default; if less than 10% defaulted the bank wasn't selling its services hard enough! The US National Debt is made of this!

Disposable goods, made of paper or card before the plastics revolution, enabled people to get on with the next job without being tied down to cleaning up after the last one. Now, with high-turnover, high-capital factories with very low-cost inputs (especially using organic plastic materials) complex but non-renewable items can be made very cheaply. This encourages the throw-away philosophy, which in turn reinforces the attitudinal changes which support such high-volume producers. Criticisms of this trend, from conservation-minded organisations or individual politicians, are countered by pointing out that it really is *less* energy-wasteful, more environment-preserving, less polluting, to make 1000 plastic items instead of 50 ceramic or metal ones.

I have, of course, chosen these examples to illustrate what I think is the central issue of decadence. Please do look over them again, just briefly – I have put in a few clues – to see whether they give you *one message*. Firstly, responsibility of teachers, and children, for children attaining competence is not stressed, and your television mechanic changes the part rather than repairing the appliance – he'd rather you bought a new one, probably. Secondly, we use cheap do-it-yourself, shoddy goods, and eat fast food. Thirdly, there is more promiscuous sex but less concern about baby-starting, which can be used to rehouse you (but you leave your pet puppy on the street). Fourthly, much public concern, and violence, is directed against "exploitation" of animals (actually, mammals), while conservation issues (or even the question of what happens to animals "liberated" into the wild) are not addressed; using numbers to persuade in these ethical arguments is not seen as "fair". Fifthly, the credit card enables you to get an instant meal, and fifteen minutes later you are free of the problem of the packaging, it's in the waste bin (there is only that moment of indecision, whether to eat the packing or the hamburger – credit to Dennis Norden).

All these decadent practices and symptoms, and I *think* nearly all such examples of what *you'd* call decadence, have something in common which I find difficult to articulate. It is something like Instant Gratification without concern for the Longer Term Effects, but it's also like Getting my Bit, and the rest of the world can Go Hang, and it's like I Want It Now, and I don't care what happens tomorrow (or in nine months). But it's also about setting up progressive situations, like drug dependency for kids, or kidney machines for more invalids than we can get transplants for, or enormous capital investment in fast-food-packing factories, all of which could escalate desires beyond any reasonable expectation of fulfilling them.   There can never be enough drugs for the addict, enough organs for transplanting, enough customers to keep all the high-output factories going.   They are something like the Oxfam village of 1000 starving people (pp 113-4); our instant "solution", give them food, leaves me with a vision of the escalating future: 1200, 1500, 2000 *starving* people!   The pornography market, like the drug scene and, of course, the National Health Service, all have this flavour for me.   The National Health Service is a marvellous part of a Welfare State, until the sums are done to pay for it.   It is a bucket without any bottom in;  it can take all of the country's work force, all its productivity, and still find it inadequate.   With AIDS on the horizon, that is a very likely outcome.   When it was inaugurated, it seemed a glorious alternative to personal health insurance, but the bills are now being presented for payment.

How does this refine my "decadence" description?   It's the instant, "macho" decision, rather than the calmer judgement, but that *is* often the wiser move. Many of the decadence examples I have given are very like, have resonance with, solutions I have approved.   It is *not* the spontaneity, the immediacy of the decision that I mistrust.   I used to enjoy high diving;  there is that moment of decision, then, very consciously.   There is the "falling in love", the decision to commit your caring in this one direction.   The contrast, for me, sits right there.   You or I can make the decision to dive, or to fall in love, or to leave (or go to) university.   *We commit our own future.*   But when Oxfam, or Band-Aid, commit us to escalating aid for the village of 1000 starving people, it's the organisation committing us to help a third party.   It allows us to be effectively unselfish, we think.   A closer look suggests that the professionals, the Illich School of Charitable Paternalist Givers, wants me as a "patient".   It's not that I think that Oxfam is evil; but I want to make my own decisions.   There *are* the bottomless buckets, but Oxfam also commits us to real teaching, construction of irrigation systems, to helping people pull themselves out of downward spirals.   This seems a reverse-of-decadent activity, doesn't it?   However, when you look at the actual, real effects of Foreign Aid programmes by rich countries, they *nearly always* turn out to widen the gap, to help the rich at the expense of the indigent[6].   They don't help the third party in the long run.

What have these Oxfam examples to do with the teachers and children, my first example?   It's again a "now" versus "in the fullness of time" situation; educational exercises have the longest-term outcomes in our society.   So directing attention to classroom activity, projects, or putative dyslexia (just as to starving villages) is more immediately rewarding, more *relevant*, than worrying about what will happen to kids ten years in the future. And this short-term reward philosophy is just the hall-mark of my "decadent" label. It always has "Someone else can pick up the pieces later...." as a rider! There is a readiness to discard the future for a solution in the present.

This concern with the now, the relevant, the instant, the escalating, at the expense of the long-term, the eventual, the conserving is, of course, a well-publicised awareness – the better newspaper editorials pick it up at least once a month. It is seen in the support of short-term research projects rather than deeper investigations; the demand for relevance, especially industrial relevance, of university science; Readers' Digest, and correspondence colleges, thrive on it. It has been blamed, especially, on the "H-bomb mentality": "Why should we care about twenty years time? They'll have blown us all up by then!"

I am proposing a different and alas more illuminating context for these demands for satisfaction *now*. It has its roots in the reproductive philosophy I've presented here. It is diametrically opposite to the explanation which proposes H-bomb insecurity; it offers *security* as the basis for decadence. We must note that it's not joy they want, but satisfaction, MacDonald's hamburgers not caviare and champagne, chipboard furniture not water-beds, council flat now (even with baby instead of puppy) instead of self-confident, well-privileged children in ten years' time. I think I know, you see, what decadence is and where it arises, and – as a biologist concerned for the future of Man – I find it terrifying.

Decadent practices are those which *can only* arise in *security*, in affluence. Of course it's worth getting out of the parental home, at whatever cost – if you don't have to pay the bill for your baby, for disposal of your puppy. It doesn't matter if the telephone table you buy today disintegrates in two years' time; the DIY store will still be there then, and you'll have money in your pocket – or credit then, just as much as you do now. Life is assumed to be *unchanging*, in the affluent city. If you're confident that there'll always be someone to clear up your mess, you can make as much as you want. Of course we can start a National Health Service now – people in thirty years' time can deal with any little problems that arise by then.... That is exactly the attitude appropriate to mammals in the nest, looked after by parents, and it's there in all of us. The city is just like the nest, because of the systematic interactions which occur without action on your part: garbage disposal, money hand-outs, cheap instant food, central heating, shops, cheap entertainment. "Society" has taken the place of Daddy and Mummy: the place to live, the food, the money hand-out, all are there and assumed to be there for all time, without action on your part. University students receiving State grants provide a perfect intermediate, which can be usefully compared with both the home and the affluent city. I was always worried about the students who didn't give my books back, or indeed who showed only the shallowest appreciation that microscopes and other hardware should be cared for. They didn't clear up their places in the lab before they went off in the afternoon – it was obviously, for them, just like home, and Mummy would clear up after them. And there was no need to give Dad his books back now, either ... If you wanted excitement to spice up your life in the home, at university or in the decadent city streets, it could be obtained vicariously through drugs, sexual competition or "conquest", barbarian sports, television, cinema or, more intimately, video-recordings.

"Bread and circuses", that's the secret, and it hasn't changed much since Rome. Exploitation by private enterprise is more-or-less successfully kept down to bearable limits (but not in Chicago of the thirties, for example) by police or other authoritarian organisations. In this atmosphere of security, mammals and especially humans have "circuits", cultural turn-ons, which set up the trial-and-error behaviour which expanded our horizons usefully when we were children. "Trying it on" is the phrase I know, but you'll have others. The experts in this kind of behaviour are the police and the social psychiatrists like Goffman. *Where the action is*[7] is a perceptive analysis of just this kind of naughtiness in security, with each of us testing the status of our (barbarian) position by trying out forbidden actions, for a thrill but also for self-establishment. As in the nest, you need to do things which are wrong, as well as those which work and reward you, to define your limits.

There really is a great variety of human activity, and inactivity, available in cities. There is a great deal of naughtiness too, just as there is in the nest and the nursery, because the city *is* the nest (as in ants' nest, too) of the citizens. Most baby mammals, and most citizens, spend most of their time effectively asleep. The tribal part of civic life does not call upon the rational mind, only upon the well-worn, almost "reflex", social responses: "Whose first round is it tonight, then, Fred?", "Let me get up, Joe, I've got to be back home for *Dallas* or my Mum worries... ", "You'll not come into my shop again unless you pay this bill..... " – watch those television series whose writers understand that ritual life so well.

The barbarian city-dweller can exploit the tribal unthinkingness, can exploit the decadence, as well in the city as he can exploit the tribalism of the agricultural scenario. Not only the Mafia, but pop artists, gang leaders, even some scoutmasters and many of the very good schoolteachers use their charisma to impress (both senses, again) a gang of followers. Then the city environments permit such a gang to achieve status by intra-gang and inter-gang rivalries and exploits. Although the tribal "background" serves for the backcloth, the privilege-pool and the source of new gang-members, it is sometimes the tribal response to the gang exploits that counts as the status-currency between gangs. It need not be rival gangs who are shown off to directly; media coverage of an event like football hooliganism, a cleverly-constructed scouting exploit, or a business take-over may signal effectively to other barbarians.

The apparent security of the tribal life in the affluent city, like that on rich agriculture, is liable to be upset by barbarian rivalry or exploitation. This is especially so when the tribal stability of the city, or its capital base, have been eroded, for example when many instant commitments have led to longer-term debts, when long-term responsibility has decayed. "Democratic" election to public office is frequently to blame for this short-term view, and to that extent democracy leads to decadence – dictators or other autocrats often think far ahead! But to both the elected officer and the autocrat, the tribal city-liver is "just a number", not involved in the "life" of the city. In the decadent city, nearly all of the tribal livers really are nonentities, as far as the "movers", "operators" are concerned. In simpler societies, all *were* more immediately involved, for good or (especially) bad. In the village, *all* the girls would have been at risk of rape by the Mongols, *all* the children could have been killed, *all* the men were often effectively enslaved or put to the sword. This happens in many African states today. In the city, even in some African cities, nearly all the tribal lives are not upset more seriously than *reading about* extortion or murder two blocks away. There are, of course, parts of all big cities where extortion, prostitution, drug peddling and murder are a real part of the lives of most folk. Here the tribal way of life includes a large measure of appeasement (see Dickens); or tribal cultural enclaves (city ghettoes) form separated villages-within-the city which can exclude foreign barbarians by incomprehension, a major social weapon. But these areas, dangerous or foreign, are only a tiny proportion of the city's life – and they are *not* the decadent parts! Quite the reverse, indeed. This is the white hope of our cities.

I believe that there is a very close causal connection between the deprivations of affluence, and the arrival of decadence; any human social system which fails to give its juveniles the abilities which will make life interesting for them, because they don't need them *now*, has failed them. Its institutions will decay, its practices will become inappropriate to its continued existence, productivity will decline below that able to support civic services, and it will become an urban wasteland inhabited by a few tribesmen and barbarian gangs. Its government will be characterised by its readiness to discard the future for a solution in the present.   Such are many decayed city centres, all over the world.   We have done that.   But my hope lies in the next step up of our evolutionary ladder, systems of cities and, especially, interactions between living cultural systems within cities.

## References

References in full are to be found from page 243 onwards. Below are listed names of authors and dates of publication

1. Darlington (1969)          5. Hardin (1982)
2. Darlington (1978)          6. Cassen et al (1986)
3. Harris (1974)               7. Goffman (1972)
4. Oyama (1984)

# 13

# DISEASE, DIVERGENCE AND THE BIOLOGY OF DIFFERENCE

We have left the cities in a parlous state at the end of the last chapter. There are few cities that have taken this road to the end, for a very good and sufficient, but not obvious, reason. If our affluent urban Apes had been alone in the world, and the tribesmen and their barbarian exploiters/rulers had made but one city, that may well have slid into affluent decline as I sketched out in the last chapter. But we are not like that. Mankind lives in very diverse cultures, and their histories have selected for different abilities under different sets of social rules. Different groups, too, have had different histories of disease, which have left them with multifarious genetic bases for resistance (p189). We have made tribes, and cities, from the midnight sun to the equator, on a basis of agriculture, of sea-fishing, of the exploitation of trade, of sex, of sin, of the beauty of temples and of the power of emperors. Each has flowered for a while, and then when it has declined its inhabitants have turned their eyes to other, different, cultures with new attractions.

The early towns were often aggregates of different tribesmen, some warriors, some priests, perhaps around a castle or a market. Darlington's evocation[1] of the magic of these places, the biological magic, is both delightful and scholarly; he set his scenes in a dense framework of historical events and illuminated them by genetical insights. More recently, Boyden[2] has drawn together Sumerian (7000 years ago in Mesopotamia), Harrapan (4500 in the Indus valley) and Olmec (3200 in Mexico) archaeology to paint a picture of early urban humanity. I envisage the street of the leather-workers, all stinks and pelts, smoke and shrill women, the men being away bargaining with the trappers; the metal-workers, proud of their offensive and defensive pieces, with one or two clever pieces hung at each stall; hunters, and butchers, in the market around the pens, stink and blood and shouting, much as a century ago in all of England's market towns; corn-and-meal, vegetables, seedsmen, fruits in season; inns full of weak beer, arguments, some women. These towns served to mix genetics and to mix cultures, to spread seeds of new plants, new dogs, sheep, cattle. They did not retain their heterogeneity, though. Some parts of our old towns still have street-names, markets, styles of old houses and shops that serve as a reminder of those days. But most towns have evolved into more homogeneous entities. As transport improved, so towns became known for one or two specialities, as spa towns or for leather goods, as a market or as a port.

Only the growing cities could serve as military and commercial, and of course religious, centres for several markets. Perhaps they were at the junction of two rivers and could live on trade, or simply on visitors, and then became the centre of power for the surrounding country towns. Each town had developed a different character, determined largely by the nature of local produce, and the cities they fed all became different again. At all levels, in each country, city, town, village, commune the people were different, the trade was different, the culture was different. Some of the differences were only quantitative, how *much* leather-work, how *many* sheep; some were truly qualitative, special ironwork or gold-leaf decoration, a potent saint's relic or miracle-working well, a new and different method of iron-working for the new ploughshares. Because of these different specialities, foods were different, patterns of reproduction both biological and cultural were different, and – especially – parasites and other diseases were different. Cities on a tropical river suffered river-blindness, malaria, schistosomiasis; a city on a northern temperate river suffered winter cold, and starvation when the river froze and the government was corrupt. Cities with harbours had good fish supplies, but were liable to attack by pirates ... You can imagine these as well as I can, and add the differences you know! The biology of each city was different; different practices had been developed, perhaps selected, which dealt effectively with local problems, and there were many compromises, many trade-offs, few ideal solutions. Each city became a human ecology, and its people were adapted to its ways and its demands.

Because of trade rivalries, because of curiosity, but mostly because of war, slavery, pillage there were always people on the move. Visitors to towns would seek out possible relatives, or people in the same line of business; very different technologies, very different genetics, very different cultures met in the market towns, in the leather towns, especially in ports. Mostly they did not stay separate, but ports particularly became melting-pots of culture which enriched the local towns with new stories, new myths, new songs and sagas. There have rarely been times, as under the aegis of Rome or of Genghis Khan, when travel was safe over long distances, through many cultures. But mostly, people did not move more than the ten or twenty miles to the next town unless there was a war, a plague, a drought. So towns, cities, even small countries developed, became internally diverse but developed a kind of overall cultural character. There are the remnants of this all over the UK, for example. Let us look at one city briefly, at its environs and its competitor, to contrast with the multicultural cities where the next evolutionary step is happening.

Hull (really Kingston-upon-Hull), has been a large port for hundreds of years, but has been concerned much more with fishing, and servicing the fishing fleets, than with international trade. Like some of the other cities on the north-east coast, it represents local people and interests, but it never had the international flavour of Liverpool, Southampton or Bristol. It recognises different kinds of village folks inland, in Cottingham, Willerby, and those, like Anlaby, Ferriby or Hedon, nearer the Humber shore. The docks, the markets, the transport centres from which fish was dispatched all over England, are very different local patches if you live in Hull. But a mere fifteen miles away, over the water, a bit further seaward on the Humber, is Grimsby, the rival port, with just as many diverse areas (although it is much smaller). Like Hull, the trade speciality has always been the fish trade, but the much more mercantile side (and this has now paid off handsomely). The Lincolnshire hinterland of Grimsby is much more determinedly agricultural than Hull's, and has had much land reclaimed by Dutch farmers. The Dutch are still a very real presence in many local towns and villages – the Lincolnshire end of the Humber Ferry was called "New Holland". No Hull man or woman would be mistaken for a native of Grimsby, or *vice versa*. However, both lots refer to the town of Goole, twenty miles further inland up the Humber, as "Sleepy Hollow"! Beverley, an old leather town fifteen miles from Hull, didn't want to know about the fishiness of its great neighbour (now, alas, in the past, as Grimsby's fish-trading expertise has ousted Hull completely). All its eyes were turned to the surrounding agriculture, and oak forests, and alum works (now in the past, too). Import of exotic skins through Hull was a very minor business, more important for Beverley. Only tens of people were involved in this import trade, but they became trend-setters who apparently changed much of the character of Beverley, and finally resulted in the demise of the local leather-trade. This is a tiny taste of Humberside, a little enclave around the estuary of some minor north-eastern rivers in England. Multiply that by all the towns and cities of England, then by all the industrial nations; add the great historic city-cultures around the Mediterranean, in China and central Europe, in Nigeria and Central and South America. Diverse cultures were everywhere on the globe, rising and falling in affluence, decadence, wealth, plagues. No other animal has had so diverse an ecology.

These human groups were not only culturally different. Deep genetic differences had appeared early among the races of mankind, and the different cultural sub-groups split and refined these still further. Cultural practices which encouraged inbreeding cleaned up the genetics of those cultures which practised it – all the dubious recessive alleles found themselves partnered, showed their dubious effects (p 90 ), failed to breed and died out.   The difference in childhood deaths, in miscarriages and misery, cannot have been great after the initial losses – people have nearly always been able to produce babies to excess, anyway.  This view contrasts with Darlington's genetic view of history[1]: his story is generally of *outbred* heroes and conquerors consolidating their family position by inbreeding and so becoming incompetent – that *was* the orthodoxy, when he wrote.  However, we now know much more about the disease-resistance polymorphisms (see below).    Another difference between our stories is that I am referring to the sub-populations generally, not only the leaders, the innovators.  The genetic base of inbreeding folk may have been smaller, and they were perhaps more liable to decimation by disease, or chronic dietary inadequacy, than out-breeders; but they *were* more likely to be adapted to their local geography, local diseases.

Other cultural practices encouraged out-breeding, and the hybrid vigour so produced gave its own characters and strengths (emphasised, indeed, by Darlington).  Most of the genetic selection, however, most of the evolution of these sub-groups away from each other, was caused by differential susceptibility to disease organisms.   In consequence, the stranger was indeed to be feared, because he brought new and virulent disease – but his genes could be valuable, not least in defence against just such disease.  Much of the history of human sexual choice sits squarely upon this paradox[3] – but that is another book I haven't yet written!

We do need, however, a short look at tissue-types and disease susceptibilities, at this major set of genetic polymorphisms, before I can come to the subject of how many species we are, and in which contexts we should use the word "species" about *Homo sapiens sapiens*.  This is indeed a vital consideration for a biological understanding of the complex life of the decadent city.  In some ways a city ecology is like a multi-species biological ecology (there are breeding barriers between the groups, for example); in other ways, however, it is like a mono-culture of domestic animals or plants (*some* diseases, some predators, can attack everybody).  In some ways, indeed, a city is like one complex colonial organism like a Portuguese Man-of-War – a biological entity called a *sociozoon*[4].  There is a whole new genetic story here, about the interactions of the individuals and about the biology of sociozoa, which biologists are just beginning to work out[5].

Until the 1960s very nearly all biologists believed that the genome of each animal of a species very generally resembled that of every other of the same species, in more than (say) 99.5% of the genes (except for the sex chromosomes, sometimes). There were a few different alleles (versions of the same gene, like those for blue or brown eyes) about in the population. Some of these alleles were on their way out, being generally bad for their carriers. Perhaps, too, there were a very few that were on their way in, towards "fixation" in the population, because they gave Darwinian advantage. These different options for a gene, these "allelic forms" of any gene, were usually expected together with the usual version in any one organism (recall that each of us has *two* versions of each gene, one from each parent). We expected them to have been received from only one of the parents, because these alleles were apparently rare. Certainly less than 1% of genes in any animal, and probably in any population, would have been expected to be "heterozygous" (different alleles received from mother and father). A few genes were known to be "polymorphic", that is to say they were to be found rather regularly as different alleles in different animals. But they seemed, like the polymorphism in blood group alleles in people, to be of not much consequence. They were oddities, and a few biologists had found little ecological stories which explained away this oddity. Blood group alleles were useful to teach some biology with personal impact, in the days before the safety rules prevented intentional blood-letting in schools.

There were a lot of polymorphisms accumulating in the literature, and population geneticists were laboriously working out what differences they might make, when a new technique appeared in the middle sixties. This permitted a detailed look at the genetics of an individual organism *without breeding it*, by seeing how many versions of each protein it had. How many kinds of that protein, that gene, were to be found in the whole population could also be discovered by sampling many individuals, without laborious breeding programmes and even sometimes without killing any animals. Each protein, of course, represented one length of DNA which coded for it, one gene, and the different versions were the effects of different alleles. These variant alleles were found to be *much* more common than the old genetic stories would have had us believe. Let me explain what was found. One animal might have types $a_1$ and $a_2$, for example, of one particular enzyme – it was heterozygous at that gene locus, having received $a_1$ from one parent and $a_2$ from the other. It might show only type $m_3$ of another protein and type $x_1$ of a third – it was "homozygous" at these loci, having received the same allele from both parents and so having only one version of each ($a_1, a_2; m_3, m_3; x_1, x_1$). In another animal, however, we might find only $a_1$ (no $a_2$), $m_3$ again for the second protein but $x_4$, homozygous but different from the $x$ which we found in the first animal, for the third protein. In that whole population, however, we might be able to find

$a_1, a_2, a_3, a_4$ and very rarely $a_5$, versions of the first one. We might only ever find $m_3$ of the second, but $x_1$ and $x_4$ of the third.

What was indeed very generally found, among all kinds of eukaryotes (including some that didn't go in for sexual reproduction) was that as many as a tenth of all the genes in one genome, one organism, were usually heterozygous. That is, two *different* alleles represented 10% of the genes of that one organism, because different versions had been received in sperm and egg from the organism's two parents. Remember that we used to think it was perhaps 0.5%! Worse, for our previous theories, was to come; it turned out that about a *third* (30% not 0.5%!) of all the genes we looked at had variants somewhere in the population.

There was, in response to this discovery, a very general division of biologists. There were those (mostly population geneticists) who believed that these allelic differences we were looking at had very little effect on the life of the organism, were effectively *neutral*. The rest of us (especially reproductive and developmental biologists) tended to be *pan-selectionist* about these differences; we believed that any genetic difference *made* a phenotypic difference, and the evolution of development took on a different, and more comprehensible, appearance. Some of the genetic differences turned out, actually, to be balanced controlling systems which prevented the organisms showing small genetic differences; but this "canalisation" had considerable phenotypic effects (even if only in *reducing* the effects of other genes[6]), so was *not* neutral. Different geographic races of organisms turned out, very often, to have much the same alleles around in the population, but in very different proportions, and different combinations were to be found in individual animals. To look back at our $a_1, a_2, a_3, a_4$ and rarely $a_5$ example above: another population might have $a_5$ as its commonest allele instead of the rarest, and heterozygotes $a_1, a_2$, which we found commonly in the first population, might be rare in the second. This was just what had been known for a long time about human blood groups. A, B and O individuals were to be found in nearly all human populations, but the proportions differed enormously, as they did for other blood differences. It turned out, then, that blood groups were typical, not odd; a third of genetic systems behaved like that, to some extent, and the genetic textbooks had to be re-written.

By far the greatest complexity, many times the number of alleles, and much the greatest difference from human group to human group was found in the tissue-type and immuno-type genes. It had been known for more than a century that only identical-twin mammals would accept tissue grafts from each other. Inbred (brother-sister mated) laboratory breeds of mice were started in the thirties and, by the late forties and fifties many had become "isogenic": they were all effectively identical "multiplets". Working out the basis of the tissue-rejection was very complex, even using these mice, but it turned out to depend upon the most polymorphic set-up yet found.    The major mouse tissue-rejection system, or "histocompatibility complex", is called the H2 system, and probably has four gene loci;  that doesn't sound very complicated.    But each gene, *A*,*B*,*C* or *Dr* is represented in the mouse population by many alleles. The "same" system in human beings (called HLA, for "human lymphocyte anti-gen") has hundreds of different alleles of the *A* and *B* genes, many tens of the *C* and at least tens of the *Dr*.    Most of these can now be determined (rather expensively) at major medical centres, and the HLA information is of course used for kidney, occasional heart or skin, and to some extent for corneal grafting.  I had myself typed back in 1980, when only a few of the alleles could be identified, and I came out as HLA-*A* 9,19;  HLA-*B* 7,Bw35;  HLA-*C* w4,?; HLA-*Dr* 1,?;  the ?s mean that I am probably not homozygous at these loci, but have another allele that could not be identified.    There are many other polymorphic loci involved with these and other immunological properties of animals.    They determine what spectrum of antibodies they can make, for example, even though antibody specificities are randomly generated within those sets.    Different populations have different whole "sets" of these immu-nological genes, with the individual animals having allelic variations mostly within the characteristic local set.

What, however, is the biological function of this fantastic array of variation? All biologists now agree that it is related to susceptibility to disease[3], particu-larly viral diseases.  But to some extent it relates to infection by bacteria and even grosser parasites like malaria (a protozoan), nematode worms (like threadworms, or filaria), flukes (like *Bilharzia*), tapeworms and perhaps even lice!  It is, in a sense, a lock-and-key system.  Each of us codes our tissues, and our special chemical defence system of antibodies, so that "self" is not attacked (usually ..., see below),  but any alien chemical signal is recognised and its bearer is destroyed.  If we all had the same HLA system, of course, an intruder could camouflage itself to look like our own tissues, and parasitise us without detection (some perhaps do, even now).  But because we're all different a para-site can't develop a "master-key" and invade a whole population.  They can and do, however, develop camouflage or master-keys that work with a large proportion of us.  When Asian 'flu struck, about one person in five seemed to be susceptible;  with other 'flu variants, a rather different sub-group of people can catch each one.

Unfortunately, this clever system has two major disadvantages.  All of our tissues have rather different key-patterns, and it is obviously possible for parasites to hit on, say, the particular code that is characteristic of special nerves; when we react against that parasite, perhaps these antibodies react against our own nerve proteins. That is why, the second time we're challenged with the chicken-pox virus, we often get shingles; the attack spills over onto our own chemical keys which "look like" the viral camouflage. Some of the tissue-types may not need a viral challenge; they may be liable to respond to a not-very-available chemical cue in our own bodies by producing an attack, as if our own chemical cue were an invader. People with HLA-*B* 27, for example, react against their own spinal column discs, which go very stiff and inflamed, producing the disease "ankylosing spondylitis". Other "auto-immune" diseases, like some kinds of arthritis and some nerve or muscle de-generative diseases, and some kinds of infertility between specific men and women (each of whom can be fertile with somebody else), are side-effects of our attack on viral or bacterial invaders. We involve our own chemistry, our own tissues by similar mechanisms, and this is associated with particular HLA combinations, particular lock-and-key "shapes". Another side-effect is our propensity to react against other common chemicals with reactions, allergies, that cause us discomfort out of all proportion to the danger of being invaded; grass pollen, house dust mites, horse brushings can cause incapacitation in some people. (A suggestion has been made that we're now *too* healthy – if the IgE, allergy, system had our normal run of parasites to deal with it wouldn't be so reactive against minor irritants.)

The other problem with the HLA system is that it does *not* give a whole human population protection against a particular disease; it only really protects those members of the population that have the right (or, from the parasite's viewpoint, the wrong) combination. If these are in the majority, susceptible people may not catch the disease because they may not meet an infected person or situation. But the usual effect of a human disease upon a fairly isolated population is of *selection* for particular HLA types, death or disability of a proportion, sometimes a large proportion of the community. The next disease selects again, so each population has its own particular spectrum of susceptibilities, relating mostly to the history of the diseases it's been exposed to – and a whole suite of other pathologies that come as part of the package with that particular HLA kit. It is supposed that HLA-*B* 27 must protect its carriers against something fairly common and fairly nasty, for example, or its tendency to ankylosing spondylitis would have cleared it out of the gene pool long ago. So too, with allergies, presumably, and with the various arthritides. Biologists do not find local populations of animals which

The transmission of <u>culture</u> from generation to generation should be part of the ~~professional~~ ~~process~~ <u>reproduction process</u> (this is "meme" territory). Otherwise sterility

implication — the transmitter of culture is the "parent" — should have an interest in the success of his offspring, should take their development at heart, should know what are their interests.

Fight against dumbing down should start from there — knowing and proclaiming the interests of the audience

This dumbing down could stem from several sources:

(a) because of the development of the self-regulating profession, that enlarges more and more and contains, according to ~~the~~ a normal distribution of abilities, all levels of competence. But being a regulated system it needs to protect its states, ~~even to~~ ~~the extent of pro~~ by protecting its members, even when incompetent. (a trade union system).

(b) economical pressures and the transformation of relationships, with pupils becoming customers.

(c) represent a natural development of cultural evolution.

——— x ———

Transmission of information from generation to generation does not involve only ~~DNA~~ genetic material but a whole host of extra-genetic material. — Cultural evolution can be seen as such extra-genetic information.

down to energy stores (yolk)

all this he calls "profit" that is "invested" as "capital" by parents ~~to~~ into the new generation.

or "privilege". In fact, in higher organisms,

all early life of the progeny is parentally protected — maternal

first (for mammals) and then by both parents with the newborn offspring
with early childhood there is then the other investment,
cultural – methods of learning and orienting into the environ
This type of parental investment is more of a Lamarckian
type of transmission of parental information – transmission of
acquired traits

have diverged as much as this.  There really is something different about the biology of human cities, in which the people in them go further up the roads to peculiar polymorphisms than almost anywhere else in biology.

Small in-breeding groups of people, then, will have their special genetic characters, in a variety of ways.  They will, of course, not only have been selected for disease susceptibility, but for their general ability to contribute children who themselves grow up and breed in the local culture.  Such selection in an iron-smelting and working town must have been totally different from that in a sheep-farming district, different again from a fishing port.  Very different diets would have selected for different trace-element and vitamin requirements and retentions.  Recurrent famines or gluts would have fostered some kinds of metabolism, just as tropical sunlight or the brief Scandinavian summer selected different skin types and pigmentation, but less obviously. Superimposed and interacting with these differences was a great number of life styles, cultural patterns refining and reproducing the social structure in successive generations.  Some of these were not stable from generation to generation, though they may have been very successful for those who practised them;  banditry (unless what we hear of Albania and Mexico has more truth than I credit) is not reproductively stable *genetically*, though it may be culturally, like other gang-systems.    Mohammed III killed  his nineteen brothers, and fifteen concubines pregnant by his father, on the same day, following the Rule of Fratricide in force at that time in the Ottoman Dynasty; the ruling Islamic families found it very difficult to carry through any coherent culture using such rules[1].  Indeed this rule fell into disuse soon after.  What is remarkable, for us to lay alongside the peculiar biological polymorphisms of city-folk, is such very odd sets of biological practices.

Why should wide polymorphism, and varied practice (including murder of one's own family), be favoured?  Why should this *ever* be found in a culture? Perhaps because specialisation within an ecology enables better use of the resources by one's own kind?   Male and female carnivores are often of very different size (either way) because they do not then compete with each other so much for food animals, and more progeny can grow up to breed.   Such specialisation of roles in cities is manifest all around us, to avoid economic competition for resources, and to give more opportunity for status.  This specialisation is the alternative to opting out, to finding a place in another human ecology;  even murder of one's congeners could be explained like this. The opposite question then arises: what holds the competitors *in* the city, in the competing situation?   What are the contrary forces which provoke cohesion in one city and prevent either the "opting out" or complete biological specialisation?

One biological specialisation comes to mind as an example. Many of the medieval cities, and some of the travelling peoples like gypsies, had a role for freaks, especially dwarfs. Achondroplasia, a condition in which the long bones of arms and legs stop growing prematurely, is a very common mammalian mutation. It has been selected for in many breeds of dogs, from dachshund to basset-hound, and turns up in other mammals too. It produces the commonest kind of human dwarfing, and these short-appendage but normal-bodied dwarfs have long been popular as circus performers, and for other more private roles as entertainers. There were many families of these people, specialised for the entertainments they provided, and with allegiance to others of their kind and their peculiar culture. Their relationships with the professional clowning families, and the other entertainers, was professional. But their allegiance to their sponsoring families, and to the city in which they were given a social place, was the major force. In the medieval Italian cities, there was apparently great jealousy and rivalry centred upon these families ; they saw themselves, if I may put it in our more fanciful terms, as a specialised organ of their sociozoan city. So did the warriors of the Greek city-states, at least according to Homer.

So, in many ways, do the people of Hull and Grimsby; indeed, most of us have such an allegiance to town or city. Even if we were reared far from urban life, the local town touched us with its stories, its fascination, and we still remember it as an allegiance when we have moved away. So the groups within the city passed on their culture within family and within trade, within guild; but the interactions between families in social and sexual life, between trades in goods and services, between guilds in restrictive practices and honours, formed the reproductive net of the city itself. All of the smaller groups seem to feel a strong allegiance to the city itself. Is this allegiance simply to the geography, to the territory? Perhaps there is a little attachment to place, to streets, to neighbourhood; but I think that the major attachment is to the cultural succession through which we grew up, that formed us in its image. The particular gang ritual, that particular cinema, the relationship with those shops, that church, this market are the items we get nostalgic about, and that gives the clue. Can our nostalgic selection of emotional attachments tell us why cities are so reproductively stable?

Reproductive stability was, obviously, one of the most desirable properties of a cultural system, for then it could be improved; its folk could adapt to it genetically, alien practices could be tested, accepted or rejected. Obviously, too, only the reproductively stable entity can be recognised, named – these are the only entities we can abstract. Because of this, the question becomes "What is it about at least some cities that provides reproductive stability, whirlpool-like continuity through time as the people pass through?". Here I must distinguish between reproductive stability of the larger entity, the city so-ciozoan, and the parts which themselves reproduce. The stable reproduction of the parts is a necessary, but not a sufficient condition for the reproduction of the whole, just as in your body. I will compound this dangerous social/ biological metaphor by reminding you that most of your cells reproduce stably, but that is not *your* reproduction; it is, however, essential to your physiology that they should do so, and so to your own whole-person reproduction. Similarly (but it is a dangerous simile) with the city. The city's character depends on the interactions of its families, its trades, its guilds and therefore depends upon their own reproductive stabilities as entities (nearly) in their own right. However, these entities belong to sub-cultures in the city, and these sub-cultures are, I think, the crucial level for cultural reproductive stability. There are two kinds, however, from the city's point of view: the city's own indigenous "organs", and the foreign immigrants.

We are all familiar with reproductively stable sub-cultures around us. In urban England in the 1980s Irish Catholicism, Orthodox Judaism, Methodism are more stable than most Church of England patterns, but not (to my eye) as stable as Cypriot Greek, Hong Kong Chinese or the Asian Islamics. English aristocracy is hanging on, but its stability comes, I guess, more from Oxford and Cambridge traditions than in the past, when their families had defined places in the culture. There are very many ways of attaining this stability in such minority groups, but they all depend crucially on the passage of culture, its fables, myths, prohibitions, courtesies, probably in the original language for immigrants[7,8], with mothers' milk. In the nursery, in later peer groups, reinforcement of the cultural models must occur to the virtual exclusion of others, which could be more attractive. It is paradoxically much easier to transmit your culture in this stable way if you are part of a minority, preferably (from the viewpoint of stability) an oppressed, discriminated-against minority. There won't be "others" in your play-groups or street gangs, the in-group customs will seem to be a much more consistent, contained set than the wild variety of behaviours out in the larger social world.

There must, on first consideration, be a lower limit to the size of the group which can transmit its culture within another kind of culture, which can form a stable sub-culture. It would seem that there must be enough people to provide outbreeding marriages, at least, and to provide the various elements of a culture: priest(s), workers, leaders, perhaps marriage-brokers, bankers, warriors. However, there have been several cases, even in my small experience, of single close-knit families succeeding quite well in maintaining their mores, and the juveniles may go far to seek their (cultural) kin in the larger world. My father's family lived in and near Dudley for many generations without (much) attrition, because they were *so* culturally different, being Jewish. The adolescents made sexual contacts mostly with other Jewish adolescents, through family and Jewish organisations (many of which had well-established networks in England by 1900). In that situation I know of occasional single families "breeding true" culturally, and I can see why. This will occur particularly if they are in a culture with whom they only interact marginally, and if they can maintain even occasional contact with "home", or with the diffuse network of their kin.

In contrast to these cases, I would have supposed most trade-restricted groups in the early towns to have been subject to adolescent impressing techniques in the street gangs. Let me give an example. I would not have bet much on the chances of a leather-working group of families from Wales retaining Welsh practices, or language, if they had come to an early Black Country town like Dudley. There would have been cross-cultural contacts with other leather-workers from Walsall, and nearly all of the locals of the same age would have been Black Country. Chapel contacts would mostly have involved the adults, and local church organisations would have been "close enough" in many cases, so the "Welshness" would have been lost in the second generation. This is what we call "assimilation", and it is generally regarded as a Good Thing; I think it destructive, and I know why my early culture has made me feel this. But I shall argue it too!

Similarly, and in contrast to the Jewish experience, the streets of different "indigenous" trades in the early towns must, in my view, have "married out" much of the time; I can so easily imagine the young copper-worker lad paying court to the girl of the cheese-sellers (and I *do* know it's a Hollywood image – but did it ring true in myth *first*?). This imaginative excursion into the sexual mores of the early towns is to point up the contrast. In towns the different trades, different districts, have become assimilated into the life of the town. In cities, however, the ghettoes have *never* been like the trade districts of the towns; the ghettoes really are isolated bits of different cultures. Even away from the ghettoes in the city, there are "distributed" alien networks. These distributed cultures within the larger city culture, like Cypriot fish-and-chip shops or "Chinese" restaurants in Birmingham, or the Chinese laundries in Boston, usually maintain a separate culture which again seems to be reproductively stable.

This contrast in reproductive stability forms a crucial part of my argument about the future of the cities. In general, trades in towns are not reproductively stable now – family firms, local industrial networks *were* stable but are not now, in affluence. Exceptions, like blacksmith families or the more aristocratic families of petty squires in the towns, are tied by specific myths, specific cultural difference, and perceive themselves as of "a different sort of people". Exceptions in the other direction are more interesting, examined in detail in the next chapter.

This question of the reproductive stability, and of necessity of the reproductive isolation, of different groups in the cities is the crucial bit of our reproductive biology – and cultural inheritance. It relates, too, to a semantic issue which may as well be considered here, while HLA, and other questions of human genetics, are fairly fresh in your mind. This concerns the question of whether human beings are all of one species, or whether it is more useful to consider our genetic and, especially, our cultural differentiation to merit consideration as several different kinds of organism. Basically, the problem is whether we grant the cultural diversity of peoples the same *status*, to delimit kinds of biological/cultural organisms, as we have done with the "regular" biological characters, differentiating "regular" species.

Classically, species in biology were defined as the largest groups of organisms which could breed with each other to produce fertile offspring. Alas, that working criterion has gone by the board in thirty or forty different ways now that modern biology has assimilated the genetic analysis I mentioned above. As in so much real science, definition won't help; what we need to see is that we all agree about some species, and then see what they have in common under the new paradigm. This area *is* problematic; it took me some time to think of some species we all *would* agree about: *Apis mellifica*, the honey bee; *Drosophila melanogaster*, the laboratory fruit fly; *Panthera leo*, the lion and *P. tigris*, the tiger – and nearly all, I guess, of the others. However, there are a lot which sit at or over the edge of our usage (and the honey-bee is a bit odd ..... some domestic "varieties" don't interbreed!). It turns out that many of the different kinds – species – of plants in the potato-and-tomato-and-tobacco family (*Solanaceae*) form fertile hybrids quite happily. So do those in many other plant families, but that doesn't stop botanists thinking of them as "good" species. Zoologists get a bit more unhappy about odd breeding properties: black-back gull and herring-gull in England are distinct, non-cross-breeding good species. *But* as you go around the Northern hemisphere you find progressively less-black-backed bird populations, all of which interbreed; then you come right around to our no-black-backed-, or herring-, gull. There are "species", like dandelions, daisies and some lizards which don't employ sexual reproduction; so each *individual* is a separate species (or each very-genetically-different clone, more sensibly).

There is a pair of species, the swordtail (*Xiphophorus helleri* old name) and the platyfish (*Platypoecilus maculatus*), which all of us in the tropical-aquarium-fish hobby accepted as separate, good species even though they interbred quite happily to give fertile offspring (often more valuable as aquarium fish than the parents!). The swordtail males have a long sword-like prolongation of the lowest part of the tail fin, and swordtails grow to twice the length of platies – not eight times the weight, because platies are much plumper. There is no reason, looking at these two species and, say, their relative the Limia, why you would put them closer than two different *genera*, never mind species. And they *were* put in two genera, named *Xiphophorus* (the sword-bearer) and *Platypoecilus* (the plump live-young-producer), each of which had other species in it which *didn't* interbreed! But, unlike the situation with inter-fertile genera of potatoes, which botanists accept happily, genetical zoologists got very upset about these inter-fertile fish and made them one species, called by the older name *P. maculatus*. This really is daft, because *apart from their inter-fertility* these two really are very different biological organisms. Even if the inter-fertility shows that they "really" have very similar genetics, and developmental programmes come to that, to some of us it only shows how important little differences can be! After all, we now know that *Homo sapiens* and *Pan troglodytes (satyrus)*, the chimpanzee, have less than 1% average difference in their DNA! Each species has a wider internal range of DNA variation, by far, than this average difference. Yet I have not heard anyone propose that we're one species (the inter-breeding experiment is, I guess, unlikely to be tried.... ). These examples persuade me that there is no biological reason why we should not consider mankind to be differentiated into many cultural, and perhaps genetic, species; *not* to do so, in fact, unfairly excludes our close chimp cousins from our company ...

There are of course all kinds of persuasive political reasons *not* to call different branches of mankind's tree by such divisive labels as different species. I want here, though, to emphasise differences and I must get it clear that mankind, as "a species", is so diverse that generic names could be applied to distinguish the cattle-blood-and-milk-eating tall thin black Masai from the littler vegetarian Hindus and the plump fish-and-aquatic-mammal-feeding Inuit (Eskimo) – were it not that we can interbreed *genetically* perfectly successfully. Like the platies, however, it's our life-styles which are so different; I think we should ask, of the fish-hybrids (and perhaps of the potato-hybrids), whether they can survive in the "real world" outside aquaria (or greenhouses). If we can't easily imagine an intermediate life-style for crosses between Masai, Hindu, and Inuit this could confirm us in our generic differences. (What? Did I hear you say that pure examples of these peoples *wouldn't* interbreed anyway, because their ideas of sexual partners don't include each other? Well, our geneticist friends would be relieved to hear about these "cross-mating barriers", *usually* found in recently-differentiated species ... ). We *are*, biologically and for all political purposes, one species. In the town and the city like Hull, we have created a cultural ecology in which different kinds of people, with different ways of life but initially from the same cultural and genetic stock (from the surrounding towns and villages), fulfil different functions. As I have argued in the last chapter, this initially-culturally-homogeneous civic system, even though it promotes the affluence of all its members, becomes decadent. I'm now (and especially in the next chapter) going to contrast these different-function natives with different-culture foreigners, and I'm going to argue *as if* the latter are different cultural species, not liable to cross-breeding and assimilation.

There are a few places in the world where most cities really have drawn only upon local peoples; in parts of China, northern India, Ulan Bator in Mongolia, parts of Russia, some Scandinavian cities like Trondheim, perhaps Stockholm, even Aberdeen and Glasgow – although the mixture from which some of these latter cities drew their peoples was a richly mixed one! I chose Hull and Grimsby as my diversity-within-the-city examples above because both do seem to have grown mostly from local roots, yet to have become affluent – Hull, however, despite several large manufacturing industries, has been on the edge of my "decadence" for some years, and is I think just being rescued. Some multicultural cities owe their very existence to their site, at the junction of several cultures which have contributed from the start:  Vienna, Istambul, Beirut, perhaps Copenhagen – and Birmingham.

In most countries which are not on islands or peninsulas, then, cities draw foreigners as well as locals, for our good and sufficient reason: from *inside*, the deprivations, the boredoms of affluence are depressing. But from *outside* the affluence of the city is seen as eminently desirable and exploitable.

In all kinds of different cultural milieux and contexts, then, the apparently affluent life of the city attracts the indigent, the lazy, the barbarian – but also the homeless tribe, the plague survivors, the part of the feuding family which lost, the starving remnants of a great culture broken by drought or warfare. Look at our present city applicants, the shanty-towns around so many tropical cities, the slums in the temperate ones. There *are* excluded peasants from the land around, often in the majority and hoping for assimilation.   But there are also refugees from far away too, jealous of their own cultural heredity and anxious to retain it in the new circumstances.   In the city's workings, these refugees bring useful new skills and frequently make their place *above* the indigenous, un-assimilable  peasants who dominate the shanty-towns.  Sometimes, and a good example here is the tailoring trades in 1930s London, the aliens are seen as a recognisable, exploitable labour source;  but then, they specialised in the area where they were exploited, and took it over from the locals!

Affluence destroys the motivations of the city-dwellers, but excites that of the have-nots outside, both local peasants and foreign imports.  Local peasants are not as excited by it, because their skills are already used in the city, there is no place for them without competition with peers.   The indigenous workers are usually (*pace* Marx) too idle to revolt, and their jobs are taken by the more desperate foreign aspirants from outside.   These aspirants usually become incorporated into the life of the city, and their children go to the city's local schools.   This is the city's protection of its own culture (p.200).   So, although the foreigners provide a continuing input of new motivation and try to keep their culture, there is little effective cultural input because the city tries to paint any immigrant child in its own colour.  Adolescents and adults, too, have many social pressures on them to conform to local mores, and it takes a very stable cultural background to resist this.   Bus drivers in Wolverhampton may *look* black, but their culture is usually much the same as that of the white kids they grew up with – they sail under false colours.   In contrast, a Jewish or Cypriot child in the same schools, the same gangs, will usually have retained a characteristically different identity.

Mixing-up of cultures occurs in many ways:  in ports, by slavery, migrant workers, missionary zeal, and by oppressed populations finding sanctuary in liberal-because-affluent communities.   Often the invading barbarians, the conquering Normans or Spaniards, attempt to organise the affluent society to their pattern.   Such conquerors either provide educators, or frighten the local ones, to devalue the local culture so that what results is acceptable to the more powerful group.   Sometimes they fail, as classically in ancient China, which was said to have absorbed group after group of barbarian conquerors;  my interpretation of this is that the affluence could provide sufficient for the invaders, too, to become sated and therefore deprived – after deprivation, their children do not contribute to history!   There is frequently more mark left on history by an oppressed minority, after the cultural take-over, than by those who attempt to take over;   they may be confirmed in solidarity by the oppression, whereas the conquerors are encouraged to relax their own cultural patterns. Such minorities as the erstwhile Christian slaves in Rome, the discriminated-against Jews in early-twentieth century Germany and England, or Scots in England, all left more of a mark on the history of their countries than their mere numbers would have predicted; they were a yeast in the social mixture. Welcome migrants, filling a niche in the society, may well not leave much of a mark, like the Irish navigators who built the English canals (and left us the word "navvy") or the doctors from the Indian sub-continent who now fill so many hospital posts in the UK. Assimilation by loss of the specific cultural characteristics of the immigrants, be they conquerors, manual labourers or professionals, only gives more recruits to the downhill bicycle race towards apathy, decadence. Eventually their children swell the ranks of tribal or barbarian urban impotents.

Symbiosis between different kinds of human systems cannot begin by minimising differences, then. This follows the same pattern as previous symbioses: when the eukaryote cell appeared, the mitochondria, chloroplasts, nuclear structures did not lose their individual characters. The new, more competent, organism used their different abilities to expand its compound versatility. There is an interesting balanced symbiosis of marmots ("prairie-dogs") with rattlesnakes and owls, which live in their burrows; and it works well for the participants (even for the marmots, many of whose babies are eaten by the guests!). But there is no pressure towards a marttle-owl! In contrast, parasitic lengths of DNA from ancient viral invasions, which became assimilated into eukaryote genomes, left parts which still persist in the chromosomes of organisms as diverse as *Drosophila*, maize and mice and men. Although they may move genes about, the host organisms are not much changed by these assimilated life forms, even though they are assimilated most intimately, into the very DNA. On the other hand, *Drosophila* depends on peculiar simplified symbiotic bacteria to define that part of the egg which will become the germ cells; a very complicated co-operation occurs by which the mother's ovary assigns these bacteria to the "pole plasm". Female fruit flies which carry a mutant allele which prevents their doing this co-operation properly have normal-looking offspring – but these have *no* germ-cells and so are sterile because the special – integrated but not assimilated - symbionts were not cosseted properly. The mutant is called *gc-*, grandchildless! The message is that symbioses work by treasuring differences.

How can assimilation be prevented, allowing cultural heterogeneity to grow and be valued? Is there any possibility of human cultures, particularly civic cultures, allowing room for other cultures in their midst, for heterogeneity[8]?

This biologist would, for good Darwinian reasons, expect not. After all, the cultures we have are those which have most successfully resisted subversion, which have proven the best at incorporating the alien *without change to themselves*. The surviving cultures are those which were best at using what was most desirable of alien-culture techniques, both social and technical, but also best at rejecting the reproductive messages. In that sense the educational establishment could well be seen as the defender of each culture, recognising the alien, alternative cultural messages and cutting their reproductive lines. Reproductive stability of cultures, then, faces a paradox: each culture must defend itself against subversion from outside, while contriving that its "buds" can subvert effectively if transplanted. The Spanish Inquisition was a dramatic example of a clerisy doing this very effectively, even if not avowedly educational in purpose! Several other world religions have also become very effective memetic systems because they have got this right (in both senses; the Islamic Gulf States, and Iran, are excellent modern examples). In contrast, several Western cultures and some (brief!) cultures of history have attempted to allow free reign to alternative ways of skinning cats – they have all ended up being skinned themselves.

"Laisser faire" systems explicitly recognise the value of incorporating different value-systems; but they usually don't defend themselves, and so face subversion from within. In the affluent, decadent, falsely confident liberal society, however, this goes even further. There is a temptation to open the floodgates entirely: "Everyone's entitled to his opinion!", "Let them go to hell in their own way!", "The missionaries were the worst face of Christianity!", "Yes, you *can* hold the bat that way if you like.", "It's only fair to give the Creationists equal time in the schools with the Evolutionists!", "Ah, but you don't know that astrology isn't ruling our lives ....", and so on. Because we feel that we *could* be wrong, it seems somehow proper to let *everyone* else be right! I interpret this in a way which shouldn't surprise you, by now: I think that we have the cultural means to *deny* someone else's culture, but we don't have any approved cultural tricks for *accepting* someone else's ideas. We all feel obliged to argue against a new thought or a new proposition, and this conservatism is obviously a good, useful strategy in any culture – most new ideas *aren't* better than what we had before, of course. "Yes, you can integrate your life with ours, but only if you become like us" has always been the cry, but we (the Liberal Left, at least) now feel guilty about this. Other cultures, based on totally different themes, obviously do have rationality behind them. What we have done, though, is to let in all the silly, dangerous, nonsensical or subversive cults because we don't feel that discrimination is proper, from our little, one-history, experience of Social Truth. I am going to develop a rule for doing this, at the end of this book, to allow you not to give house-room to followers of Kali or the unwashed, and not to give headroom to scientologists, astrologers, or simple creationists; I even tell you how to recognise those who open more options, rather than offering culs-de-sac!

Because I am now approaching the climax of my argument, let me attempt an ordered recapitulation of the steps so far, less discursive than the attempt at the beginning of Chapter 11. This, then, is the bones of this biologist's social message, so far:

1. Man's innovation is reproduction of life style through *shared* cultural inheritance, each child receiving "privilege" from many adults of previous generations – hence "Privileged Ape".

2. Simple "tribal" forms of this (e.g. Eskimos, Tsembaga) can be eminently successful, and stable ecologically. That is why they're still here.

3. Simple " barbarian" forms (e.g. Norsemen, Mongols) could be success-ful predators or organisers, and apparently often formed stable systems with tribal agriculturalists.

4. Early technological affluence, resulting from the barbarian/tribal sym-biosis, gives the possibility of true citizenship, and this can enable cultural inheritance of more diverse kinds, specialisation to reduce competition and enrich each citizen's life. All citizens provide security for each, by division of labour, including police and educator functions.

5. This is not stable, for the specialised educators soon (possibly when common technology is beyond most of them) form "schools" (Illich) which renders formal education progressively less relevant to society, transmitting cultural privilege less and less faithfully. This loss of transmitter function arises because it is in the immediate political and personal interests of both pupils and teachers to drop standards (*set* by educator examiners and not then tested by doing, but by saying) and decrease the diversity of what is taught.

6. The technologically competent cadre, especially its "barbarian" ele-ments, then confirms its political power in the cities (e.g. contemporary UK, USSR, USA, even China); but technology brings affluence and apathy to the majority.

7. With more effective transport, different cultural modes rub shoulders. The first generation of immigrants to a city finds privation, stimulus and a new cohesion (ghetto-structure) in their new world. They may specialise into a new, useful function. But the further generations pass through the hands of the edu-cators, and their specific cultural inheritance is devalued, despised by the native "establishment". The parental generation see the educators as the local

"clerisy", respected members of the local establishment. They are thus robbed of their heritage, and salt is rubbed into the wounds of this deprivation by demonstrations (e.g. by Jensen) of their inferiority in the areas most respected – by the educators, whose standards they adopt in the mistaken impression that they are the universal standards of the culture. The educators have succeeded in defusing another invasion by foreign memes!

8.  The immigrants now compete for the same, narrow, educator-defined privileges and status as the natives, making a much more homogeneous and easy-to-teach school system;  this is a great loss to both immigrants and the native culture, for they could have complemented, instead of competing.

In the last chapters I ask whether there is a politically and individually viable route towards a society which values the differences among the cultures of its co-residents instead of destroying them.  Can we make a real symbiosis, working with cultures that have produced *either* intolerance or wet liberality, neither of which will serve our purpose?


## References

References in full are to be found from page 243 onwards. Below are listed names of authors and dates of publication.

1. Darlington (1969)
2. Boyden (1987)
3. Joysey (1984)
4. Serebriakoff (1987)

5. Harper, Rosen and White (1986)
6. Cohen and Massey (1984)
7. Bullivant (1987)
8. Modgil *et al* (1986)

# 14

# IMMIGRATION AND THE RISE OF THE MULTICULTURAL CITY

In these last chapters I must try to pick up all the questions I have left through the text, pick up the threads of my several arguments, and try to make clear my reasons for optimism. If you have been persuaded that there are suggestive similarities, at each advance in biological organisation, with the sequestration of the social group whose job has been to pass on our cultural heredity, my job is nearly done. If you are not persuaded that the educators have withdrawn from social involvement, or that they indeed are the group which has taken to itself the job of passing last generation's wisdom to next generation, and that this wisdom is the most valuable part of our inheritance, I have failed to persuade, or perhaps to communicate. If you are unsure of how much weight my biological analogies can carry into the social arena, we are together; I am unsure, too, and hope either that my points will carry because of their links with each other (independent of their foundation in biology) or that the links are there even if I haven't communicated them well.

I tried, at the end of the last chapter, to summarise the argument as a series of steps, leaving the affluent city receiving immigrants from different cultures and painting their children to match its own culture. I finished up by asking whether there was any route from here to heterogeneity, from competition to complementarity of cultures. I think there is, and that it's already happening in all the major, truly multi-cultural cities. But I think that if we don't see it in a biological way we will either discount it or feel threatened by it. When I first came to this conclusion it surprised me. So I tested it, because it seemed to bear on my social – and educational – philosophy. I have spent weeks in San Francisco, many odd days in New York City, three days in Tokyo, years in Birmingham, weeks in Hull (but I was at university there too, and some of my family live there), a few days in Sydney, Brisbane, Glasgow, San Diego and New Orleans, many days in London, asking questions of people in cafes, on the street, in bars, at school gates, at parties held by (usually biologist) friends to which they invite (often biology) teachers. I have been doing this since my tutorials (pp 126-7) in the 1970s, about 15 years. I have had several fights, but nothing serious, and people have been prepared to discuss, compare, criticise these ideas. I have not read nearly all the anthropology and sociology I should have, and I have not been to Africa or South America.

The picture I have achieved is a little different from the one I started with, which was much more like the African Lake parallelism example I describe below. The whole picture only took shape during a singing-for-my-supper world tour in 1986, and crystallised during my discussions with colleagues about my reasons for leaving the teaching profession yet remaining a professional biologist.

I choose a biological, rather than cultural, ecological example to illustrate the evolution of cadres, and the contrast with complementing cultures, in cities. This is a favourite evolution-in-action teaching example I've used for many years, the evolution of cichlid fishes in the African Rift Valley Lakes, and I must lay a bit of foundation for you. Cichlid fishes are advanced, perch-like (for Americans bass-like or sunfish-like) fishes, ranging from a couple of inches to about two feet in length, say from about half an ounce to forty pounds – quite a range. There are about 1,200 species (out of about 24,000 of all fishes), *not* counting all the ones in the African Lakes. All of them guard their eggs and babies, and most have a monogamous sexual choice system, both parents holding a territory in which the eggs are laid and the young are reared. However, in a large proportion, especially among those we will be considering in Africa, one parent holds the eggs and babies in its mouth for some weeks, starving the while. Some are exclusively vegetarian, eating only microscopic algae or scraping the leaves of water-plants or chomping whole plants including the roots; others are exclusively carnivorous, eating molluscs or sieving tiny crustaceans from the water or eating only other fishes. Some of the latter are specialised to a diet of the young of other fishes, which they get by sucking them out of their parent's mouth; yet others have specialised to a diet of other fish's eyes, or scraped-off scales, or tail fins. Still others grub about on the muddy bottom, passing large quantities of mud through their digestive systems (like earthworms or sea-cucumbers) and getting a small proportion of nutrient from it. The above list of food habits describes what they do in the wild – in aquaria they mostly eat prepared commercial fish food!

So what is so special about the Rift Valley Lakes? We will just consider three, Victoria (about 0.5-1 million years old), Nyasa (Malawi, 2-3My) and Tanzania (Tanganyika, 5-10My). Lakes do not form suddenly, even in a Rift Valley (unless we make them, as at Kariba). They are formed of backing-up rivers, pools, natural dams which change their connections and isolations over a long period. In these lakes and river systems nearly all of the original fishes were cichlids (others have been introduced, see below). There are several very common, rather generalised river species which, we know from comparative anatomical and some fossil evidence, are the evolutionary origins of the "species flocks" in each of the Lakes. There are about 750 species in Victoria, all probably descended from one species like the commonest riverine one today (*Haplochromis burtoni*). These differently-specialised forms will often interbreed in tanks, but apparently don't in the wild (see the discussion about what we mean by species on pp195-6). On the same criteria there are about 2000 species in Malawi, and nearly 3000 in Tanganyika.

The interesting thing to us is the remarkable parallelism in the three lakes: all of them have the standard fish and algae eaters, but all also have fish species specialised to a diet of eyes, or of fins, or of other fish's babies. Each of the lakes started with a *different* founder species (or several in Tanganyika) yet all have produced much the same ecological spread. There are even little black-to-blue forms with three broad gold longitudinal lines in each lake, whose bony structures reveal that they have evolved from quite different forebears. Biologists call this parallel evolution, and the species which so resemble each other (but with very different histories, different ancestors) are called "convergent". I could have used the better-known parallels between marsupial mammals and the eutherians, in Australia and North America, but I prefer the enclosed lake-environment to compare with the cities. Then I can compare the more primitive cichlid fish stocks, still in the rivers which run into the lakes, with market towns and peasantry around the cities.

Cities, in my comparison here, should be thought of as like these Lakes, centralisations of the ecology. Within such centralisations, new competitions and new opportunities spur differentiation of the stocks, producing complication of the ecology and stability of the overall system. For me, this cichlid convergence story parallels the production of the various urban posts (policemen, teachers, priests, engineers, poets and so on) from Frenchmen in Paris, Germans in Frankfurt, Scots in Aberdeen. There always were a few species of catfish in the rivers as well as cichlids, when they found themselves in the young lakes. Equally, different cultures were included as minorities in the young cities, and like the minority catfish, could have had their specialities set up from the start: Jewish enclaves may have had a disproportionately large financial role, Chinese in restaurants, and so on. The African Rift Lakes are mostly cichlid-dominated, though, just as nearly all cities are dominated by the mass of indigenes. This is the expectation, indeed, of most of the indigenes themselves. The average Parisian still expects his service engineer, his waiter, his boss and his mistress to be French, I think. Certainly, from what we read (and so far as I could see in three days walking about and talking with people!) the Japanese expect their cities, their urban lives, to be Japanese right through.

Foreigners are "outside", still (again, though, I could well have missed other Orientals – but I did *ask*, and I was usually with another biologist, a local).

The African Lake cichlids are atypical, and show a very young evolutionary ecology, even in Lake Tanganyika. In older bodies of water, different fish families, or even sub-orders, show the different ways of life: barbs or characins swim in the open water, catfishes and loaches grub on the bottom, lung-fishes and cichlids eat snails and clams. A variety of families has produced fish-eaters, all with different tricks: stalking, rapid swimming, darting, camouflage and the quick gulp, a speciality of fishes like the pike.

In most complex symbioses of this number of diverse species, like coral reefs or tropical rain-forests, even savannah, there are *very* different kinds of organisms filling the different niches. It is very rare, indeed, in biological ecology to find versatile organisms *of the same basic kind* having ways of life that impinge on each other, that compete even a bit (remember that all the Lake cichlids eat fish food, given the chance!). It is usual for "contiguous niches" to be occupied by very differently specialised organisms, not ones that are *nearly* the same. The well-known exceptions, Darwin's finches, the species of *Dendroica* warblers that have specialised into the different niches a tree provides, the fruit flies of Hawaii – and the African cichlids – are all famous, useful teaching examples, because they show evolution *in process*; it hasn't settled down to an efficient system yet.

Actually, there is some alarm among evolutionary ecologists, because other very different species have recently been introduced into the African lakes, often by local people wishing to increase the commercial worth of the crop (but usually having the opposite effect, see p114). It is what happens then that is most illuminating for our comparison: as soon as real specialists in algal feeding, bottom-grubbing or even a clever kind of predation come along, the cichlid "amateurs" lose out to the newcomers. Specialised as the cichlids appear to our eyes, especially in comparison to all their cousins with different specialities, they are all just "cichlids" as far as a real specialist like a catfish is concerned. A catfish has a very long evolutionary history of specialising for bottom-grubbing; he is a match, *at that trick*, for any cichlid, with his special sense-organ whiskers, his special uncloggable gills, his loss of air-bladder, his armour against leeches and all the other tricks catfish have now. He has these *to start with*, as soon as he finds himself in the new lake environment! It is not at all surprising that introduced catfish displace cichlid bottom-grubbers, or that specialised characin streamlined piscivores displace the cichlid who is only better than *other cichlids* at being a fish-eater! So, too, in my comparison the Indian businessman displaces the locals in Fiji, and in

East Africa; the Jewish businessman displaced the German; the Italian or Chinese restaurant displaced the English café, and the Cypriot fish-and-chip shop displaces most of the others in the English Midlands.

These latter may seem the most trivial of examples, but are excellent first steps towards true multi-racialism *without* assimilation. After a while, the Parisian expects the occasional Chinese meal, even the Bostonian accepts the Chinese laundry. In England today many junior hospital doctors seem to be Asian, most bus drivers West Indian (Caribbean). Unfortunately, these rather less prestigious societal niches have often been filled by the obviously foreign, "coloured" applicant, because colour is a convenient marker of the alien for the locals. Originally, there may be exploitation (but see the next chapter), as with Jewish immigrants being used in tailoring establishments, "sweat-shops", in London's East End in the '30s; they had taken over three-quarters of the trade in the '50s!. It is interesting to me that the junior hospital doctor post, the bus-driver job, are by no means bottom-end in status *now* – both positions carry great responsibility and above-average wages/salary, and high status in the re-spective communities. There are very many indigenes who would not aspire to these heights[1], like the local peasants in circum-city shanty-towns.

I am not very convinced about the multicultural basis of this situation, though. A little investigation frequently reveals that the apparent heterogene-ity denoted by the colour actually is unreal: these people are often "sailing under false colours"! Their culture owes more to Bradford schools, then Middlesex Hospital Medical School, or to a Tipton junior school and a Wolverhampton Comprehensive education. They are assimilated persons, who have lost much of their rich cultural heritage and become cloaked in the drab gray of English lower-middle-class. How much more exciting, for all of us, and how much more fulfilling for them, if they could come back in the evenings to the richer, more colourful intimacy of their fellows-in-culture instead of *Coronation Street* and the sullen muttering of frustrated children who have not found joy at school or in the home. To some extent, the Indian sub-continent or Caribbean immigrant to England or America has already made a commitment to our culture, and has often, if not usually, cut ties with the old ways. When they arrive, they usually don't wish to get into the ghettoes but actually try to assimilate quickly; studies of this phenomenon[1], at least in Australia, agree that it is not unitary. Different cultures differ in this too. Islamic commitments are not easily lost by the Asiatics, for example, and these can draw them into contact with ghetto life, and hold them there. Even the Islamic children are too often seduced by the apparently richer MacDonald's culture, however, and they then take a pale imitation of indigenous routes.

The Irish Catholic, the Jew and the Sikh have to some extent retained their culture in exile. So have Poles and some Chinese families, but less obviously. San Francisco is a city whose verve is said to be derived, not from the mixture of races, but from the presence of many different immiscible full-blooded cultures (and many people with little recognisable culture at all!). To some extent, indeed, this *is* only appearance, in San Francisco or indeed Birmingham. They may look like Poles or Chinese to the indigenes, or wear turbans or other un-Western garb, but the culture they have over here, or in San Francisco, is very little like what their friends and family do back home. If it was, they wouldn't be here – when they do go back, they are "our English relatives", remember. The Greek restaurant owner, no less than the Scottish gynecologist, is branded as alien if he attempts to go back to his "home-land" after two generations abroad. Recall the British who came back from the British Raj in India, how different they were even though they had been running a little sub-culture, "more English than the English", for generations. It may be in this case, and possibly in some others, that the home-land had changed more than the ex-patriates. That last is certainly true for some groups: the Japanese, called Sansei, third generation in California; East German families who came out to set up restaurants or steel factories in Cleveland, Ohio in the early thirties; New Zealanders who come "back" to Scotland after the family has been gone for eighty years.

It's really a bit like the argument-to-ancestry (p65); just as in the case of the man-like ancestor of the apes or the ape-like ancestor of man, we wouldn't know whether the ex-patriate or his cousins who remained have changed more. Whether he or his cousins more closely resemble the culture which he left must differ from case to case. Indeed, because human societies all change, and some of the changes are going on in both places, there is built-in evolutionary convergence. There is another way in which this emigrant situation is misleading, nearly always: we fail to present our culture in its entirety; when we're among aliens, we edit. We don't, in fact, behave as we do at home. The Caribbean bus driver and the Indian doctor *try* to be English in their roles in English society. Perhaps they are indeed more "ethnic" when they get home to the family! Some of our roles depend upon "fitting in", painting ourselves indigene-coloured, but others require that we emphasise our special other-cultural characters. Just as we develop special faces when we're growing up, for home, for school, for lovers, and special accents and styles, so we all have a special *foreign* face – or several of them. If your trade depends on your behaving "properly" Chinese, too, then you exaggerate those characters your host culture thinks of as Chinese, whether *you* do or not. Equally, if those

Jewish characters are the things you believe got the Germans all steamed up in the twenties, you'd be unlikely to parade them in modern Berlin!

If we actually can't get the *genuine* culture from ex-patriates then why, you may wonder, am I making such a fuss about keeping it "pure"? Why does it matter that it might get painted over, taken over by the indigenous educators? Because I believe that the multi-racial society is nevertheless more interesting, more able and more stable than the unitary, assimilated culture – even if its exotics are a little bogus or a little over-painted or painted-over. That's why.

To the extent that local "education" has replaced exotic culture and substituted the local standards, ambitions, and abilities all the parties concerned have lost. A new competitor has appeared, whose complementary abilities have been lost; the indigenous (English) Bradford secretary whose job has been taken by a (local) Sikh blames the Sikh, who had nothing to do with it – his *parents* brought him over. He should blame the educational system, which in the name of anti-racialism turned the potential young Sikh into a Bradford lad, competing with indigenes for jobs. The fire and colour of West Indian culture has largely been replaced by a hopeless quest for Jensen-esque equality; the sari has largely been replaced by the Marks and Spencer's blouse and skirt; it would not surprise me to hear that the muezzin has been replaced by a tape recorder and loudspeakers. The loss is literary, artistic and technical, both to the indigenous culture and to the assimilating culture's children. This is mostly because the replacement culture must always be at a low, "pidgin", level: the cultural basis of the indigenous culture is not there in the stranger's home; the kids don't have *my* picture of Little Red Riding Hood (still less do they have the original English one). It takes several generations for the indigenous myths to take hold in the stranger's house, so that the children have an indigenous cultural base on which to build. But until that happens, the acceptance of local culture by alien children must be very superficial. Sometimes I wake up at night, truly, trembling at the thought of the replacement of the Kama Sutra and other Hindu love tracts (and courtesy-between-sexes stories), the lovely way this knowledge passes between the generations in some Hindu societies ... with *True Love Stories*, or Mills and Boon books! These railway-station snippets are perfect in their way, beautifully adapted to catch and inculcate the adolescent Bradford boys and girls. They work well with adolescents who are the heirs of a culture that included chivalry, Shakespeare, Victoriana and Empire, then rationing and utility furniture, Cindy dolls and Monty Python. The Bradford culture has all the little unconscious hooks that the names and situations of the Mills and Boon books hang on to. But the first-generation Hindu in Bradford has very few of these, and can only pick up this bit of culture at the most superficial level.    And the Hindu girl has not her extended family to instruct her in her own culture's myths and manners, nor the books, nor (usually) the language(s).    So she picks up only the "pidgin" level of our culture, and we all lose.

Why doesn't the system simply "add", you may ask.    Why must the Sikh lose his ancient stories and prescriptions, proscriptions if he goes to a Bradford school?    Why should the young Hindu girl get her tips on flirting only from *True Love Stories*;    why can't she have intimate conversations with her unmarried aunts as she would have done in Delhi?    There are two separate answers to this, both rather depressing.    Firstly, there seems to be a kind of "Gresham's Law" about culture: just as with money, bad culture chases out good!    It actually is much more fascinating for the Sikh children to watch *Coronation Street* or *Dallas* on the telly.    It also has the social advantage that they can talk about them at school the next day.    These programmes *are* superbly made social documentaries, with a real moral purpose and a real place in our present culture.    They are the modern technological Mills and Boon!    It is, I think, totally wrong to dismiss them as "trank pills", chewing-gum for the eyes (lovely phrase, not original to me).    *East-Enders*, a modern television soap-opera about (nearly) multicultural London working-class life, exposes urban life, for the first-generation alien parents, in a much clearer way than any number of courses in "The English Way of Life" at evening classes!    The local cultural system inevitably attracts the young teenagers, and if they have grown up watching *East-Enders* they are probably acceptable to the adolescent gangs, in school and outside, as impressionable material.    This is particularly so because these programmes *show* assimilated people of their own kind, taking part;    indeed part of their moral message is that it's a good idea to get assimilated into the culture – "You've come here to live, after all, haven't you, Achmed?".

More insidious, however, is that the very lax, *secure* culture of *Coronation Street* or *East-Enders*, the grey-painted indigenes and their grey-painted "coloured" (but often indigenous too) friends is in such deep contrast to the constraints of the embarrassingly "foreign" home life.    It has always been very difficult for all of us, but especially juveniles, to act in defiance of an accepted peer group cultural norm[1,2.]    It is very emotionally rewarding for these initially-foreign children to have some of the catch-phrases, the in-group language, gained from last night's episode of what all the locals watched.    I saw this very clearly among university students: if there is nothing attractive to weigh against a socially-acceptable but low-value activity, that activity is of course pursued.    "Leave that f... essay, come out for a drink with us!" is enormously binding on our actions. Most university students find it irresistible, because they have nothing to put in the other balance-pan – perhaps if they were paying for themselves at university, they might think "Add £5 for the tuition fees I'm wasting" and choose not to go – but I doubt it.

The foreign kids really want to behave like their school-friends, and at that age it's very difficult to maintain a deep secret different-cultural life which has few rewards. It was for us, in the East End of the late forties, when nearly everyone we *knew* was Jewish, to differing extents, and it was very much a ghetto situation (we had not taken the walls down from the *inside*, yet). It was difficult for me at school, at swimming-baths, in the tropical-fish-breeding circles, even at the cinema, to feel that the concerns of the synagogue, the dietary laws, getting home in time for prayers, was valued by the people I respected. Some do it, nevertheless, and their culture-in-exile is both strengthened and changed thereby.

However, the second reason for the failure of imported culture is much simpler, more "mechanical" and even more devastating than the "Gresham's Law" of culture: there has always been a break in the cultural tradition. Even if our young Sikh friend comes to Bradford and goes to the local Sikh Temple, it's a different one, one infected by the local mores to some extent, even if only that it has central heating and draught-excluders. He must see his relations, his elders in the culture, compromising a bit with local conditions, and it is very difficult for him to see why he should not. The problem with our Hindu girl is much simpler, much less quantitative: there *are* no unmarried aunts about for her to hear stories from. Even if there are relatives in somewhat that relationship, they won't be leading the kind of life (often semi- or total prostitution, we're told, in Delhi – how else can they contribute to the family budget?) that makes them expert on matters sexual. We do things differently here, after all, and any aunt can probably only tell English-city stories, or pass on obviously inappropriate stories from *her* youth. There is, of course, the nurse, or the family-planning doctor; but they can only give local advice, mostly warnings, and cannot provide expertise in sexual relations, if that is what the girl seeks from them. Local boys, however, are only too anxious to oblige, and little of the Hindu survives that interaction.

Everything seems to be stacked against the maintenance of foreign sub-cultures in cities, then. How have the sub-cultures which *are* successful survived these two problems? Firstly, I think, by being discriminated *as* different, usually discriminated against; that results in the feelings and behaviours of mutual support which are well developed, *and make us feel rewarded*, in all cultures. So external discrimination adds points for the ex-patriate culture, because the support behaviour usually gets high status marks from the outside, indigenous culture, too.   When Sir Oswald Moseley's following held anti-Jewish meetings at Ridley Road market, even after the '39-'45 war, those of us Jewish kids who went along, shouted and scuffled, were always helped by police, by shop-keepers, in ways we'd never have deserved without those fights – and when you met these people later, they told you what had happened before the war with Moseley's gangs, and you gained acceptance and status. You felt, then, that you were valued *because* of your difference, not despite it. There have recently been some equivalent scuffles with other ex-patriate groups, or identifiable aliens, in much this way, and they have produced the stories, parables, myths for their sub-cultures.   (Note that I use "myth" in the anthropological sense[2,3,] referring to meaningful, usually prescriptive stories, which may *or may not* be based on historical fact – Lesko[2] has a dramatic description of the Challenger disaster evolving, in the space of 12 hours media treatment, from news item to myth.)   *That* is, I think, the most important part of the Ridley Road episodes for me; I can tell you this story, but I can also re-live it with my friends who were there, and pass it on to my children.   The foreign cultures come over here with a full pack of their old myths, mostly of little immediate interest to their juveniles, who are quickly immersed in their new culture (not least because of mandatory schooling).  The juveniles slowly acquire a set of new ones. Without doubt, the quickest way to accumulate them is to be persecuted – but the costs are usually considered too high;  there are benefits, but they are longer-term and abstract.   They will not be chosen over risks of mutilation and death as xenophobia mounts.    More realistically, elected representatives will not find myth-provoking dangers vote-catching so will promote tolerance (and its bed-fellow assimilation), rather than ghetto-production and the integration of new, strong complementary cultures into the city's structure[1,2.]

The successfully integrated cultures we have in British cities are the results of historic myth-productions at least as much as locally-produced discrimination. The most fruitful of these was the Nazi holocaust, for Poles and Russians as well as Jews. In Israel, of course, those myths arising from the holocaust threatened to take over the whole culture in the fifties, but have now been generally superseded by tales from the successive Arab-Israeli wars. There are few modern myths as potent as Entebbe, are there?  That action has been well-documented and exhibited by the media, too, so it serves as myth for other cultures. It has taken its place with Shane. I believe the whole modern Israeli society to be as strong as it is because of the rich diversity of myths upon which it is built;  it is as different from the old ghetto-Jewish society as is possible in our world.  Yet, and very informatively, that very ghetto-society is included in modern Israel as a viable sub-culture – it even finds, indeed provokes,  the persecution it needs for its own maintenance in the new anti-ghetto, anti-religious Israeli society!  The many other cultures in Israeli society have peculiar status too;  for Israel, in my view, is an *urban* stratified society with many cadres extending over the whole country.  Kibbutzim, moshavim are ways of making a good ("family") business out of (intensive) agriculture, while benefitting by economies of scale.  All the cultures find their place as in a great city, not as in an ancient agricultural community at all;  the cities don't feel to me different from the communal farms, and kibbutzim are a *city* trick, not a tribal, agricultural one!

The Soviet take-over of Hungary produced a rich set of myths, which have settled in among the complex set carried by Hungarian ex-patriates everywhere.  These Hungarian sub-cultures in other societies, like many with roots in central Europe, carry some of their myths as aphorisms, as jokes, available to de-fuse present passion.  The late George Mikes analysed and exposed many English myths in *How to be an Alien*[4] and flavoured it with many Hungarian ones.  The wry wisdom exhibited in this book, and its successors about other cultures and sub-cultures (especially *How to scrape skies*, about Americans) is one of the best public expositions of sub-culture maintenance.  That it is very funny demonstrates one of our major de-fusing mechanisms – and increases the pleasure of learning from it!

The *other* recent holocaust, the virtual destruction of the Ibo peoples by, among others, their fellow Nigerians the Yoruba and the Hausa (the "Biafran Wars"), has not contributed to our myths at all.  The media coverage here, as I recall, was of the "African tribes murdering each other again" variety, with comments that news was difficult to come by in a war zone.  Certainly the number of people who died was comparable with the Nazi killings, yet even the Ibo themselves have not found it a rich source of stories;  all concerned, even the Yoruba, seem to need to put that history behind them.  There are, of course, many persecutions in all histories (but England has less than most).  Few, however, have been as well-documented, from all sides, as that shame-provoking three hundred years of slavery of the African blacks in the Southern States of America.  This was a break in cultural reproduction, for each of the people taken from villages, towns, cities in Africa and dumped, after grotesque treatment, on the shores of the New World.  Some of their re-established cultures have been ones of which the rest of us are not proud: Haiti, the Rastafarians, some of the more naive Hot Gospel-ing peoples, are something of the kind of culture we might have expected to rise from the ashes of slavery.

But *Jazz*? That whole musical tradition, *and* the strange version of Christianity it was embedded in, has changed everybody's life, all over the globe, and has overwhelmingly enriched rather than degraded the older cultures it has invaded. Its roots were in misery, in poverty, often in degradation, but its flower stands tall with, and as part of, Man's finest cultural triumphs.

Some of the inter-cultural politics which inform this book, and nearly all of our thoughts about racism, about differences, about one culture living and giving freely within the bounds of a host culture, come through Martin Luther King and those who have been continuing his work. That philosophy also derives from black slavery in America, or more accurately to the subsequent dialogue about it. The Black Experience, as we are learning to call it, has become part of all cultures, as widely spread as the Jewish Experience (or at least the Woody Allen version of it). Black myths, Jewish myths, even the mythical myths of our destruction of the Neanderthal peoples as invented by William Golding[5] and Jean Auel[6] enable us to relate to other peoples, other cultures. They provide a common set of myths for the older city culture and the immigrant sub-cultures. Further, because these myths are "larger" than those of our little sub-cultures, they enable us to shelter together under the umbrella of a larger vision of Man. There is the seed of hope in this larger vision, rooted in the grand myths we share.

Nearly all of the sub-cultures I now associate with have acquired this larger vision. Because people have nearly all gone on foreign holidays, even if only coach tours or cruises; because people's work, even the most mundane, entails working with Islamics, or Hindus, or Wolverhampton lads of Caribbean stock; because our boss may be Japanese, our secretary may be Jewish; because your work-force, Ibrahim, may be Welsh miners' wives; because of all these, in Europe especially, we see ourselves as part of a very heterogeneous "world culture". Surprisingly at first sight, both Russia under Gorbachov and the new People's Republic of China seem to me to be more open to these internationalist ideas than is the United States under Reagan. The USA is in a peculiar position; it seems to have "contained" the problem (as most Americans saw it) of having such a mixture of immigrants. These have mostly now called themselves Americans, and indeed America is the great assimilation culture in many respects. It is very unwilling to take any value-in-difference political stance, however, because most Americans are not very willing to talk about its great social experience, slavery. Although assimilation, all-Americans-together against the foe, is the usual stance there are some cities which are paraded as "multicultural". San Francisco is supposed to be the great "melting-pot" city; well, yes, but how many of its cultures actually *reproduce* there? The Chinese one does, through that beautiful Chinese High School – but the Germans and Italians all seem to have been born in the mid-West, the Poles come from the East coast (all the ones I found came from New Jersey, with cousins in Minnesota), the Hungarians came from ... Hungary, the Californians came from Los Angeles and Monterey, the Japanese and Koreans I couldn't understand well enough to find out more than that. But I certainly *didn't* find a great metropolis of reproducing cultures, as I had been led to expect. Even Hangzhou, in the People's Republic of China, had peoples of different origins, Mongols, Southerners, black people from the far West, in its crowded suburbs; they were all talking different languages and eating different foods – and with dwellings whose different styles were apparent even to my occidental eye! I *think* they breed their cultures there, but my culture is too far from theirs, still, for me to tell. My guess, though, is that I may come to feel "of one people" (a Mongolian woman's phrase to me) with them again, easier and probably earlier than I will do it with Californian strangers in San Francisco. I got the strongest feeling that the people of different cultures *there* were visitors, like me; they did not reproduce their cultures there, and all were far from their cultural roots except the San Francisco Chinese.

I have been arguing that a real multicultural society, with the different cultures supplying different kinds of people into the complexity of the city – Chinese restaurants, Cypriot fish-and-chip shops, Japanese-run factories, English playwrights and policemen, Irish publicans (I invent wildly) – is not only desirable and possible, but almost here. Birmingham, New York, Hangzhou are beginning to show this kind of structure, and politicians in many countries are taking actions to promote multiculturalism. Sometimes these actions promote capitalism, sometimes socialism, but there is a strong de-centralising movement in Russia, China, Eastern US, even Argentina and Brazil, and recently in the UK autocracy.

This is the time of decisions. If our cities *are* becoming multi-cultural, if we are beginning to value *differences* in culture, how can we take steps to foster this for our children and for their children? Should we? If we believe in the "Invisible Hand" of Adam Smith, we can sit back and let "market forces" do the deciding for us; equally, if we believe that Little Green Men from Arcturus II have been watching over Earth, we can leave the deciding to them (I incline to the latter rather than the former, as you'll see). But who will transmit the values of the multicultural city? Surely not *us*? Most of the readers of this book will probably be "soft liberals" – like me – of the kind I've been deploring; many of you will be teachers, or otherwise in the educational system. Do we want only our liberal, top-of-the-head, namby-pamby, internationalism-with-

out-guns to be taught to our children?  I fear that this is the perfect recipe for
the meek inheriting the Earth ...  Fine, but how long will they keep it?  The
Israelis, or the Japanese, will take it away from us, not by force but by effectiveness; effective selling, or take-over of our services, supplies or customers
– or the Israelis just by saying "Boo!".  Who can run such an enterprise, the
multicultural city in a multicultural world?  The British *nearly* ran one for a
long time, but only by keeping all the bits apart.  The British Empire did, to
a greater extent than any since Genghis Khan and Rome, foster its sub-cultures
– but only because the English sahib was always there on top, keeping the
natives down.  The international consensus is, I am sure, that we did it better
than the Spanish or the French – whatever "better" means in that connection.
But I do not, indeed, propose to give the running of multicultural cities to
English aristocrats, or German organisers, or Italian politicians, or Japanese
paternalism.

   I want to do what I have done all along, to look at *what is actually happening
successfully*, to learn from the biology of the real world[1,2,3,7].  Because this is
at the highest level of complexity reached by life so far, because indeed it is at
the top level of the "morphostat" concept invented by Serebriakoff in *Brain*,
the "sociozoon"[8], I cannot use lower-level examples, among animals especially, but even in simpler cultures, to point our way.  There was no way to
search among the proto-mitochondria, proto-centrioles, proto-chloroplasts to
see the future plan of the developed eukaryote cell with its nucleus.  There was
no way to look at the early multicellular eukaryotes to see which bit would
become the germ-cell line; *Drosophila*'s special bacteria to mark them was,
I'm sure, unpredictable.  However, this is cultural evolution, introspective if
not predictive evolution, and perhaps we have much more of a chance to see
where we're going.  My tactic is to look and interpret, to spot the sociozoon
in our future.  I have to look and see what works *now* in this kind of system,
if I'm right that we have achieved general rules for evolutionary jumps by
symbiosis.  You may have different answers here, because your experience is
different from mine, and I'd like to look at a lot of answers because I know my
experience is inadequate too.  All my experience as a reproductive biologist,
though, tells me that we are about to take a step up by cultural symbiosis, and
that a new hereditary system is emerging, and will take us all in a new direction.
I can even guess what it is.  That's what the last chapter is for.

# References

References in full are to be found from page 243 onwards. Below are listed names of authors and dates of publication.

1. Bullivant 1987
2. Lesko (1988)
3. Malinowski (1963)
4. Mikes (1959)

5. Golding (1964)
6. Auel (1980)
7. Boyden (1987)
8. Serebriakoff (1987)

# 15

# CULTURAL SYMBIOSES CAPTURE THE FUTURE – THE NEW CLERISY

This book is in many ways a celebration of symbiosis. This last chapter picks up, expands and weaves this thread into a pattern which I trust includes all those elements you found interesting in my previous chapters.

My crucial point about biological symbioses of all kinds has been that they involve disparate biological organisms – or cultures. Advantage to the partners is achieved by retaining these differences and capitalising on them, not by minimising them: the very different prokaryotes which co-operated to make our eukaryote cells, the algal cells in the cells of *Hydra*s or giant clams, the fungus and the alga which combine to form the amazingly hardy lichen, the bacteria and protozoa in the cow's rumen, the myriad partners on the coral reef or in the rain-forest all live more successfully because their adaptations include other, very different organisms. Difference is promoted, too, in the Lake ecologies exploited by the cichlid fishes – adaptation in different directions permits less competition, more stable exploitation of food sources. This must be a generality about symbioses, and the thought behind it is very similar to that behind all specialisations, ecological and social. Biologists used to call this the "division of labour". Adam Smith used the same term, I believe.

The Bloomsbury Group, at the root of English Socialism, saw clearly that the different roles in society were symbiotic. They pinned their hopes for the future firmly on "political pluralism", *not* equality. Indeed they hoped for two representative bodies, "political" and "social", representing bankers, engineers, even housewives[1]. Marx had clearly seen that the different elements of affluent society were complementary[2]; what he inveighed against was *exploitation*. (He would have enjoyed, I think, George Mikes' comment on Capitalism *versus* Peoples' Socialism: "In the former, one group of people exploits another; but in the latter, it's the other way round!".)

The concept of exploitation is a difficult and dangerous one, very relevant for the acquisition of symbiosis for organisms *and* cultures. Many reproductive biologists even see males as "exploiters" of the females' investment in production, fuelling, and care of *their* offspring. There is clearly a sense in which this is so, and many kinds of organisms have lost sexuality and thereby freed themselves of that exploitation. Such all-female animals are very successful, at least in the short-term[3], although it is not clear that they can keep up in the evolutionary arms race with their parasites or produce diverse offspring for patchy ecologies[4]. Indeed, we still do not have a general answer to the biological question "Why is sexuality so widespread and so successful?"[4]. (It is clear enough that there *are* advantages, so that I can even imply a similar – but unknown – advantage to cultural recombination, by exchange of verbal children, on p 57).

The "exploitation" of parents by offspring, or of females by males, is a measured use of the word. Between animals of different species, the issues are usually clearer, but symbiosis muddies the water. We would not, I think, speak of either the alga or the fungus in the lichen as an "exploiter" of the other. We might think that it was a bit unfair of the coral, or the *Hydra*, to keep the algal cells in its tissues, take photosynthesised food from them and even digest them sometimes. But these algal cells do benefit by the light-seeking mobility of the *Hydra*, or the coral's calcium/phosphorus metabolism. The cow's rumen bacteria *exploit* the cow's grass-seeking-and-processing mechanisms, after all, don't they? This is, I think, a fair alternative description to "The cow exploits its bacteria to enable it to digest grass."; don't you agree?

There are, of course, many between-species associations which genuinely are exploitation, at least in the early evolutionary stages. We call this parasitism. Such parasites harm the hosts less, of course, as evolution proceeds, both because they regulate their demands and because the hosts adapt to their presence. Zoology students were always surprised by how many parasites are *normally* carried by wild sticklebacks (the commonest small fish in small British ponds); a fair proportion of the little fishes have more than thirty easily-findable species, and in some apparently healthy sticklebacks a quarter of the weight is well-adapted parasites! Most of "our" harmful parasites, like the sleeping sickness organism *Trypanosoma*, tapeworms, most roundworms, do us damage because they are not primarily "our" parasites. We and our domestic animals catch them from their natural hosts, who generally are not much bothered by them; the *Trypanosomes* live harmlessly in eland and other game animals in Africa, and harm (immigrant) cattle when they are transmitted to them by tse-tse flies. A few kinds of African cattle are already less troubled by sleeping sickness, I understand. This is the common history of biological symbioses, with early pathology succeeded by degrees of tolerance (commensalism), often followed by the establishment of dependence in *both* directions (mutualism).

This progression surely occurs in cultural evolution too. I have rehearsed a story of early barbarians "parasitising" tribal agriculturalists, then the two cultures coming to accept each other as the barbarian conquerors became protectors (p 73).    I am sure you can see where I'm going: can the immigrant cultures of affluent cities, which are always seen initially as foreign parasites, be brought to such a mutualism?

Mexicans coming into California, Pakistanis coming into England, even Pommie Englishmen coming into Australia now, are usually seen as parasites on the affluence of the host country, taking from the indigenes what is rightfully theirs.    In the affluent cities, this is often initially the pool of free hand-outs;  but resentment mounts as the second-generation immigrants "take jobs from" the indigenes.    I have a nice cartoon of a pair of well-dressed Asian young men, passing by a gang of resentful, smoking and drinking, English layabout youngsters;  one Asian is saying to the other "I don't know what they're complaining about, we're only taking the jobs *they* don't want – doctors, lawyers, accountants..... "!    This is seen as the immediate and urgent social problem where affluence, immigration, and cultural decadence meet, and the question usually asked is "What can we do do about it?".    I think we should welcome it, in a very special way (see below) because it holds the symbiotic solution to the other problem of the affluent city.

This other problem is decadence itself, the breakdown of the vital life of the cities as they become affluent.    Then tribalism and barbarism take over from responsible citizenship, in the new richer ecology, with the city's capital to live off or to exploit.    That leaves the city centres destroyed, and the suburbs un-interesting.    If, then, we could foster an appreciation of the foreigner as a source of pleasures rather than competition, we might begin to make the city's life more complex as an ecology, therefore with more rewards and pleasures both for the indigenes and the immigrants.    This has begun, as we've seen.    Chinese restaurants, Cypriot fish-and-chip shops, American hamburger chains, other "ethnic" restaurants, even the humble delicatessen have changed the eating habits of most Western citizens.    The importation of foreign foods, especially fruits in Western cities, has been proceeding profitably for many centuries.    It has added variety *without* the embarrassment of the foreigner in our midst;  in the street markets of British cities, "barrow-boys" selling fruit are usually aggressively local.    Imports of Japanese and Korean domestic electronics are only tolerated, I suspect, because there is similarly no foreign-cultural connec-tion.    They are sold in "our" shops.

There is relief mixed with considerable resentment, however, when these same Far Eastern businesses set up their factories in the consumers' own country.    There is often relief because the Eastern businessman will choose areas of high unemployment;  but there is resentment because the "business methods" of the Far East look remarkably like exploitation to the ineffective poorly-educated Western adolescent. This is seen to be more like the biology of the predator than of the symbiont! The effective business methods of the West Germans, especially the Japanese but even the Americans are definitely seen as predatory by many British "working-class" adolescents and their trades unions (from the vantage of the city-nest security, "hawks on the horizon" is a real threat, indeed). Can we, then, devise ways to make these apparently less attractive aspects of foreign cultures appreciated by our city-dwellers? We must consider the poor Mexicans or Bangla-Deshis on the one hand, and the Japanese factory owners-and-organisers on the other. Both must add to our multicultural mix.

We should, to continue my practice of observation, ask where, in the affluent city societies, have multicultural activities been most apparent and useful? Communal activities of the cities may generate very impressive monuments, using a great variety of expertise, much of it imported. York Minster took some 20,000 man-lives, about the same as was required for the Apollo project, which put a man on the Moon (about a million man-years)! But in essence, this is perhaps not very different from a market town building a church or a Town Hall. Those are only quantitatively different as human associations get bigger. What activities are fairly *specific* to the urban associations we call cities, and are there qualitative differences? The organisation of business, as in a Chamber of Commerce or other convergence of Guilds, is one level up from a Guild, and can include much more diversity of interest. Its members and existence, its rules, are not so different from the town guilds, village trade associations. The important difference *is* the much higher proportion of people who are not associated with specific trades but with Trade, not with any profession but with Professionals. The stockbroker, the exciseman, the agency for courtesans or for warehousing, and especially the lawyers of all kinds fit into the upper status levels of the city Society.

Most of us would agree that there *is* a real difference here. Let us not be confused by a misleading similarity. In the towns, and before that in the parishes, the baronies, the wards, there were aristocrats who did little, usually descendants of previous conquerors (or other "barbarians"). Many members of "noble" families lived lives of leisure, effectively as parasites upon the agriculture and its organisation, mine-working, shipping and commerce organised/exploited by their kin. Conspicuous consumption became a mark of high status in these families, and this has carried over into most human urban cultures. However, the lawyers and stockbrokers, who have inherited this mantle and wear it ably and obviously, *do* have functions in the cities' upper levels. So there developed in the cities a cadre of high-status, well-paid professional administrators, middle-men or tithe-takers from much of the city's wealth. Unlike the aristocratic layabouts, these men had positions not only of influence but of effect; they made policy and promoted the city's image abroad. They were, surprisingly often, foreigners; many aspired to work in the administration. Many more junior administrators worked for them, and in some cities a real "Civil Service" appeared, an effective administration for the city itself through which its polities worked. This is the "City Machine" of the Americans, recognisable in the old Italian cities, but not in ancient Rome or Athens which were run (often alternately) by aristocrats and generals. The organisation of the police, of taxes, of parades and festivals came under the aegis of this diffuse cadre, and it used its unique access to city wealth to co-ordinate large projects. Sports stadia, animal collections, public parks, public theatres, markets, public holidays are invitations by the city to all its sub-cultures, and a proportion of each sub-culture partakes of them in its own style. Parades, particularly, are invitations to express cultural strength in acceptable ways, and to admire the efforts of other sub-cultures. There is nothing remarkable, I suppose, in that description. But there is one arcane activity, characteristic initially of European cities but now infecting them world-wide, which is so odd that it must be illuminating.

The world of operatic music, so often played in the original language, was very popular among the top status levels, aristocrats and intelligentsia, of all the civic European cultures of the last three hundred years. Most European cities built great, very costly opera houses. It is amazing that this peculiar pretence, with highly ritualised singing and usually with very complex and frequently unintelligible stories, should have been the art form most highly regarded by most of the top-status groups in civil society. It was almost totally an art form of the Court, the aristocracy and especially the organising cadre of the big cities until the invention of the gramophone. Now a few arias celebrating classic situations, like "La donna e mobile...", "Che gelida manina...", and especially the Clown's song "Vesti le giubba..." from *Pagliacci* are in millions of homes, having been bought as "78s" between the wars. Caruso's "Vesti le giubba" was the first disc to sell more than a million copies. *Why* were they bought? Why did everyone know the name of Caruso, then of Gigli? What was so special about Mimi's tiny hand? What did people want? Why did all the big cities in the Western world compete to have enormous, expensive, opera houses which were always a vast burden on the public purse? I didn't know until I came to write this book (but operatic music has been my favourite since my college days).

What is so remarkable about this activity which made it the high status art?

I think it provided ready-made "deep" cross-cultural connections between disparate people. Previously, a knowledge of Classical literature had formed a common background of accepted common culture. Indeed, this has remained true for a dwindling English sub-set to this day. There were other super-cultural connectors. Sephardic Jewish international financiers had a common language in Hebrew, likewise, and a common classical (Spanish) background as well as the Biblical stories – Maimonides, as it were, added to Moses. Later (Ashkenazi) Jewish immigrants into Western Europe and America had Yiddish, and a rich lode of ghetto myths. This is my own cultural base, and I have many times engaged in, and observed, the intimacy-building rituals. "Oh, from Poland? Your mother's people? Are you related to the Cable Street Grodzynskis, from Lodz? What, you know what happened to Sophie after her man left the grocery business? Yes, I must agree he was a bad lot, that one." And so, like two dogs walking around one another, the ritual connections have been made; each is now anchored, given a place, in the other's cultural base. The world of reproductive biology, of course, has exactly the same ritual. "Oh, you did your Ph.D. in Whittingham's lab? Was Paul Burgoyne there at the time? What happened to that girl who was doing her post-doc with xxxxxxx? Yes, I must agree – he was a thoroughly bad lot, that one." And again the connections have been made. If the biologists are from disciplines which are further apart, they call upon old great-uncle Haldane, uncle Waddington, bad old cousin Lysenko, even old Grandfather Darwin to establish a family of common, "deep" connections.

Opera is very like cricket or baseball, or philately, in just this one peculiar property. If you like it, you know its "deep" rituals and you can talk in depth to *anyone* else who knows them. Let me give you a very personal example: I have co-authored a couple of text-books, and a complex theoretical paper, with Dr. Brendan Massey, whose culture is Irish (very – he is a Kerryman!). Our cultural backgrounds are very different indeed. We have much of modern developmental/reproductive biology in common, of course; but our attitudes to teaching, to reading both in and around the subject, to experimental design and to the animals themselves – as evinced by the keeping of pets, for example – are poles apart. Our most intimate communication is certainly in our shared interest in operatic recordings. By building on that, from our first acquaintance, we have contrived to work very profitably together, to *use* our differences productively, so as to extend the scope of our joint abilities.

Opera, *because* of its highly artificial and ritual structure, is a very high level social glue. Very different people, able in different areas but in different styles from different cultures, can meet in the foyer during the Interval and cultural cross-fertilisation can occur.  A better simile than with adhesives, perhaps, is with those multi-pin plugs-and-sockets which enable complex independent electronic items to communicate.  A reference back to an earlier idea I floated can tie up one of my links: early cross-cultural connections, social recombinations (p57) were perhaps achieved by the interchange of verbal children. Cross-fertilisation between modern civic sub-cultures is achieved by linkage through a super-culture like opera.

So why do people buy opera records and play them at home? They enjoy the music, of course;  but *why* do we enjoy such contrived, ritualised music?  Do they think "Perhaps I'll meet someone whose abilities I'll need and who'll also think the Schipa/Bori death of Mimi is the most marvellous performance ... "? Of course not – or at least less so than the teenager collecting tapes of the Top Ten, who may be quite explicit about the social glue effect. Opera – or philately – enables you to transcend your own parochial culture.  English-speaking people felt that it was supernational, and discriminated against MacCormack, a superb tenor, in favour of Italians of much less ability (Caruso was a special case, of course). In order to evoke this emotional difference *for you*, how would you have felt about Guiseppi Verdi's music if it had been written by a Bromsgrove lad called Joe Green, who started writing for his local town brass band? (Busseto, Verdi's home town, is not much bigger than Bromsgrove.) Does this example help you to distinguish your social obligations/prejudices/ rituals from the enjoyment of the music and the drama?

There are many of these cross-cultural allegiances that all of you achieve. Opera has simply been one of the most obviously and dramatically civic, and one I'm interested in myself.  You could perhaps substitute philately, or Esperanto, or Mensa.  But you should *not* substitute a religion or a political stance;  these are both always wedded to sub-cultures, they do not transcend them. Professional pursuits may or may not transcend culture;  in the two I am concerned with, it seems to me that sperm biology does, but ovarian biology does not.  Art forms often transcend culture;  I heard the members of two symphony orchestras, crossing in an airport lounge, do the "Have you been under Mehta?  We were in Tel Aviv, and...." (I forget what);  then they talked "Jet-Set": "The breakfasts on Swiss-Air, simply divine, you haven't tasted muesli unless..... " (I made that up, but you get the flavour).  The jet-setting language, like Yiddish, Maimonides, or Mimi's tiny hand, is of course another of these super-cultural systems.  It joins disparate cultures, it is a glue of social symbiosis.  Much great art does seem to transcend culture, but – apart from opera – I'm unclear how much it carries of sub-cultural bias (like religions). There is a vast amount of not-so-great art, however, which I think is the real symbiosis soup, the real social glue, the resin matrix in the fibre-glass of our interwoven cultures. It includes a few films, a substantial minority of TV soaps and series, and especially science fiction; I'll come back to it from a different direction in some pages time.

The parochial/universal character of the different pursuits illuminates the sub-cultural relationships in the city. In the sub-cultural hobby groups I do know (for example tropical fish breeders, anglers, koi-carp keepers, rabbit fanciers), there have been a few Caribbean members, but almost no Asians, few if any Greeks or Jews, before the fifties. The last ten years may have seen a few permanent Asian-background members joining these clubs, but they will be assimilated, second- or third-generation from the immigrants, who have effectively become locals. Where *does* one see the unassimilated cultures?

The Extra-Mural lectures from local universities, the evening classes at the local Technical College, will often have a great mix of cultures. This is especially true of the "arty" ones, not nearly so true of the handicrafts. It has not been true of the ones I've run on tropical fish breeding or freshwater ecology, but it certainly has been of animal handling and contraception.

So, you may well ask, what? How does running these classes, or the constitution of sub-groups like rabbit-breeders, illuminate super-culture/sub-culture differences and connection? I seem to have a clear idea, when running these classes, if the class are wanting within-their-culture, eyes-down, mind-on-the-job-in-hand teaching or whether they want a mind-expanding, taking-to-new-thoughts, universalist approach. I seem to have two modes, as a teacher; but I now realise I also have at least two modes as a civic person. Driving out with the pony and trap for some shopping just now was a quite different Jack Cohen from the one who is writing this with *Andrea Chenier* on my record-player. Universal now, parochial then. In Lewis Thomas' essay *Lives of a Cell*[5], he says of his symbiotic mitochondria: "I like to think that they work in my interest, that each breath they draw for me, but perhaps it is they who walk through the local park in the early morning, sensing my senses, listening to my music, thinking my thoughts." In writing this book, I am communicating across cultures, I am pretentiously drawing breath for Man; but, like the mitochondria, I – as little me – listen to Your music.

We are getting there. There are cohesive, integrative activities of the sub-cultures which may enable the city to behave as a city, as more than a conglomerate of sub-cultures. Even in our multicultural cities, however, we are not yet making stable symbiotic entities. They always include some dying, assimilating cultures which lose their special character in one generation of schooling, and some reproducing sub-cultures, mostly uneasily integrated into the city's life.   The city's cultural defences are effective against the former, but only partially so against the latter;  these are usually walled off, except for their special, *low cultural level*, trade function – Chinese food, or Jewish tailoring. This trade function enriches the rest of the life of the city, improves conditions for the indigenes, but there is little real cultural communication except at the very lowest, material-and-money-exchange, level.     Indeed, much of the character of the trading situations seem to be set up to permit *no* exposure of the cultural backgrounds of the participants.   The formalities, from business letters to restriction of conversation in "ethnic" retail outlets and restaurants, prevent intrusion of sub-cultural flavour.   Furthermore, there *are* some high-level cultural communication systems, like operatic music, which are so artificial, so ritual, that they do not serve as contamination channels from one culture to another either.   Neither Brendan Massey's Irishness nor my Ashke-nazi Judaism is exposed to change, to conversion or assimilation, when we discuss different recorded versions of *Otello*.  Nor do I, as a customer, interact with the Cypriot nature of my fish-and-chip shop or the Chinese nature of my Cantonese restaurant.    Nor do you, and that's my clue.

These are the *protected* low-level and high-level communication-lines of the super-cell, the cultural symbiont, and it is in these terms that we must seek the germ lines of the multicultural city.   Just as these important between-culture civic interactions hide their nature, and require or forbid certain behaviour so that sub-cultures remain inviolate, so we should expect that the germ lines of the multicultural city will not be obvious.   For them to perform their function they must be discreet.    Rather than tear off this last veil dramatically, then, I shall lay bare the highest-level reproduction this planet has yet achieved – delicately.

As a first step, let us return to the concept of a "clerisy", that group of people which transmits the bones of the culture to the next generation – the meme transmitters.   Let's look to see who's already doing the job, or trying, and see what a job they're making of it.   Perhaps surprisingly, we have some maps of possible future societies, and the ones which have become popular surely represent credible futures.   We can use them to compare the jobs being done by different groups in our societies and the guessed-at, fictional ones.   We have Utopias guessed at, invented, built and we can do our thought-experiments on them.   We also have a great variety of Dystopias, which can serve as horrible examples.

Several of them[6] see the advance in communications, especially the televi-sion screen watched by the torpid billions, as giving power to the media.   Do we think that it is the media bosses, who are more and more the final arbiters of what our children see and what paints them citizen-coloured, who lead the flock, who keep all the culture-strings together?  Do you think they promote Welsh television *because* it is different and not (only?) because it attracts different advertisers?

Others, notably Aldous Huxley versions, see the educational establishment[7] as doing the job – doing it ineffectually, except in *Island*[8], but doing it. Certainly most science-fiction authors see the Big Science[9], the Big Technology[10] too sometimes, as housed in the  universities, and they have not really made any sensible suggestions about it coming out.  I don't include pastoral[11], or all-things-to-all-women Utopias[12] because they've copped out on our question; they're usually Americans, sometimes anarchists or *real* socialists, with much more on the ball and much more technology – but the story exposes just one sub-culture in detail[13].  That's not useful to us.

If we really ask, as biologists, what is the structure of this new clerisy, we come back to our alternative evolutionary stories for getting to Man, two versions of the Ladder of Life (p25).  One starts "Once upon a time there was a nerve cell...." and the other "Each mother gave her offspring a little something more.....".  The nervous system, with its centralised brain and ramifying communication lines, is a seductive model and would lead us to see the media, I suppose – or even perhaps the post, telephone and computer networks – as the integrative system of the multi-culture.   The reproductive "system", with all those communication lines carrying information or capital from one generation to the next, provides seductive models, and this would lead us to the educators, university and school, and to the investors, stock-broking organisations, as mediators.  But if what I have built up in this book is so, then reproductive philosophy should seek out the real clerisy *by its tendency to wall itself off* from the physiology of society.  We should not seek it by its nervous-system-like integrative properties, or by its control of the basic education, or of the capital privilege, of the next generation.  If myths are the binding, building elements within cultures, they must be changed to permit cultures to live together[14] – and such change will *then*, secondarily, change education[15] and media choice and where the capital is put.  The change will be subtle, but we may recognise other signs of the effective new clerisy;  one sign may be its internal feedback system, as we'll see.

Various Utopias (some referred to above) have figured the Communications Industry, the World Intelligentsia (in universities or as the "Establishment"), the Politicians/Diplomats, the Civil Service, or the International Organisations (United Nations, UNESCO, WHO and the other acronymic – but not myth-generating – institutions) as that group which will force, coerce, and promote the New Society. Let me now propose an unexpected one. These very people who give us our Utopias, our maps to the future, are our myth-generators. These give the communications industry, and the media, and our educators, the models and the myths which enshrine, and perhaps generate, our concepts of the Future. They are the Science Fiction community, authors, editors, readers and critics. They are unique among literati, too, in that there is a very strange feed-back mechanism in their society, which I expose below (and which has uncanny resemblances to the biology of nuclei and gonads).

Let me set up the technical-future novelist, from Mary Shelley with *Frank-enstein* through Wells' *War of the Worlds* and Huxley's *Brave New World* to Clarke's film *2001*, as the myth-creators[16]. You, *whoever you are*, have incorporated those myths into your own making. I have already advocated the view[17] that the continuity of character of a society is marked by its continuing myths (using "myth" in its anthropological sense – they are usually based in perceived reality). I used modern Israel as an example of a multicultural city-like society with a newly engendered set of myths. The most helpful way to identify the new clerisy, the germ-plasm of the new symbiotic society, must surely be to examine the generation of our new myths. We know that the media distribute them, make some fashionable and others disreputable; mothers, play-group organisers, and then Educators pass them on. Who engenders the myths of the New, Multicultural Society? Vance Packard? The Beatles? Bronowski? Ronald Reagan? Alastair Cooke? Superman? H.G.Wells?

It is not the ordinary, everyday (mundane) television series. *Coronation Street* and *Dallas* are the old, nostalgic re-runs, parading our previous values, the last generation's fairy tales. The science documentaries, particularly the "pop" ones, have done much more to add to our general knowledge-base, but have not, I think, changed myths or provided new and potent ones. Desmond Morris with *People-Watching*, David Attenborough with *The Living Planet*, the sex educator Martin Cole, have given people new images, and this may have influenced many judgements, perhaps decisions. They, and their Media promoters and editors, producers, have done more to change our society, to influence the direction of future change, than the politicians who have claimed to have done so! But I don't think they've provided *new* invention; these scientists have, like other media presentations and like the politicians' presentation of policy, put new labels on much the same goods.

Superman[18], as a concept, a wish-fulfilment, a shining new *myth*, has done much more – and Buck Rogers, Flash Gordon also, because the thirties comics in which the strips appeared were read by virgin minds. How many of you know the name of the fifties myth-maker who invented Dan Dare? Batman and

Robin? *These* have made many of our contemporary myths, you know. We may point to many recently minted myths, and suggest messages: Sherlock Holmes and the Saint, making intellect and wit admirable; Dennis the Menace (and other boys' comic-strip heroes – and swots) making reading-to-learn despicable; Marilyn Monroe, making stardom uncomfortable; Tarzan, reinforcing back-to-Nature for strength and naive virtue; Churchill, making obduracy (pig-headedness?) in the face of evil a real saviour-of-civilisation. Add to this list yourselves, but don't include J.R. in *Dallas*, or Princess Leia in *Star Wars* and its sequels; don't include Luke Skywalker and Han Solo, who were old fairy-tale stereotypes, even to Luke, the *hero*, turning out to be Leia's, the heroine's *brother*! (And the villain, Darth Vader, is his *father*!) Jabba the Hut, the Wooki, the aliens in the bar scene in the first film, were all only venerable s-f images finding their way to wider exposure; Ewocks, of course, were just Teddy Bears turning on the small-and-cuddly other-peoples'-babies emotions. So was E T, and *Alien* was the other side of the same coin. They were not what I meant by the myth-making effect of s-f. These are *not* the new myths of the multiculture.

*Star Trek*, in contrast, has provided many brand-new images, now well integrated into popular and political culture: the musical "Pop" world produced *Stop the World, I want to get off!* but the much more potent "Beam me up, Scottie!" is a *Star Trek* contribution. Even a musical spoof of *Star Trek* (*Star-Trekking!*), originally produced by musicians who were not fans of the show, rose to fame in the last few weeks and has entered the collections of many pop musical sub-cultures.

If you are making a mythogenesis list, don't forget the Westerns, either. As books, and especially as films, they have left their mark on all our cultures, so that the morality of man-with-a-gun is now part of our common heritage. It determines the thoughts of the bank robber, and of the bank teller, of the policeman and of the judge (though a bit of Perry Mason comes in there too!). But it has also affected toys, children's games ("cowboys and Indians" has set cross-cultural patterns for generations), the status of the Maoris as well as of the Cherokees. Many television series are built simply on this pattern, with "goodies" and "baddies" and a car chase which ends the moral tale. Much of so-called "science"-fiction and fantasy is the Western transplanted to Mars or Elf-land – but conscious copies, like Clarke's *The Deep Range*, about herding whales with dolphins, or the *Dungeons and Dragons* stories and games, have indeed added to our stock of new and original cultural myths.

When seeking the myths upon which your cultural prejudices are based, those which have made you what you are, don't forget the Great Dinosaur

Demise, the Great Neanderthal Scandal, the Great Conservation Ethic, The Third Reich, Chernobyl, Entebbe and the other Big Stories of our times. All these affect all your prejudices and mine, determine our responses to our fellow humans to a large extent. To some extent all of these *are* the common myths of the multiculture. Who initiated them? To a first approximation, most people would believe that Hitler and Idi Amin, meteorites from space and human sewage in Lake Erie were the important causes of some of the above events. However, only a very few important events become Important Events like the above list, become Myths. Who makes the new myths, who chooses the Important among the events, even fictional events like Utopias; who determines their potency, their longevity?

The first answer must be our friends in the media, particularly film and television. However, even the most superficial second look shows that they *follow* the public myths, and only very rarely create them. J.R. and the rest are the latest versions of very ancient models, given a new lick of paint but with much the same profiles; the archetypes are alive and well and are re-issued periodically by the media. Compare them with Don Giovanni, Mimi, Rigoletto and his daughter Gilda, La Dame aux Camellias, Faust, Figaro, Otello (and Iago), who all weave their threads within, between, across our cultures. Who, then, generates new models of the world? Do they "just appear"? Are they dependent on the outside event, after all, or are they generated by intrinsic processes of the cultural ecology? If the latter, are they "accident", or are they generated by a process which monitors their effect on the culture? If the former, they cannot be related to my theory; but if the latter, then there is a good case for considering this self-conscious mythogenesis to be at the centre of the reproductive system of the multi-culture.

The biggest difference in everybody's world view over the last thirty years, I guess, is actually a difference in our mental picture of The World. For all of us now, it's not a "place", it's a planet! Earth is not Mother Earth (picture of pair of Shire horses pulling a great plough through the soil) but a lonely planet in space, a sphere, a dot. Where did that picture come from? One view would point to satellites, and television pictures. But I am suggesting that the satellites are there, and so is television, because Dan Dare, in Eagle Comics in the fifties, reinforced some myths in the children of those exposed to Wells, to Verne, to Buck Rogers in the thirties[16]. Of course most people's image of Earth, now, comes from pictures of Earth from outside, *finally*; but *initially* it came from Dan Dare, and Buck Rogers, and from a succession of more-or-less realistic films, cartoons, stories which put the Earth firmly in its place as just another planet, and the Sun as just another star. This is an odd, and oddly scientific, kind of *realism* which appeared initially in the service of fiction, often of fantasy.  Here I must digress again, even in this final chapter, to consider the history of realism in our stories and our myths.

The place of fantasy, truth, science in our world-myths would take at least another book.  Let me crib from the guest author's speech given by Doris Lessing at the World Science Fiction Convention in Brighton in 1987.  She was asking why people are now surprised at fantastic fiction, prefer "realistic" fiction.  To an author with an interest in history of story-telling the facts were clear; *all* of the early stories we know, from sagas to children's tales to creation myths to moral tales for adults, were fantasy.  They were known by both teller and listener to be allegories of the world, at closest, and were usually accepted as exciting tales of a different system, with different rules.  Biblical stories, for example, were woven around the real historical events but were given miracles, prophecies, angels, devils to make the morality more exciting.  The 1001 Nights, with their djinns, ogres, giants, rocs are exciting for children in just this vein; I first came across them, as you probably did too, in the Andrew Lang version[19].  The Burton is much nearer the original, and is a gorgeous set of myths for adults; but it's certainly not realistic, especially in the sexy bits[20]!

Only in the last three hundred years or so has the realistic story, what the science-fiction or fantasy author would call a "mundane" story, been around. The recent twist, anchoring the story plot to one sub-cultural pessimism, has its roots in Russia but its feet in the kitchen sink; it has lost the bold fantasy of its Russian model, and now simply gives a realistic version of what could be happening in the next street, next house.  Even the constraining rules of the detective story, or the Western, or other "cult" fiction like the Mills and Boon romance or the pornographic novelette, have been dropped.  In its attempt to be mundane, most threads of the modern novel have lost the myth-generating ability or function.  It has become smaller-minded than its readers, in the hope that its small embittered world will attract those fearful of the large empty spaces in the new scientific world view.  It holds up the mirror to the reader, a small mirror, whose self-consciousness as literature lessens its engagement with the technical world-culture.  Its "heroes" and "heroines" do not grow; they learn their limitations as they battle with bureaucracy, casual cruelty, outside forces, political conspiracy, or the uncontrolled (read "uncontrollable") desires of their own – unimprovable, "given" – Human Nature.  The modern novel is indeed mundane; it inhabits the world of the television soap-opera, often cruelly warped to give sick humour or to permit a relaxation of tension at the climax.  Browse on your local railway-station bookstall – these are the books of the civic culture.  If they can be said to hold a mirror up to life, the reflection given back is smaller, tighter, a clenched view of a squeezed-out world, from the inside.

In contrast, most science-fiction stories are set in the open, scientific world-view that sees the future as larger, more open to possibilities than the present, sees the Earth *optimistically* as a tiny planet: "Look what we've done with it, what we can do with it ... ". Most important for our present purpose, there are many, very popular, kinds of science-fiction which see the social systems we have *from outside*. They have a larger ambience than any one of our sub-cultures, so can generate myths which can hold relations-between-sub-cultures within them. Let me give some examples, because I need to establish the existence of this kind of social-reflexive myth in *your* minds before I can argue that it could be the single most hopeful social sign in our society.

I will choose four kinds of science-fictional myth-maker. There is the Future story, looking at our cultures from a time when they have been subsumed by a larger culture, or destroyed in a holocaust. There is the Alien story, looking at our cultures from an apparently different evolutionary viewpoint, to emphasise the difference between necessary and contingent, universal and parochial, aspects of the reader's culture. There is the Robot story, looking at our society from the viewpoint of our artefacts, looking at human culture from inside but nevertheless from a different viewpoint again. And there is the Utopian story, which initially seemed to be the most useful for our purposes, for finding the germ of the future in our society; however, we shall see that it turns out to be least useful in the end.

The Future story may take either of two routes to place our present culture in the reader's context, but from "outside". It may be an "After the Bomb..."[21,22] (or other punctuation in human history) or it may be from a successful future development of our present society[23,24]. There is a genre of stories which uses time-travel as a plot device to put modern man in the new context[25,26], to open his mind to the possibilities of our own culture, or to put a future person into our pivotal times[12,23]. Wells' *Time Machine* produced the new myth of the Morlocks, below-ground socialist workers of the future, and the Eloi, "useless" artistic cattle upon whom the Morlocks fed. The other stories I've referred to have all become classics because of such contextual enlightenment, too, and have all provided *you* with myths[16]. The details aren't important here, and I don't want to take time here to abstract plots of any of these stories. Read them (that's why I've referenced them), recognise the bases of some of your thoughts!

The Alien story, again, comes in two main versions. There is the Contact[27,28] story, in which an aspect of the contacter's culture turns out to be congruent/

antithetic to an aspect of the contactee's. The other kind is the "working-and-living-together" story; initially (in the 30s and 40s) this was an "Earthmen (for which read "Americans"!) of several disciplines get together to solve problems caused by alien cultures", of which the paradigm was probably van Vogt's *Voyage of the Space Beagle*[29] in the early fifties. This was very widely read, and gave the concept of the "nexialist" (one who specialises in building bridges *between* disciplines) to our language – but, more importantly, to our thought. Then there was a spate of "alien-and-human-team solve problems neither could solve on its own"[30,31]. These ranged from Jim White's *Sector General* series[30,32], in which sundry alien medical/social problems are dealt with by a multi-species hospital in space, to various expeditions[33,34] in which a multi-species team solves alien problems. More recently, the *Uplift Wars* series by David Brin[35] has dolphins and (improved) chimpanzees forming a team with humans in a vast web of alien polities across our galaxy. The probabilities are not at issue here; the interest for us is that the "Alien Terror" story-line of the Thirties has given place to value-the-difference stories in the last ten years. Even the inimical aliens of recent years[36,37] have their own rationale, are shown sympathetically – again their culture illuminates aspects of ours *from outside*. There are all kinds of "nearly-alien" plots too: my reptilian Yilane[38], for example, competing with different species of "humans" on a world from which the giant reptiles were not wiped out (no, they are not intelligent dinosaurs!), or even the Neanderthalers in Jean Auel's[39] prehistoric sagas. All these expose human sub-cultures as inadequate, and promote world-visions of rewarding co-operation between disparate sub-cultures or species.

The Robot sub-genre, too, has promoted many pervasive myths in our – your – society. Isaac Asimov has certainly been its main exponent, promoting human/robot co-operation in his series of short stories about their development[40], and in the Lije Bailey novels[41]. Forerunners of contemporary robot stories, Capek's *RUR*, von Harbou's *Metropolis* and so on, were like the early Alien stories: the protagonists were of one, dominant culture and were *against* the robots. An early sympathetic robot was Jenkins in Simak's *City*[11], certainly one of the most beautifully wrought of these myth-makers: Man has gone, and the Dogs remember him by a set of tales in which different *kinds* of men, and Martians, and robots, make an interwoven future history of great dignity. In contrast Stapledon, when he wrote *Last and First Men* in the early thirties, was in tune with his times; his species of men succeeded each other, they did not co-operate – and his images did *not* produce lasting myths. But now, almost all of the potent robot stories have co-operation, complementation as their theme. From "Robby the Robot", the only memorable element of the film

*Forbidden Planet*, to R2D2 and C3PO in *Star Wars*, android mechanicals have caught the imagination of the public. One of the great Works of Art in this genre is *The Hitch-Hikers Guide to the Galaxy*, with Marvin the "Paranoid Android" producing trenchant, because witty and wise, comment on the human situation!

The "mundane" makers of Utopias and Dystopias are not convincing to me, bye and large; like those who advocate revolution – at least in words on paper – I find them faintly pathetic in today's world. The real revolutionaries are *responding* to myths generated by fin-de-siecle philosophers; these were re-interpreted in the sixties by Derrida and Foucault, and form some of the bases for present utopian thought. So the combination, revolutionary utopianism, even the dignified French educational model of Marcuse and Foucault, doesn't ring the bell for me. I can't find a handy source of civilised – amused – supermen and superwomen to run it. I agree that the French provide a lovely – and loving – model for civilisation, but they are not a source of myths for Utopias which could work.

My choice of science fiction Utopian/Dystopian myth-makers begins with those I have found unconvincing, too, but who have been picked up by the literary or philosophical establishment[42]. Asimov's futures have been read by many people, and they mostly have an explicit trio of symbionts: robots (of course), intellectual/artistic philosophers (e.g.the Second Foundation) and proletariat (this last being "our" culture, writ denser). Neither he nor Harrison (*Make Room, Make Room* which made the film *Soylent Green*) addressed the problem of human cultural diversity exactly, but nearly all Harrison's other serious work explicitly lauds symbiosis between cultures; *Deathworld* and its sequels did it explicitly. Heinlein's futures are firmly set in an American frame, for all their variety, and are full of "assimilated" people; they are very different, they complement, but even the Lazarus Long sagas don't address the diversity of peoples. (They do, however, clearly show the dependence of different styles of living, different periods of history, upon each other, and contrast beautifully with Stapledon.) Niven's *Known Universe* series is full of co-operating aliens and humans, including some culturally odd humans, but even *Ringworld* is populated by American philosophies, bye and large! His Pierson's puppeteers are odd "aliens", but only in one or two ways do they differ from his human protagonists.

Some of the women writers, especially Le Guin, portray real differences; in *The Dispossessed*[13] she shows two cultures, superficially socialist/anarchist versus capitalist/monetarist, apparently in opposition. Her protagonist comes to realise how each has a real need of the other, neither can exhibit, expose its social philosophy unless the other is there; and both systems are necessary, too, for the complex economics of the system. Bester's *The Demolished Man* and *Tiger, Tiger* both have diverse societies, and the plots weave in and out of strange cultures which don't understand each other, but work together. All Delany's works do this too. All of the above examples have been widely read by the general public, judging by their sales. Gordon Dickson's *Childe Cycle*, including *Dorsai*, are among the most highly regarded of these utopian futures, and depend for their ambience on *specialisation* of the human species along different cultural pathways (soldiers, philosophers, religious fanatics, pragmatists); the dramatic end of the cycle, however, could well underline the sterility of these individual paths and return to our grand theme of evolutionary symbiosis (we discussed possible ends in 1987).

But the new myths are exposed as obviously in the lower-level media productions. *Star Trek* exploits the five cultures of its team in *every* episode: Scottie, the "ship's engineer",is the caricature Scot familiar as engineer – and gynecologist – throughout the English-speaking world; "Bones" McCoy, the chief medic, has Irish connections; Uhura, Caribbean woman Communications Chief, is usually less involved in the macho adventures but is always present in body; Jim Kirk is the Captain, a slightly over-done all-American WASP; and the half-alien (very difficult for a reproductive biologist!) Spock, has pointed ears, copper-based blood (!) and an inability to feel human emotions. The plots quite often exploit this simple-minded caricaturing of human *differences* in their resolution, and in their interaction with other cultures the moral is (nearly) always co-operative. "Bop the bug-eyed monster!" plots are very rarely seen now – and contrast this with the Dan Dare team.

That excursion into science-fictional themes has probably persuaded you that much of your prejudice is indeed rooted in these themes, or at least that all these are familiar tropes in your society. What you do not know, unless you are a true fan (and you're probably not, because the germ cells take up only a tiny proportion of the body-mass, and the clerisy is always a small minority...) is that the organisation of the s-f community is unique. It has no resemblance to the Detective story, the Romance, the Thriller, the Western or any of the other genre fiction (with the exception of its half-sisters, Fantasy and Horror fiction). The others have conventions of a kind, meetings with one author and acolytes, or even a group of authors and critics under the aegis of, for example, *Ellery Queen's Magazine*. But they do not have conventions, Conventions, of the s-f kind, with several world-name authors, many small-time authors and hundreds of very verbal fans. A "Worldcon" (held annually) usually has about

4-7000 attendees, perhaps forty well-known authors. All the names I've mentioned above, from Asimov, Clarke, Harrison, LeGuin, McCaffrey, Niven to Zelazny go to several conventions every year, where they meet comment, criticism, adulation – all *feedback*. The feedback comes at all levels, from literary criticism through matters of scientific or sociological theory to issues of film and other media presentation (I discussed this philosophy with Gordie Dickson at a Worldcon). These feedback loops involve, note, only a small, monitoring, segment of the audience of the authors concerned. Nearly all the readers *don't* come to s-f conventions. At the conventions the tropes, the cliches, the myths meet critical exposure to many cultures – *sub-cultures are over-represented*! There are *more* Jews, Asians, Carribeans at English conventions, and Swedes, Germans, Americans too.

As in the opera house, the sub-cultures meet productively; but there is a vital difference. In the opera house the myths are assumed (everyone is expected to know the *story*) and the techniques and rituals form the topics of conversation ("A magnificent high A, but I thought a touch sharp ..."; "These Chicago sets are not convincing for *Don Giovanni*, are they?"). But at s-f conventions the myths and mythogenesis are specifically addressed ("You *can't* do another *After the Bomb*, Larry; how about a *Zoo keeper saves the world from bandersnatchi*!?"; "How about the *only* cure for AIDS being *very* expensive, Bob?"). It sounds pretentious, but there is a strong sense that the myths of tomorrow, the framework of tomorrow's society, is being made and monitored. If it is the case that the technology derives from the ideas (as well as the converse, of course) and that the media only promote existent myths, then a major part of tomorrow's world is conceived in the s-f communities' get-togethers.

How does this relate to the criteria I have set up for recognising the germ plasm of the multi-culture? I am sure that this is where very many of our societal myths originate, especially those which relate to co-operating diversity, to promotion of the multi-culture. I hope to have persuaded you of this too. But this is not enough, by itself, to identify a heredity. It does have two other properties, and an unexpected third one, which identify it for me unambiguously as a major part of our clerisy, our nucleus.

The first property, additional to mythogenesis, is withdrawal from the *working* of the organism. S-f conventions *are* private functions, with little interaction with the wider world, and s-f authors, however famous, are not involved in decision-making. They are frequently asked to commemorate some event, like the landing on the moon, the passage of Halley's comet, the achievement of human "test-tube" fertilisation, because they are identified as having presaged or publicised it. But, in their capacity as authors, critics, publishers they are not involved in the events themselves. Some of us, and I am an example, combine work in publicly-promoted science with the generation of science-fictional ambiences, backgrounds to stories[32,37,38]; but these are fairly separate personae, and in any event my s-f activity is supportive, rather than generative. The esoteric language and practices of science fiction fandom, like those of Freemasonry in the past, confirm its "private" nature, again perhaps because it is a part of the established cultural heredity. This esoterica exists mostly as privately printed and circulated magazines, perhaps 30-50 in the UK but with virtual continuity with those in the USA, France, Australia, and even Poland and Russia; this continuity is assured by reprinting articles, commissioning critical works, reviews and even stories. A typical fanzine has a circulation in the 800-2000 range, and will often include correspondence with authors (most of whom were fans in their time). Names like *Speculation, Concatenation, Gonzo, In Defiance of Medical Opinion* show resemblances at one end to pop-science and pop-art mags and at the other to the Underground Literature papers. This is a vast, active and effective network of s-f discussion, which is not usually considered in "proper" political, literary or even revolutionary ("Underground") surveys[43] – it is "walled off".

The second way in which this body of myth-generators can be identified as the clerisy concerns the popularity of their myths, what they call (slightly naughtily) their tropes. There was a newspaper headline "Two-headed Mutant Baby Plague" passed around at a recent convention (occasioned by two pairs of Siamese twins joined abdominally), which caused wry laughter and a useful listing of a variety of such tropes. Chernobyl was, of course, mentioned in the article, as was a scientist ("Scientist"?) who "refused to comment"! "Computer takes over World..." is another such, and you can add your own. How about *Dr. Strangelove*? S-f myth-based references are everywhere, they are ubiquitous in our popular culture. *Dr Who, Star Trek, Battlestar Galactica* are all very popular (not only with your children), and Gerry Anderson's series of cartoon versions continue the moral myth-creating functions of the early Dan Dare comic strips.

The third clue is for me the most impressive. I have been worrying for some years about the common properties of eukaryote nucleus, metazoan germ cells, reproductive individuals in colonies, the reproductive parts of systems. Their isolation from day-to-day function is impressive as a common property, and the s-f community shares that. Another property, however, concerns their control of some of the facets of the larger system, those which are reproduction-related, by an *internally-controlled* feedback regulation. The most familiar example of this is the production of sex hormones by the gonads of man and other mammals; this production is modulated by hormones from the pituitary gland, itself controlled by releasing hormones from parts of the brain. In the past this has been seen as a hierarchical system, with each successively higher structure/function being hailed as "controller". I learnt in the fifties that the pituitary gland was the "conductor of the endocrine orchestra", for example, before the releasing hormones which control *it* were discovered. The modern view, however, is beginning to see the gonadal system as primary, with all the external hormones and "control" from the pituitary and brain a *result* of events in, for example, the Graafian follicle in the human ovary. In such a complex feedback network, of course, no part is isolable. Nevertheless, many workers are now showing that local effects of the ovarian products (especially steroid hormones, inhibin and probably small growth-factor-like proteins) have priorities over endocrine secretion for ovarian function. Equally, chemical control by the queen bee of the workers' activities has been emphasised in the past, but more recently her own internal physiology has been shown to be a "balance-wheel" for the whole colony. Whereas control of the cell workings *by* the nucleus was the usual model until the fifties and sixties, internal control of the nucleus by its own products is now the fashionable image. Just as the ovary modulates its own activity *via* the pituitary and brain as well as by internal feedback, so nuclei control development by responding to earlier nuclear products in the cytoplasm (p27).

An image I have not used so far can be brought in now. The Board of an industrial company is in *some* respects like the systems I have been describing. I am now suggesting that in these other systems there occurs an interaction between Board members which is a central part of the functioning of the Board both in its reproductive and its controlling aspects. I am not denying such internal control systems in the firm's sub-systems like the secretarial pool, in the kidney or in the mitochondrion. I am directing your attention to the contrasting *kinds* of regulation which occur in such a central or sub-system. The sub-systems seem to me always to be *homeostatic*: they act in such a way as to preserve their short-term state, their identity. In contrast, the Board, the nucleus, the germ cells, the queen bee show *homeorhesis*[44]. They act in a *progressive* way, with a goal-different-from-now built into their working; they maintain a path, not a position (by both internal and external, from the "organs", feedback). Puberty, ovulation, or swarming, or industrial take-overs or differentiation are not part of the function of each sub-system I've introduced; they are changes of state, controlled centrally, which *re-calibrate* the homeostatic mechanisms of the sub-systems.  The nucleus, queen bee or clerisy, then, can be recognised by its homeorhesis, and distinguished from other sub-systems which only show homeostasis.

The science-fiction community is one of the few which show such homeorhesis, self-controlled guidance towards new states.   Such systems have been called *teleonomic*, goal-directed.   Many artistic factions change "self-consciously" through time:   the cinema, the novel, television production are examples.   But these do not do so by self-direction;  their own change is only occasionally a part of their processes directing change.  Recursion of this kind may be exposed, utilised as part of the art form (all art forms show self-reference), but it is not integral.  In science-fiction it is.  In the sixties a new, more self-consciously literary and inwardly-directed movement appeared, calling itself the New Wave.  The literary side of the genre spouted buckets of praise, *but* this did not take over.  Some elements of that fashion can be found in many modern stories, but looking-at-our-cultures-from-outside is still what sells to editors and readers.   If I am right that this self-and-culture-conscious, self-regulating super-cultural phenomenon is beginning to serve as the myth-generator and the myth-reproducer for the new multi-culture, this would be expected.  It has a larger part to play than as one form of literature:  the future of your children has "Big Brother is Watching You" written in it, whether you have read Orwell or not.   My message is simple:   we are all watching Big Brother, Little Sister and all the other sub-cultures, and the Family of Man has acquired a communal conscience.

The Family of Man is also rapidly acquiring a new, world-spanning organisation. Extensive travel, pervasive communication on local and international level, and easy reproduction of both informative and artistic information has made the deep structures of city life available to all who want it. (The real costs of tape-copying, even paper-publishing are approaching Third-World peasant availability.)   As more and more of the city's business is done from "home" by computer link, the resemblance to a human super-organism becomes more apparent to those, like the communications media, who think in terms of nerve links.  I have, I hope, sensitised you to the alternative view, the reproductive view.    This sees the multi-national corporations[45], run as they are by homeorhetic Boards of Directors, as *alternative* symbioses to the cities.  They run their own education systems, generally (called "Management Training Schemes" or other euphemisms ...);  they have their own myths[46], which give their internal cultures strength.   They use multi-cadre or, very frequently, multicultural future planning systems because they *work*.  The Japanese have apparently not yet adopted a multicultural system within their corporations, but they have, of course, taken the education of their workers' children out of the hands of the city's educators.    These educators are, I believe, everywhere losing their ancient position as guardians of the city's mono-culture against immigrant cultures, and their central role as clerisy.   The former has largely been taken over by urban or industrial training-schemes, and the latter by the new myth-makers, of which the most effective (even in the large technology-based multi-nationals) are those who generate new world-views, the science-fiction community.    This is very effectively promoting multiculture and symbiosis now, in *opposition* to the educator/administrator stance which promotes non-recognition of differences ("anti-discriminatory practice").

The urban systems could perhaps learn from the multi-nationals, who use different cadres, different cultures, to educate their different communities. Perhaps the urban symbiosis would work better if each culture reproduced its own kind, *including the cultural apparatus for integrating with other kinds*. So, in the city, such de-centralisation of control could return cultural reproduction to the clerisy *within each culture*[15].   In most Western cities now, secular so-called "education" goes on during the week, and a few of the stronger sub-cultures have "Sunday School", "Cheder" (for Jewish children), a variety of Islamic schooling systems, at the week-ends.   In the USA[47], increasingly in Europe (including Britain) and Australia[14], even in the USSR[15], "ethnic" schools are taking back the children of parents disillusioned with public, "grey", education.  My view of urban cultural reproduction is happy with this; I would even go further:  the sub-cultures should educate the children during the week, and the optional – but prestigious – integrative education should be available at other times.  Ideally, this should be paid for by the sub-culture as a group if it is group-oriented, but by the family or by the individuals themselves (perhaps on a loan basis), in the more individual-oriented sub-cultures.  Such a reversal would permit a change in prestige for the integrative educators – city administrators, multinational managers could be required to take selected groups. They would not object. Eminent figures in the business, scientific, entrepreneurial, artistic life of the city would be happy – *as they are now* – to involve selected groups of such juvenile representatives  of the sub-cultures in their own special areas.  This way of passing the cultural life of the city to the next generation, with interest, is consonant with the view of human reproduction I've given in this book.  What we do at present, mostly, isn't. But there is hope.

The multicultural city symbiosis, and the multi-national company, are showing a large proportion of our multi-species a new, more effective and more demanding way of life.  Because these systems treasure difference, and because human differences complement whereas similarities only compete, these symbioses are the future. In the past, we have treasured our differences but mostly for ourselves, as soloists on the cultural instruments of Mankind. Now let us treasure our differences and those of others, so that our new myths of spreading out from this little planet can lead to new symbioses, to give us all more joy.

# References

References in full are to be found from page 243 onwards. Below are listed names of authors and dates of publication.

1. Hsiao (1927)
2. Marx (1975)
3. Bell and Vasiliki (1986)
4. Bell (1982)
5. Thomas (1980)
6. Spinrad (1974)
7. McIntosh (1961)
8. Huxley (1962)
9. Huxley (1955 [1932)
10. Brunner (1971)
11. Simak (1981 [1952])
12. Russ (1975)
13. Leguin (1975)
14. Bullivant (1987)
15. Modgil *et al* (1986)
16. Aldiss (1975)
17. Levi-Strauss (1975)
18. SiegelandShuster (1928)
19. Lang (1898)
20  Burton (1985 [1890])
21. Mead (1960)
22. Miller (1961)
23. Heinlein (1986[1962]
24. Pohl and Kornbluth (1953)

25. Asimov (1958)
26. Wells (1922 [1898])
27. Dickson (1965)
28. Niven and Pournelle (1986)
29. van Vogt (1959 [1951])
30. White (1962)
31. Mitchison (1964)
32. White (1983)
33. Clement (1964)
34. Niven (1970)
35. Brin (1987
36. Niven and Pournelle (1976)
37. Niven and Pournelle (1987)
38. Harrison (1984)
39. Auel (1980)
40. Asimov (1968)
41. Asimov (1960)
42. Moylan (1986)
43. Smith (1977)
44. Waddington (1974)
45. UNESCO (1986)
46. Peters and Waterman (1982)
47. Lesko (1988)

# REFERENCES

Aldiss, B. (1975) Billion Year Spree; the history of science fiction. London: Corgi
  Books.
Ardrey, R. (1969) The Territorial Imperative. London: Collins.
Asimov, I. (1968) The Rest of the Robots. London: Panther Books Ltd.
Asimov, I. (1958) Pebble in the Sky. London: Corgi Books.
Asimov, I. (1960) The Naked Sun. London: Panther Books Ltd.
Auel, J. (1980) The Clan of the Cave Bear. London: Hodder and Stoughton.
Bantock, G.H. (1975) Progressivism and the content of education. In Black Paper 1975
  (Ed. C B Cox and   R Boyson). London: J.M.Dent.
Bell, G. and Vasiliki, K. (1986) The cost of reproduction. *In* Oxford Surveys in
  Evolutionary Biology (ed. R Dawkins and M Ridley). New York: Oxford University
  Press. 83-131
Bell, G. (1982) The Masterpiece of Nature. London, Croom Helm.
Bigelow, R. (1969) The Dawn Warriors: Man's evolution towards peace. London:
  Hutchinson.
Bourdieu, P. and Passeron, J.C. (1977) Reproduction - in education, society and culture
  (trans. R Nice). London: Sage Publications.
Boyden, S. (1987) Western Civilization in Biological Perspective. Oxford: Clarendon
  Press.
Brin, D. (1987) The Uplift War. London: Bantam Books.
Brunner, J. (1971) Stand on Zanzibar. London: Arrow Books.
Bullivant, B.M. (1987) The Ethnic Encounter in the Secondary School: ethnocultural
  reproduction and resistance; theory and case studies. Lewes, East Sussex: Falmer
  Press.
Burton, R. (1985, orig pubn 1890) Antonio's Tales from the 1001 Nights. New York:
  Stewart Tabori and Chang.
Cairns-Smith, A.G. (1985) Seven Clues to the Origin of Life. Cambridge:
  Cambridge University Press.
Campbell, J.W.Jr. (1961) Tribesman, barbarian and citizen. *Analog Science Fact/
  Fiction*. XVIII 9 (Br Edn., Sept '61) pp2-3 et seq.
Campbell, J.W.Jr. (1961) On the selective breeding of human beings. *Analog Science
  Fact/Fiction* XVIII (Brit. Edn. Feb.). 2-4 et seq.
Carter, M.A.and Thorp, C.H. (1979) The reproduction of *Actinia equina* L. var.
  *mesembryanthemum. J. Mar. Biol. Soc. U.K.* **59** 989-1001.
Cassen, R. and Associates (1986) Does Aid Work? Report to an Intergovernmental
  Task Force. Oxford: Clarendon Press
Clement, H. (1964) Close to Critical. New York: Ballantine Books.
Cohen, J. (1977) Reproduction. London: Butterworths.
Cohen, J. (1979) Maternal constraints in development. *In* Maternal Effects in
  Development (ed. D R Newth and M Balls). Cambridge: Cambridge University Press.
  1-34
Cohen, J. (1984) Contraception. In The Encyclopedia of Medical Ignorance
  (ed. R Duncan and M Weston-Smith). Oxford: Pergamon Press. 189-202.
Cohen, J. and Massey, B. (1984) Animal Reproduction: parents making parents. *Studies
  in Biology No.163*. London: Edward Arnold.
Coleridge, S.T. (1938) The Political Thought of Samuel Taylor Coleridge; a
  selection by R.J.White.   London: Jonathan Cape
Coleridge, S.T.(1830) The Church and State, according to the idea of each. London:
  Hurst, Chance and Co.

Comfort, A. (1973) The Joy of Sex. London: Quartet.
Cox, C.B. and Boyson, R., eds. (1975) Black Paper 1975. London: J.M.Dent.
Darlington, C.D. (1969) The Evolution of Man and Society. London: George Allen and Unwin.
Darlington, C.D. (1978) The Little Universe of Man. London: George Allen and Unwin.
Darwin, C. (1871) Descent of Man and Selection in Relation to Sex. London: Murray.
Davidson, E.H. (1986) Gene Activity in Early Development. 3rd edn. New York: Academic Press.
Davies, N.B. (1988) Dumping eggs on conspecifics. *Nature* **331** 19
Dawkins, R.(1976) The Selfish Gene. Oxford: Oxford University Press.
Dawkins, R. (1986) The Blind Watchmaker. Harlow: Longmans Scientific.
de Beer, G. (1971) Homology, an unsolved problem. *Oxford Biology Readers* **11**. Oxford: Oxford University Press.
de Vries, L. and P. Fryer, eds. (1967) Venus Unmasked; or, an Inquiry into the the nature and origin of the    Passion of Love. London: Arthur Barker Ltd.
Dickson, G.R. (1965) the Alien Way. New York: Bantam Books.
Djerrassi, C. (1979) The Politics of Contraception. New York: W.W.Norton and Co.
Dobell, C. (1911) The status of the protista. *Archiv fur Protistenkunde* **21** 269-310.
Dunbar, R.I.M. (1984) Reproductive Decisions: an economic analysis of gelada baboons' social strategies. Guildford: Princeton University Press.
Elia, I. (1985) The Female Animal. Oxford: Oxford University Press.
Fisher, H. (1983) The Sex Contract. London: Granada Publishing.
Foley, R. (1987) Another Unique Species: patterns in human evolutionary ecology. Harlow: Longman Scientific.
Ford, C.S. and Beach, F.A. (1965) Patterns of Sexual Behaviour. London: Methuen University Paperbacks.
Foucault, M. (1978) The History of Sexuality; 1: An introduction (trans. R Hurley). London: Allen Lane.
Foucault, M. (1986) The History of Sexuality; 2: The uses of pleasure (trans. R Hurley). Harmondsworth: Viking Penguin.
Fremlin, J.H. (1985) Power Production; what are the risks? Bristol: Adam Hilger Ltd.
Galton, F. (1869) Hereditary Genius. London: Macmillan.
Gilbert, W.S. (1885) The Mikado. D'Oyly Carte Productions.
Goffman, E. (1972) Interaction Ritual: essays on face-to-face behaviour. Harmondsworth: The Penguin Press.
Golding, W. (1964) The Inheritors; a novel. London: Faber School Editions.
Gould, S.J. (1977) Ontogeny and Phylogeny. Cambridge, Mass: Harvard University Press.
Gould, S.J. (1981) The Mismeasure of Man. London: Penguin Books.
Gould, S.J. (1983) The Panda's Thumb. Harmondsworth: Pelican Books.
Greenwood, P.J., Harvey, P.H. and M. Slatkin (1987). Evolution: Essays in Honour of John Maynard Smith. Cambridge: Cambridge University Press.
Guillebaud, J. (1985) Contraception: your questions answered. London: Pitman Publishing Ltd.
Hamilton, W.D. (1963) The evolution of altruistic behaviour. *American Naturalist.* **97** 354-6
Hampshire, S. (1956) Spinoza. London: Faber and Faber
Hardin, G. (1982) Naked Emperors: essays of a taboo-stalker. Los Altos, Ca: William Kaufmann Inc.
Hardy, A.C. (1960) Was man more aquatic in the past? *New Scientist* **7** 642-645
Harper, J.L., Rosen, B.R. and White, J., eds. (1986) The Growth and Form of Modular Organisms. *Phil. Trans. Roy. Soc. Lond.* B. **313** 1-250.
Harrison, H. (1984) West of Eden. London: Granada Publishing Co.
Harris, M. (1974) Cows, Pigs, Wars and Witches: the riddles of culture. New York: Random house.

Heinlein, R.A. (1974) Time Enough for Love. New York: Berkley.

Heinlein, R.A. (1986[1962]) The Door Into Summer. London: Gollancz.

Hofer, M.A. (1978) Hidden regulatory processes in early social relationships. *In* Perspectives in Ethology **3**: Social Behaviour (ed P.P.G.Bateson and P.H.Klopfer) New York: Plenum Press. 135-166

Hrdy, S.B. (1981) The Woman That Never Evolved. Cambridge,Mass: Harvard University Press.

Hsiao, K.C. (1927) Political Pluralism: a study in contemporary political theory. London: Kegan Paul, Trench, Trubner.

Huxley, A. (1955, first edn. 1932) Brave New World. Harmondsworth: Penguin Books.

Huxley, A. (1962) Island. Harmondsworth: Penguin Books

Illich, I. (1973) Deschooling Society. Harmondsworth: Penguin Education.

Isaac, G. (1981) Archaeological tests of alternative models of early hominid behaviour: excavation and experiments. *Phil.Trans.Roy.Soc.Lond.* B **292** 177-188

Jensen, A.R. (1969) How much can we boost I.Q. and scholastic achievement? *Harvard Educational Review.* **33** 1-123

Jensen, A.R. (1975) Race and mental ability. *In* Racial Variation in Man (ed. F J Ebling) *Symp Inst Biol* **22** 71-108

Johanson, D.C. and M.A.Edey (1982) Lucy: the beginnings of humankind. London: Granada Publishing

Joysey, K.A. (1984) Sexual choice and disease. Lecture to Univ of B'ham Evolution students, not (yet) published.

Kawai, M. (1965) Newly-acquired pre-cultural behaviour of the natural troupe of Japanese monkeys on Koshima Islet. *Primates* **6** 1-30

Langness, L.L. (1977) Ritual, power and male dominance in the New Guinea Highlands. *In* The Anthropology of Power (ed. R D Fogelson and R N Adams). New York: Academic Press. 3-22.

Lang, A. (1898) The Arabian Nights Entertainments. London: Longmans, Green, and Co.

Leacock, S. (1916) Essays and Literary Studies. London: John Lane,The Bodley Head.

LeGuin, U. (1974) The Dispossessed. London: Victor Gollancz.

Lesko, N (1988) Symbolizing Society: stories, rites and structure in a Catholic High School. London: The Falmer Press.

Levi-Strauss,C (1975) The Raw and the Cooked: introduction to a science of mythology, I. (trans. J and D Weightman) New York: Harper and Row

Lillegraven,J.A., Thompson, S.D., McNab, B.K. and Patton, J.L. (1987) The origin of eutherian mammals. *Biological Journal of the Linnean Society* **32** 281-336.

Lorenz, K.Z. (1981) The Foundations of Ethology. New York: Springer-Verlag.

Lovejoy, A.O. (1936) The Great Chain of Being. Cambridge, MA: Harvard University Press.

Luthi, M. (1976) Once Upon a Time: on the nature of fairy tales. Bloomington: Indiana University Press.

Malinowski, B. (1963) Sex, Culture and Myth. London: Rupert Hart-Davis.

Margulis, L. and D. Sagan.(1987) Microcosmos: four billion years of evolution from our microbial ancestors. London: Allen and Unwin.

Marx, K (1975 [1880?]) Wages, Price and Profit. Peking: Foreign Languages Press.

Masters, W.H. and Johnson, V.E. (1966) Human Sexual Response. London: Churchill.

McIntosh, J.T. (1961) World Out of Mind. London: Transworld.

Mead, H. (1960) The Bright Phoenix. London: Corgi Books.

Mead, M. (1971 [1928]) Coming of Age in Samoa. Harmondsworth: Penguin Books.

Mikes, G. (1959, 29th impr.) How to be an Alien. London: Andre Deutsch.

Milgram, S. (1974) Obedience to Authority. London: Tavistock Publications.

Miller, W.M. (1961) A Canticle for Leibowitz. New York: Bantam Books.

Mitchison, N.(1964) Memoirs of a Spacewoman. London: Four Square Books.

Modgil, S., Verma, K.G., Mallick, K., and Modgil, C., eds. (1986) Multicultural Education: the interminable debate. Lewes, E.Sussex: The Falmer Press.

Morgan, E. (1972) The Descent of Woman. London: Souvenir Press.
Morgan, E. (1982) The Aquatic Ape: a theory of human evolution. London: Souvenir Press.
Morgan, L.H. (1875) Ethnical periods. *Proc. Am. Soc. Adv. Sci.* **24B** 266-274
Morgan, L.H. (1958 [1877]) Ancient Society; or, researches in the lines of human progress from savagery through barbarism to civilization. Calcutta: Bharati Library (J.C.Saha Roy).
Morris, D. (1967) The Naked Ape: a zoologist's study of the human animal. London: Jonathan Cape.
Morris, D. (1969) The Human Zoo. London: Jonathan Cape.
Morris, D. (1985) Body-Watching: a field-guide to the human species. London: Jonathan Cape.
Moylan, T. (1986) Demand the Impossible: science fiction and the utopian imagination. New York: Methuen, Inc.
Mumford, Lewis (1961) The City in History. London: Secker and Warburg.
Nefzawi (1967) The Perfumed Garden (Trans. R Burton) London: Panther Books.
Niven, L. (1970) Ringworld. London: Gollancz Ltd.
Niven, L. and J.Pournelle. (1976) The Mote in God's Eye. London: Futura Publications.
Niven, L. and J. Pournelle. (1986) Footfall. London: Sphere Books.
Niven, L. and J. Pournelle. (1987) The Legacy of Heorot. London: Victor Gollancz Ltd.
Nixon, M. and J.B. Messenger, eds. (1977) The Biology of Cephalopods. *Symp. Zool. Soc. Lond.* **38**. London: Academic Press.
Ogan, E., ed. (undated, c.1925) The Wonderland of Knowledge: an up-to-date illustrated encyclopedia. London: Odhams Press Ltd.
Oldroyd, D.R. (1980) Darwinian Impacts. Milton Keynes: Open University Press.
Opie, P. and I. Opie. (1959) The Lore and Language of Schoolchildren. Oxford: Clarendon Press.
Opie, I. and P. Opie. (1969) Children's Games in Street and Playground. Oxford: University Press.
Opie, P. and I. Opie. (1974) The Classic Fairy Tales. London: Oxford University Press.
Oyama, S. (1984) The Ontogeny of Information. Cambridge: Cambridge University Press.
Peters, T.J. and Waterman, R.H. (1982) In Search of Excellence. New York: Harper and Row.
Pohl, F. and C.M.Kornbluth. (1953) The Space Merchants. New York: Ballantine Books.
Prentice, A.M. and Whitehead, R.G. (1987) The energetics of human reproduction. *In* Reproductive Energetics in Mammals. *Symp.Zool. Soc. Lond.* **57**. 275-304
Rajchman, J. (1985) Michel Foucault: The Freedom of Philosophy. New York: Columbia University Press.
Rifkin, J. (1985) Declaration of a Heretic. Boston: Routledge and Kegan Paul.
Rousseau, J-J. (1941 [1753]) Discours sur l'origine et les fondements de l'inegalite parmi les hommes. Cambridge: Cambridge University Press.
Runciman, W.G. (1966) Relative deprivation and the concept of reference group. In Sociological Perspectives (ed. K Thompson and J Tunstall,1971) London: Penguin Books. 299-315
Russ, J. (1975) The Female Man. New York: Bantam Books.
Sahlins, M. (1976) Culture and Practical Reason. Chicago: University of Chicago Press.
Sahlins, M. (1977) The Use and Abuse of Biology. London: Tavistock Publications.
Serebriakoff, V. (1975) Brain. London: Davis-Poynter.
Serebriakoff, V. (1987) The Future of Intelligence, biological and artificial. Carnforth: Parthenon Publishing Group.
Shepard, P. (1978) Thinking Animals. New York: Viking Press.
Short, R.V. (1976) The evolution of human reproduction. *In* Contraceptives of the

Future (ed. R V Short and D Baird). London: The Royal Society. 3-24
Siegel, J. and Shuster, J. (1928) Superman. New York: DC Comics Inc.
Simak, C.D. (1981, orig. 1952) City. New York: Ace Books.
Singer, I. B. (1963) The Spinoza of Market Street. New York: Avon Books.
Smith, M. (1977) The Underground and Education. London: Methuen
Smith, A (1976[1776]) An Enquiry into the Nature and Causes of the Wealth of Nations. (eds. R H Campbell and A S Skinner) Oxford: Clarendon Press.
Spinrad, N. (1974) Bug Jack Barron. New York: Bantam Books.
Thomas, L. (1980) Lives of a Cell: notes of a biology-watcher. London: Allen Lane.
Tiger, L. (1970) Men in Groups. New York: Vintage.
Turnbull, C. (1961) The Forest People. London: Jonathan Cape.
   UNESCO (1986) Science, high technology and the multinationals. *Impact of Science on Society* **151** 1-84
van Vogt, A.E. (1959 [1951]) The Voyage of the Space Beagle. London: Panther Books.
Vatsayana (1963) Kama Sutra (Trans. R Burton and F F Arbuthnot, ed. Archer) London: Panther Books.
Waddington, C.H. (1975) The Evolution of an Evolutionist. Edinburgh: Edinburgh University Press.
Weissmann, A. (1904) The Evolution Theory. (Trans. J A Thompson) London: Edward Arnold.
Wells, H.G. (1922[1898]) The Sleeper Awakes. London: Collins' Classics.
Wells, H.G. (1935) The Time Machine. London: Dent (Everyman).
White, J. (1962) Hospital Station. New York: Ballantine Books.
White, J. (1983) Sector General. New York: Ballantine Books.
White, T.H. (1939) The Sword in the Stone. London: William Collins.
Willmott, P. (1969) Adolescent Boys of East London. Harmondsworth, Middlesex: Penguin Books.
Wilson, E.O. (1984) Biophilia. Cambridge: Harvard University Press.
Winfree, A.T. and S.H.Strogatz. (1984) Organizing centres for three-dimensional waves. *Nature* **311** 611-5
Winfree, A.T. (1974) Rotating chemical reactions. *Scientific American* **230** No 6, 82-95
Wolpert, L. (1985) in "Genesis", a British Broadcasting Corporation "Horizon" television programme, produced by J. Palfreyman assisted by J. Cohen.

# INDEX